THE MAGICAL SUMMER OF PROFESSOR SIMON

A novel

Robert Masson

ISBN: 0692823476
ISBN 13: 9780692823477
Library of Congress Control Number: 2016920968
LCCN Imprint Name: Robert Masson, Chula Vista, CA

PRELUDE...THE TIPPING POINT

Homer, the fat-assed dog, waited by the door, blowing puffs of putrid air from his distended underbelly. "Woof, woof." If dogs could talk; aren't we glad they can't.

"Is that you, Al?" Gloria called.

Alec, please! In all these years, my protests were never taken seriously.

"Take Homer for his walk, will you? I'm finishing the beef stew." Gloria came through the hallway twirling a wooden spoon slick with gray grease. Gloria; tall, slender, pointed jaw, pale eyes, and parentheses on either side of her mouth. She wore her hair swept to the top of her head, held by a tortoiseshell-colored comb. Her apron blushed brilliant-colored rings and angular designs, all colorfast.

She turned away. "How was your workshop?"

"Fine," I said. "Just fine." I reached for Homer's leash.

"See anyone you knew?"

"No one in particular."

"It's amazing. The State is broke but has money to give all you *pro*fessors a day off for some silly conference. Must have cost us taxpayers a fortune."

"I'm sure it did," I said.

Homer danced, overgrown toenails clacking against the linoleum floor. He farted again, then sneezed, rubbing his snout against my pant leg.

"Jesus, take him out, will ya. I'll have to change his diet. I think it's the liver that causes the farts, what do you think?"

The leash snapped into place. I held my breath as I wrestled the door open. Homer clacked his way over the threshold and down the slick blacktop to the edge of a neighbor's lawn where he sniffed until he found the precise location to squat.

Although *I* wouldn't choose to crap on a neighbor's lawn, Homer had his own moral code. We never discussed the matter.

When he finished pawing the grass, I bent to scoop his droppings into a plastic baggie. As I stood, I felt my neighbor's gaze measuring my performance.

"Get it all, did you Al?"

Brody Fine served as neighborhood watch in these and other matters.

"You could truly eat off this grass," I suggested, tugging Homer's leash to prevent him from getting shit on his snout.

"Homer clearly thinks so. So what's going on at that university of yours?"

I edged Homer onto his own turf.

"I hear your president is looking for work."

"Indeed," I retorted.

"Well, I didn't think he'd last long. He has that lean and hungry look about him. I suppose they'll have one of those searches, won't they? You'd think finding someone to run that place was tougher than sending a man to the moon. If you ask me, I think those searches give your buddies a chance for a free meal at our expense."

Brody Fine was not someone I'd really ask that question of, but I secretly agreed that there was a good deal of interest among faculty when it came to serving on search committees. Maybe he was right about the free dinners. Before I could offer a defense, Brody turned to an article in the evening newspaper and wandered inside, giving me the opportunity to admonish Homer that if he continued to sniff his own shit, he might return in his next life as Brody Fine. Homer scratched a patch of fresh grass with several strokes of his hind legs, then farted and gave me his limpid-eyed look that suggested I mind my own business.

⟻⟦ ⟧⟼

The dinner table was set and the stew served. Our teenage son, Rodney, ambled in. He was a winsome, easy going and charming skateboarding youngster. We chatted amiably about the day, mostly from Rodney's perspective. When he had finished and excused himself, I brought the dinner invitation to Gloria's attention.

"I ran into this young man at First Federal," I began. "A former student. We had lunch and, well, that's how the invitation came about." I passed over the part about my apparent attempt to rob the bank.

"Jesus, I don't have a thing to wear." She mopped her gravy with a slice of Wonder Bread.

"We really don't have to go," I said expectantly. "This was a chance meeting." Pause. "Did I mention that his father is president of First Federal?"

"I'll poke around my closet." She looked up, her pale eyes locking onto me. "Maybe I'll buy something new. Jesus, it's a chance to see the inside of a house on Sycamore. Those places must go for seven hundred thousand, if they go for a penny. What do you think?"

"There are some very nice houses on Sycamore," I replied.

I finished the stew. In spite of our marital incompatibilities, most of Gloria's meals were tasty. And thoroughly prepared. I had never consumed an underdone meal at her table.

Dinner over, I joined Rodney on the front lawn where he coaxed me into tossing the Frisbee. After several exchanges, he said, "Dad, do you ever think of leaving Mom?"

The Frisbee hurled toward me and I shut my eyes just before it clunked me on the forehead. "What makes you ask that question, son?" Scrubbing the sting with an index finger, I checked for blood.

"I don't know. I just wondered."

"Something must have caused you to bring it up." I bent forward to retrieve the Frisbee.

"I overheard Mom talking to a lawyer today, that's all."

"Really? Well, it may have been about settling Grandma Carson's estate."

"No, I think it was about getting a divorce."

⊷+⊶

That night, I felt the mattress shift, now sloping toward the outboard side of the bed. When I had stabilized myself, I said to Gloria, "Do you really want to go to dinner on Sycamore Saturday night?" Pause. "Or shall we skip it?"

Gloria sat propped up with a bundle of catalogs. "No, I'd like to go," she replied.

We hadn't had sex in four or five months, perhaps six. I'd lost track. Something about a vaginal cramp.

"I don't really know these people."

"Mmmm."

"We could do something else Saturday night," I said. *God forbid.*

"No, I'd like to see the place on Sycamore."

"We could tour one with a real estate agent."

"If you don't want to go, just say so."

"It's not that." It was *precisely* that. "It just seems like a lot of trouble for people we really don't know." Trouble with a capital *T.*

"Suit yourself. But I'd still like to go."

A car drove by. My ears perked up. The car slowed, stopped in front of the house, then sped up. I stepped to the window and watched it make a wide turn at the far intersection. It paused, headlights dimmed, then cruised slowly back along the block toward the house. I could see only shadows and an occasional flicker of color. After a moment, the engine raced, and the car pulled out of sight.

Glancing at Gloria, I searched for a sign of curiosity. Nothing. As I slipped back into bed, she folded her catalog and turned to me. "I've been meaning to ask you something, Al," she said.

I wondered: Had the sound of the vehicle triggered the impending question?

"Have you ever had an affair?"

I gulped. Whatever had I been saying in my sleep? "No."

"Ever think about it?"

"Elizabeth Blumberg," I blurted out, as if about to be threatened with a full rotation of the thumbscrew. "When we first moved here, a faculty member's wife, someone in the music department, befriended me. I went to her home one afternoon for tea."

"You don't drink tea," Gloria said. Gloria could by a very literal person.

"Precisely. I told her that, but it didn't seem to matter. She said the invitation stood."

"And?"

"She served tea and we talked for several hours."

"About?"

"I don't recall. Maybe about my being unhappy."

"With our marriage?" She laid the catalog to one side.

"With our transition to a strange town. Trying to adjust."

"You had the chance and you didn't screw her?"

"The thought crossed my mind."

"Was she pretty?"

"She was buxom. She wore a tight black skirt and a snug white blouse. Her hair was swept up and her skin very pale. Her earrings were silver, heavy. They tugged at her lobes. She seemed very balanced in her black spike-heeled shoes." I amazed myself at the recall, a full description of someone I hadn't thought of in over twenty years.

"Did you see her again?"

"No." That was true.

"Why not?"

"I was afraid, I suppose."

"That you'd give in?"

"Yes."

Gloria dumped the remaining catalogs onto the floor, then pulled the covers over her shoulder as she rolled further to her side of the bed. "You should have gone for it, Al. It might have been better for both of us."

I turned out the light and drifted into a restless sleep in the center of my exact half of the king-sized mattress thinking, not of Gloria's comment, but of Elizabeth Blumberg. She had been older, perhaps by ten years. Her nature had been kind and soothing and confident. While I had found her attractive, it was her self-assuredness that had nearly seduced me. I was young, assuming my first university appointment, alone in my career, intimidated by the responsibility that getting an advanced degree had foisted upon me nearly overnight. I now lived in an unfamiliar town, standing out in the university community as fresh fodder for the aging, corrupt academicians whose tenure had outlived their fervor. She was strong, capable, sophisticated, and exotic. In truth, it hadn't been my commitment of faithfulness to Gloria that had kept my pants on that afternoon, but my sense of terror at the thought of standing before the threshold of erotic desire from which, once crossed, I might never return.

CHAPTER 1

THE EULOGY

When does a person realize that the time they have staring them down is less than the time they have already lived? Maybe it's similar to putting on weight or turning gray. One day you mount a scale or glance in the mirror and there you are, ten pounds heavier with streaks of age and jowls. My day had arrived and I felt old. Maybe that's why I signed up for a professional development workshop sponsored by the university.

There I sat into the first hour of the workshop, glancing down at the sheet of paper where I had written the opening line of our group exercise: *Alec Simon will be remembered best for....*

There were seventy, maybe eighty of us, all members of the State University faculty invited to participate in the retreat, a chance to examine our roles in higher education. That's what the brochure had said when I'd signed on months earlier. Now, as I sat detached, watching, I wondered what possessed me to offer myself up for this emotional autopsy. I couldn't get past the first hurdle: *The Eulogy*. That's what they called the exercise.

In twenty-eight minutes, there had been introductions, an overview, and information about breaks and lunch. As I had listened to the instructions, I grasped the location of the hotel dining area, a left, two rights. *Don't be fooled by the alcove.* I had mastered the schedule; break times, along with the location of the coffee urn, and most importantly, the handling of the evaluation forms to be completed at the end of the day to ensure proper feedback for the conference sponsors. I *got* all that.

What I couldn't figure out was the tombstone. We had each drawn one, the old-fashioned kind that show up on Halloween cards, and were instructed to write within the lines what we wished said about ourselves upon our deaths. A grand and glorious statement, the impact of each and every academic footprint on this earth. Was this a not-too-subtle way for the citizen-participants of the University Community to evaluate our performance? Was the message obvious? *What you've done for the past ten, fifteen, maybe twenty years, that's fine. Well, maybe not fine, but we let you keep your jobs. The point is, you can do better. What we want now is to know what you will do for us in the future? Ante up. Make your commitment. Produce to our expectations and we'll bury you beneath a larger paper tombstone.*

Free associate, the workshop leader had said. *Let your mind undress itself.* Forget that. I had trouble undressing my body. In the dark. I'm just not the kind of person who can undress any part of me in front of anyone. Certainly not my mind. That is the most private part of me. I had rather be caught naked running through the streets than tell anyone what I was really thinking.

Alec Simon will be remembered best for.... I looked around the room. The others continued to write. I turned my yellow-lined paper over. *Okay, think! You can do this.* I did the next best thing to free-associating; I made a list.

Position? Full professor, History Department.

Tenured? Unto eternity.

Married? Twenty-two years.

Children? A boy.

Books written? Three, all about the new Russia and the threat of World War Three.

Articles? A hundred plus, all titled *Publish or Perish.*
Classes? More than I could ever count.
Students? Hundreds, thousands.
Outstanding? A few. But where were they now?
Committees? Too many, too useless.
Fantasies? Enough.
Cat? Murdered one night by an angry neighbor.
Dog? A short, fat-assed mongrel named Homer.
Car? A five-year-old Nissan.
Pastimes? Secret prestidigitator.
Primary fault? Dullness.

I flipped the paper back and wrote within the awkwardly sketched arch of my tombstone; *Alec Simon will be remembered best for his dullness.* There. I'd thought it. And had written it. I had undressed my mind in public.

The hairs on my neck prickled as I realized what I'd declared: *dullness.* Impulsively, I scribbled an overlay of purple ink until the paper glowed and the word *dullness* blended into an oily slick that even the forensic lab at FBI's Quantico headquarters couldn't extract.

Did I deserve even that distinction? Could there be far duller professors?

Having taught at State U for twenty years, I would be known for absolutely nothing. Undistinguished. Flat. Mediocre. Sure, I'd stuffed history into sleepy brains like Lucy Ricardo stuffed candies into boxes. And like Lucy, I sometimes got behind, students slipping by despite my frantic efforts. But people liked Lucy and laughed at her ineptness. I wasn't sure they noticed mine.

I had squeezed out enough history in my lifetime for there to be plenty of facts spinning through space, popping out at cocktail hours, batted about like badminton birdies on sunny afternoons in the park, arguable among inebriates at late night gatherings. I had crammed history into narrow spaces; behind physics, adjacent to English 1 and trig, wedged into inverted crevices formed by the converging of philosophy, psychology and German 2. And that's *all* I'd done.

Glancing about the room, I watched as they finished up, completing their assignments, most likely with considerable mastery. No failures in this group. All successful university professors, glowing with prominence and self-esteem. Assuredly high achievers as children, they sat anxiously waving hands in the air, silent pleas; *call on me, call on me.* Finally, the selection. A colleague stood to eschew his own virtues in revered tones befitting the occasion.

My stomach sank. I pushed back the uncomfortable chair and skulked to an exit.

Outside the hotel's revolving entrance, the festooned doorman tipped his hat. *"'Fame always brings loneliness. Success is as ice cold and lonely as the North Pole'."* He beamed. "Vicki Baum. That's from *Grand Hotel.* Taxi, sir?" I think he had played the lead role in *Hamlet* the previous year at summer stock.

I shook my head. Shoving my hands in my pockets, I chose a direction, the doorman's salutation heightening my sense of mediocrity. *He* had made something of *his* life. He had become an actor *and* a doorman. What of me?

Pausing at the display window of a bookstore, I gazed through the plate glass at my ghostly reflection, then focused on an aisle of magazines written for people who did things, who mattered. *Airplane pilots. Yacht owners. Snowboarders.* The transparency of the glass reflected a barely discernible figure. That was me, barely discernible. Barely discernible at work, at home, even to Homer, the fat-assed dog. Except when Homer had to piss, any hand was as friendly as any other, discernible or not.

I crossed a downtown street, marching mindlessly, indifferent as to my destination. Traveling several blocks, I found myself before the imposing doors of the First Federal Savings and Loan

Association. I needed cash for lunch. After a moment, I took a deep breath, and thought, *Why not! Make someone notice me.*

Inside, the vaulted lobby ceiling rose three stories. Customers' footsteps echoed across the slick marble floor. What I was about to do next came upon me as impulsively as the urge of a bratty child on the playground to snatch another kid's toy, or an adolescent's move to steal a kiss on a first date. Before I could restrain myself, I had reached for a deposit slip and scribbled a note across the back. Striding to a window where a young teller waited, I shoved the note through the slot beneath the grill.

The woman studied the note, her expression of concern more obvious by the moment. Carefully mouthing her words, she said, "You want money?"

I nodded.

"Do you know your account number?"

I reached beneath the grill and snatched the note. My written words: *I want to make a withdrawal.* I held the paper for her to read, pointing out each word.

The young woman's frown intensified. "Do you sign?" she asked, accentuating the mouthing of her words. "I think one of the managers knows sign language."

Time for a little bit of magic. I wadded the deposit slip into a ball and popped it into my mouth. Chewing and swallowing, I held my hands out, palms open. *Empty.* Reaching behind my ear, I proffered the neatly folded slip. As I displayed the paper and held it for her to see the writing once more, the note burst into flame. I devoured the fire, licking my lips as the last of the flames rolled from my tongue. With a slight bow to the amazed young teller, I was about to tell her that I wanted to withdraw fifty dollars for lunch money, when the expression on her face captured the one thought on her mind: *HOLDUP.*

As she reached for the telephone, I made a beeline for the door.

A man followed. Not *any* man: A bank man.

Outside, I glanced quickly across my shoulder, my heart pounding. Shielding my eyes from the sun, I hurried along the street, putting several blocks between myself and the bank, but not the man. My pursuer was young, vibrant, swift, waving arms, hollering, now but a half block back. I panted, my fifty-something body out of shape from loitering against dusty blackboards and breathing chalky silt.

Dashing down the avenue, pursued by a bank employee, was not how I had planned spending the break from my self-development workshop. I should have been with the others, in the washroom of the elegant old hotel, studying the patterns of tile clinging to the walls as I encouraged nature at the urinal. Then waiting in the coffee line, brushing shoulders with superb colleagues from chemistry and psychology, watching bearded chins mouth clever and urbane chatter, arms folded across chests, leather patched elbows setting body boundaries, oval-rimmed eyeglass frames sliding down nose bridges, balding pates gleaming, bobbing. *That's where I should have been.*

The young pursuer drew nearer. Now a voice joined the animation; talkies on the road. The voice projected through space, an elongated hook formed of air molecules, reaching, grabbing at my ear, like a nasty fourth grade teacher's cuffed hand grasping at the recalcitrant bully on the playground. *Missed.* Again. Articulation now, a sound forming into a syllable. Words. A name. My Name! *MY NAME!*

"Professor Simon," the young man called.

'*What will you be...remembered most for?*' I thought for a moment that's what he had said.

"Professor Simon, will...you remember...?"

Exhausted, I slowed to a trot, the consequences of my actions about to descend. My heart pounded. My brain gulped huge volumes of air, compressing the inside of my skull.

Okay, let's get this straight. Burning the deposit slip with the inane scribble was only a joke. Perhaps not clever; perhaps stupid, a middle-aged adolescent's attempt to impose a moment of insanity upon an otherwise boringly ordered life. But still, a joke. Only a joke. I wanted fifty bucks for lunch.

I pictured the hearing. *Your Honor, I never meant it seriously.*

Tell it to the judge.

You ARE the judge.

Well, a lot of them say that.

I never meant it.

That's what a lot of them say.

What?

ALOTOFTHEMSAYTHAT. INEVERMEANTTODOIT.

CHAPTER 2

"YOU WON'T REMEMBER ME, BUT..."

"Professor Simon, you won't remember me, but I want to tell you how much I enjoyed your class on European History. Jeffrey Ryder. Two years ago." Jeffrey Ryder sported a shaggy moustache to hide a thin sensual lip, to age a young face, a beautiful woman's face. He was perhaps twenty-three.

Whirling to face the young man, I extended my hand, grasping slender fingers, a graceful, gentle touch. *Be regular*, I thought. *Don't be crazy*. Take a breath. *Be regular*. "Yes, I remember."

"You're obviously in a hurry," the young man said. "Forgive me for chasing you down, but I thought of you only two days ago. I'm planning a trip to Europe this summer and actually considered calling you at your office. Now you suddenly appear in my father's bank. This is like a sign.

"My girlfriend and I are taking a leave of absence and spending the summer traveling overseas." The young man with the beautiful face was breathing shallowly, sipping small draughts of air between sentences. "This is so awesome. Here you are."

"Yes, I am," I said. My brain spun inside the globe resting on my shoulders; with each rotation, my eyeballs caught glimpses of the outside world through the eye sockets in my skull. There was no place to lie down, so I decided not to faint, or throw up from exertion, or buckle to the sidewalk and scrape the knees of my Wednesday-go-to-workshop-trousers. "How nice to see you again."

"You actually remember me?" young Ryder asked. He looked down the block, then back at me, as if to emphasize his amazement. "I can't believe this."

I can't believe it either. Say it with me: *I can't believe it.* Come on, that's what we're both thinking. *I can't believe this is happening.*

"Traveling to Europe," I gasped. "What a nice way to spend the summer. I hope you have a marvelous time." You won't be in town to testify against me.

"I've got to tell you, Professor Simon," young Ryder gushed, his lower lip engorging with blood, "your teaching was really inspiring. Your lectures were the best. I really mean that. I was about to drop out my senior year when I had your class. That's what kept me in school."

"Well, I'm really glad," I said. Breathing, nearly normal. Pulse, approaching normal. Blood pressure, anything but normal. "I hope you have a marvelous trip." *You said that already, Professor. Just say goodbye.* "If I can be of any help, give me a call." Thank god, I'll never hear from you. My eyes glanced down the block, not for emphasis but for an escape route. A deer trapped among concrete buildings.

"My parents were so excited to hear I was going to stay in school, they suggested I invite you to dinner," the boy said. "Not wanting to appear to be a brown-nose, I blew them off. Now I'm sorry." His look down the block had grown familiar. "If you have time, I would sure like you to meet Dad. He'd love to meet you. It won't take long. But then I don't want to impose. I know you're in a hurry."

"On the contrary, I'd really like to, but I don't want to impose on your father," I said, politely dismissing the invitation. Of course, neither of us wished to impose. No imposing. No *announced* imposing. All genuine imposing was unannounced. *That's what imposing is about, isn't it?*

"You know, he's just up the block," Ryder said. His moustache curled around his upper lip as he smiled. "He owns the bank. He'd really love to meet you." A pause, well timed. A social grace, a pose, most likely derived from Mother.

I processed what young Ryder had said: *He what? Owns the bank?*

"I'd really hate to disturb his busy day," I said. Witnessing a lengthy police interrogation can ruin anyone's day.

Young Ryder took my arm and, before I could mount serious resistance, led me down the street. "I can't believe this. My father will be so surprised. And this will give you a chance to meet Armand."

"Armand?"

"My girl friend. Your History 460 course was full when she returned to campus that semester." The beautiful boy hesitated, then blushed. "She was late. That is, she had to have an abortion." He fell silent for a moment, as if in reverential reflection.

We stood at the gateway to the scene of the crime.

"I really don't think this is a good idea," I said. Breathing; rapid. Pulse; racing. Blood pressure; astounding. "Your father has many important things to take care of as president of a bank. He really won't have time to meet me."

"Of course he will," young Ryder said. "Besides, he'll do anything for me. He's just that kind of dad. Come on in."

As we entered the massive lobby, my vision narrowed to a single cage across the expanse of marble from which I expected to be visually confronted by the young woman. Instead I caught a glimpse of a middle-aged man in shirtsleeves and suspenders counting money behind a sign that read, *Next teller, please.* FBI? They were counting the money to make certain the young woman was telling the truth. She would have to tell the truth in her position. And the security camera can't lie. It witnessed the entire fiasco, read the note, photographed my face. *The digital recording was in the back room at that very moment, lighting up a cigarette, lingering over the stale dregs of coffee, going over the scenario one more time with the cops. 'It was like this, you see. I'm scanning the place as usual when this frumpy guy walks in and ....'*

Young Ryder was a ploy; a tranquilizing dart intended to bring me back alive. I'd walk into a room, purported to be the office of the president of the First Federal Savings and Loan, but it would be an interrogation room. A common thief would never be allowed into a bank president's office, anyway. I'd be greeted by the FBI, bank examiners, rough and tumble lowlife detectives waiting to get me alone in a jail cell, my wife, my son, the Dean of the College, the poor of Rangoon, a sick child with cancer, the pimply-faced girl I stood up in high school, my sick Aunt Harriet who died while I was vacationing in Bimini, and the fat-assed dog, Homer, bladder distended from insufficient walking's.

My legs nearly buckled as we waited by the bronze-engraved elevator doors, the needle clocking my remaining moments before discovery, young Ryder spinning an effusive adolescent gush about a mediocre class, an average semester, one in which I had low back pains and hemorrhoids and had developed a particularly strong dislike for Homer for pissing on the rear seat of the Nissan.

The elevator clunked to a dead stop and the doors swept open to display a wrinkled face, a purple uniform, gold trim, steady hands with manicured nails, a warmth radiating, not from body heat, but love of duty, prince of the six by six conveyer, almost God, certainly St. Peter, guiding travelers skyward in the heady atmosphere of the ancient building. We stepped aboard.

St. Peter nodded. "Mr. Ryder," the gentleman spoke. His voice, deep, rich, vocal cords embossed with fibrous gold strains resonating like a bass guitar.

We rose skyward, staring at the doors that I feared would swish open to reveal a stairway of clouds upon which I alone would ascend to Judgment Day. Instead, the elevator discharged us into a carpeted channel that funneled to an anteroom. We paused before a mahogany gate that divided me from my impending fate. I followed mindlessly into the inner sanctum. *Behind the desk, Ryder Senior sat, penning his name to documents that would put Professor Alec Simon in prison for the rest of his natural life.*

Senior Ryder smiled, rose, extended a hand and chatter went on. I waited behind my mask, bobbing and weaving, ahhing, lying.

"I can't tell you what a debt of gratitude we owe you," Ryder Senior said as my tuner kicked in. "Jeff would have never finished State and who knows what would have become of him. Now he has the union card, yes sir." Like father, like son. A slap on the old back. Hip, hip, hooray. "And we expect big things of him."

"Now Dad." False modesty? "You know I haven't decided exactly what I want to do yet. Peggy and I are traveling this summer."

I thought her name was Armand.

"Yes, yes," Ryder Senior humpfed perfunctorily. *We'll discuss this over drinks and I'm not giving you one dime to ferry around that one-abortion-already trollop. It's bad enough the bitch works for me. She just wants to marry into the family, play in the vault full of money, wrap her damp thighs around velvety barrels of gold bullion, lie panting on soft sacks of negotiables.*

Young Ryder slipped from his father's grasp and smiled sweetly. "You'll have to meet Penny before you leave," Little Ryder gushed. "She'd love to meet you."

I thought her name was Peggy.

Disapproval on the brow of the CEO. *Mix one hot trollop with one mediocre professor and you'll waste more time than I have to give.* "Perhaps dinner sometime, Professor," Ryder Senior said. "I'll let you and Jeff determine a mutually satisfactory time. Martha would love to meet you as well."

Yes, Martha.

And then we drifted downward in the cage, St. Peter having been relieved by a gum- chewing lad whose presence defiled the atmosphere. No more heavenly scent. A carnivorous earthling farting to the ditty of an all-beef-patty, jerking to stops short of the floor line, oblivious to the glory of the lustrous machine, the controls of which he held in his untrained, hairless, snot-encrusted fingers.

We reached the lobby. I stared at the clock; ten forty.

Break had ended, the coffee urn now dry. The urinals had caught the last of the flushes. Lights dimmed for act two. The presenters, shuffling papers, look about, coats unbuttoned, perhaps off by now, ties loosened. One presenter, leaning into the crowd, a hand in his rear pocket, about to say, smiling: "Small group time."

There she stood. I froze like a gazelle in the gaze of a wily lioness. Now moving, coming toward us, my nightmare about to be realized. Of course, it couldn't happen any other way. A mediocre person does a very stupid thing, and pays by being skinned alive. Flayed, that's what it's called. Flayed, then salted, then skewered over the rotisserie. Superb people exhibit their creative impulses and slop into the next level of superfluity; mediocre people succumb to paper cuts.

"Professor Simon, I'd like you to meet Penny. Penny, my former history professor."

Our eyes met. I had never looked at her eyes, or her face, not really. Nor her hair, nor her breasts, nor her hands. My desire had been only to perform a bit of magic. To make someone smile. To excel for one small moment in time, at a time when I had felt transparent. The impulse had swept over me. A rare moment of disarray in an otherwise orderly, boring life. Not to hurt, nor harm. I had not wished to startle or frighten her, but rather to regale her, to garner her attention, to offer her a story to pass along to another generation, perhaps grandchildren, about the stranger who entered her life for a matter of mere moments and performed a wondrous illusion. I had wished no more than to take her to the edge of doubt, disbelief, amazement, then allow her to swing back, feel the exhilarating joy of suspense released. And collect my fifty bucks for lunch.

Armand, *the Lioness*, smiled. In that smile, was there recognition? There was social grace, warmth, deftness, titillation, a set of gorgeous teeth, a pair of lips spread across her mouth like cranberry jam, glistening in the muted light from multifaceted edges of gilded applique. But was there *recognition*?

Seemingly not.

I sighed. Respiration slowed. Pulse, softened. Blood pressure, dropped. "I'm very glad to meet you," I said.

"The pleasure is *mine*," young Armand said. The words, the voice, the violet eyes. An inflection on *mine*? Or was it, 'The *pleasure* is mine'? My brain was too addled to make the distinction.

"This is *soooo* great." Young Ryder. "What do you say we all get Chinese? It's still early for lunch, but Dad won't mind if we take the time under these circumstances. I'll give the manager a call, tell her it's a special occasion. Professor? What do you say?"

Armand's violet eyes glowed like liquid crystals. I felt caught. *Don't disappoint Young Ryder, you nasty old man*, those eyes said. The rhyme formed despite my efforts to clear my head:

Come on, fellow, whatdayasay.
You weren't doing anything, anyway.
Running from your meeting,
Hanging out on the street,
Go on with the kid, get something to eat.
Make his day.

"Sure," I said. "I have a few minutes to spare." *That wasn't so hard, was it?*

"Fantastic. Just great. You two wait right here. I'll only be a sec." Young Ryder scampered across the marble floor, arms and legs flailing, tie flying, feet clacking on stone like cockroach legs tap dancing karaoke on the surface of a microphone.

The pause.

Looking down, I studied the marbled pattern on the tile, brown, black, gold, cream, flowing together in slick ribbons like some delicious gelatin dessert. My eyes followed the free form, guiding my gaze to the edge of her shoe, black, patent-leather, high instep, heel narrowing to a dagger point, ankle of flesh-colored flesh, purple veins weaving delicately beneath her skin.

"So Professor, do you come here often?"

That was my line, an all-men's line. In a barroom, in Toledo... *Lucille....*

"I actually have an account here," I began my absurd explanation to this woman-child-lioness, "and being in a hurry to return to a workshop I'm attending at the Lorelei, I popped in." Confession time. She *had* to remember me. What did I have to lose?

"I was so foolish to pull that silly prank with the deposit slip and the fire." I paused for some response, a smile of recognition or perhaps one tendering approval; better yet, forgiveness. "Then I realized that you thought perhaps.... That you thought it was some gimmick on my part to...." I couldn't bring myself to say the word: *STICKUP.* "So I turned and headed out, now having lost some time and found myself running down the street when Young Ryder caught up with me. What a heck of a surprise." Whew.

"I would imagine you *were* surprised," she said, a womanly voice now speaking for her, of stockings and garter belts, jewels and furs, late nights, sophisticated settings, hot breath, passion. *What was happening to me?*

'*I would* imagine *you were surprised?*' But when? When I realized you thought I was about to rob the bank? When Young Ryder caught up with me? Or when we were finally introduced properly? This young woman was the Lady Litton to my Inspector Clouseau: "Yes, indeed, I was *very* surprised." Be silly. Look down. Brush lint from your wrinkled suit.

15

Clack, clack, clackety clack. Saved by young Ryder, if but for the moment.

"Is Chinese okay, Professor?"

Those violet eyes were unrelenting.

"Just a cup of coffee is all I really have time for," I said. "I was telling Armand, or is it Peggy? I'm a little confused."

"Armand," she said. "Jeffrey likes to call me Penny because my last name is Pennington and I work in a bank. The name Armand embarrasses him. He thinks it's a man's name and he is embarrassed at the implication he could be dating a man." She paused. We were walking along the street, a street with a name I couldn't remember, though I knew it as well as I knew my own.

"I was telling Armand that I really must get back to a workshop the University is sponsoring. I only slipped away during a short break, well actually just before the break, to go to my bank. Actually, your bank. I was in such a hurry, I actually forgot to fill in the deposit slip properly. Then I left." *Isn't that silly? Am I the absent-minded professor, or what?*

"Fate," Young Ryder said. "Fate." His arm shot confidently into the air, grasping the ornate brass door handle shaped like the wing of an ancient bird of prey. The swinging door revealed a tunnel of dark leather booths, an atmosphere drenched with the aroma of hot cooking oil.

Had I finally cracked and gone to hell?

An early lunch. Pointless chitchat. Fortune cookies all around.

"'You have a kind nature and a winning way'." Young Ryder looked for confirmation. No takers. I had my own excuse; I hardly knew the boy. *But Armand?*

Next. I reached for a cookie in its cellophane wrap and ripped a corner with my teeth. How unseemly.

"Professor, what does yours say?" young Ryder asked earnestly. This was a game he obviously loved to play. I detested it. Gloria *always* wanted to go around the table and systematically hear from each and every diner; and she was *al*ways surprised by the message. And when she disagreed with the assessment, she invariably exclaimed, "I wonder why you got *that* one?" as if the gods and fate and all the demons and the baker had conspired along with the wait person who had laid the cookies across the oil soaked check to defraud her of her own appraisal. And when she was *very* put off, she clucked her tongue and said, "I would *never* have said that about *you*".

I snapped the cookie, it's edges crumbling beneath the pressure of my fingers. The message, in red ink, uncoiled. I glanced across the table. The violet eyes were upon me, watching.

"It says...." Upside down. I turned the slip over, straightened the coil, and read: "'Long life and happiness, always'." I smiled. Six numbers for the lotto. I had never played.

"That's good," young Ryder said with envy in his voice. A serious player. I briefly entertained the thought of introducing him to Gloria. "Penny?"

Snap. Clean. Crisp. No crumbs. No slip of white paper with red markings. No fortune. Cranberry lips smiled in delight. "What does it mean when you have no fortune?" she asked. She looked directly at me, violet eyes in two straight beams holding my gaze. *The Lioness and the Gazelle.*

"It means that you live for the moment," a booming voice responded.

Ryder Senior entered, stage right.

"Dad, what a great surprise. Come sit down."

Shuffle, shuffle. The great Senior Ryder sat, exchanged gazes, eye blinks, tilts of the head to one side, then the other. "I hope I'm not intruding." *Ho, ho. Listen to him.* "I decided to take an early lunch and join you. So, Professor, have you and Jeff arrived at a time for dinner?"

Stammer, stutter. Spill lukewarm tea from the handle-less cup onto a greasy plate. "Well, we really haven't talked about it. I really don't want to impose. You have a busy family and I know how precious time can be." I couldn't believe I had used the word *precious* as I glanced at the violet eyes. I was lying, of course, and everyone knew it. "I really appreciate the thought, however."

"Nonsense," said the man accustomed to getting his way. "We'd love to have you over. Let's make it this Saturday night. If there is a Mrs. Professor Simon, please bring her along. Or any friend, for that matter. And, of course, we'll have Armand for dinner as well. It will be a very nice family affair. Martha just loves to entertain. Gives her a chance to try out the new recipes she and cook have been working on."

"Saturday night," I said. That sinking feeling. The violet eyes encircled me. "Well, I'm sure Gloria will be delighted. She always likes to get out." Bumbling full professor; Gloria is obviously working away in *The Cave*, always anxious for a chance to better herself, to see daylight, to be in a real house, running water, flushing commode, momentarily safe from the gnashing jaws of Tyrannosaurus Rex. "I'll have to check, of course."

"Of course. Well, how about real dessert. My treat."

CHAPTER 3
THE DINNER PARTY

"So what are your many *other* former students doing these days," Senior Ryder asked from the head of the table as he worked over his dinner with the precision he might give to reviewing a bank ledger.

Where have all your hundred dollar bills gone? I thought. *Who knows?*

Small birds, Cornish hens, had been dispensed from what I imagined as the culinary ATM and deposited around the table. *Cook obviously had the PIN number.*

"Well, I actually don't know," I said. My first comfortable moment in the entire conversation. *Truth.* I really *didn't* know, couldn't know. Who on earth would know? There were hundreds. Thousands. "I suppose some have gone on to graduate school. Others I would imagine have taken jobs." Actually finding employment after exposure to history? I had quite an imagination.

"Don't you wonder, though?" Senior Ryder asked. His face glowed from the effect of the string of scotches he'd consumed during cocktail hour. "Wouldn't it be fascinating to follow-up your former students? You ran into Jeffrey by chance, but a concerted effort might reveal all kinds of fascinating information. Some of your people may actually be famous." His tone is sounding like a

60 Minute lead in, a Dan Rather. *How old I felt.* And what did he mean, 'some of *your* people....'? *Did that imply a cultural or a genetic link?*

Gloria had visited the upstairs bathroom twice, fingered the gilded picture frames in every room, and hung breathlessly by the rear window taking in the view of the sculptured garden, the pool and patio. Now she tackled her hen with a knife and fork, splaying the carcass, pinning both sides to the porcelain slab supporting it as if doing an autopsy.

"I had never thought of it quite that way," I said. I had never thought of it *at all*.

Young Ryder rallied to the cause. "I can find out what several of the students in my class are doing," he said, gnawing like a puppy on a leg of hen.

Martha smiled boldly, a set of choppers dazzling the crowd. "What a wonderful idea."

I grew uneasy at the building momentum. Distracting myself for the moment, I watched Gloria examine the small bones, deliberating as to whether they were edible. Perhaps she recalled Homer choking on a chicken neck; she decided to have seconds on spuds. Eating for Gloria was a focused, full-time undertaking. Besides, to her credit, she had made her contribution to the conversation with her accolades on the sumptuous surroundings.

The Lioness sat quietly content, her violet eyes sweeping across the scene like a swishing tail, from time to time pausing on each diner.

Mercifully, dinner ended and the others adjourned to various rooms of the house. Martha joined cook in the kitchen to prepare dessert; Senior Ryder ushered Gloria into the library for the ritual of pouring after dinner brandy; Young Ryder rushed to his bedroom with several postage stamps from out-of-the-country, compliments of Dad. The Lioness and I stared at each other.

"Fine dinner," I said awkwardly.

"Do you like eating little birds?" the Lioness asked, her tone sanctimonious.

I recalled she had not touched her hen. "Are you a vegetarian?"

"Not entirely," she said.

"I was hungry," I said lamely, my excuse for an act of cannibalism against a hapless creature with whom I must share at least *some* DNA.

"Yes," she said. "You seem hungry."

Seem? Or seemed? *There is a difference*, I thought.

We stood in the hallway of the over-stated house, momentarily looking for a direction. The Lioness took a step, her ankle buckling. She reached for my shoulder to lean on.

"Hardwood floors can be slippery," I said.

"I was clumsy," she replied cryptically. Regaining her balance, she tested her ankle, then whimpered. "I must have sprained it."

Looking down, I studied her ankle for a moment. Sinewy blood vessels wove crochet-like trails beneath the pearl-white layer of silk. When the inappropriateness of my fascination hit me, I stepped back. "Would you like to sit?"

"Yes, I would like that," she said, somehow conveying tones of both stoicism and sensuality.

I glanced at the well-carpeted staircase only a few feet from us and then at the Lioness. "Will this do?"

"If you will help me," she said.

Steadied by my forearm, she sat. I moved some distance away. "Your ankle may be swelling."

"It is," she said. "Do you mind?"

"Mind?"

"The shoe. Do you mind removing my shoe?"

Stepping up and bending forward, I reached for the back of her shoe with one hand. The shoe slipped easily from her foot. My fingers grazed her stocking-encased arch. I felt an embarrassing tingle in my crotch. "There," I said, as if setting the stage for my withdrawal.

"Will you rub my ankle?" she asked.

"Your ankle?" I replied.

"Where it is beginning to swell."

I reached forward, dumbly, the tender flesh beneath her stocking moving in response to the pressure of my fingertips. My eyes were momentarily drawn to those of the Lioness. Violet eyes. They were on me, watching without discernible emotion, following my movements. "Is this alright?" I asked.

"It's fine." Violet eyes held mine. "Thank you." The act had been perfunctory.

My fingers snapped open as if her flesh had turned to molten iron. What was she thinking? What did she suspect? Had she truly misconstrued my intentions? A line of perspiration formed along the edge of my collar.

"Would you kindly replace my shoe?"

I picked up the black heel and slipped it on her foot. The smell of leather and perfume nearly overcame my senses.

She held her hand toward me and I took it dutifully, allowing her to brace herself as she stood, feeling her hip brush against mine as she rose to nearly eye-level.

A whoosh of air overhead. I glanced up the staircase to see young Ryder racing toward us, imposing with a sense of adolescent glee. "Well, that's that," he said. "I now have two stamps from Zaire."

The Lioness smiled at Young Ryder and offered him a cheek to kiss. Her violet eyes held me in their gaze as the boy's thin, sensuous lips barely grazed her skin. Then he raced off to his computer to log in his new acquisitions and trace their history somewhere through the vast virtual world of the internet.

Senior Ryder burst from the library with a tray of drinks, Gloria smiling in his wake. I wondered if they had made out, if she had offered up her breasts to fondle, panting as she sometimes could, perhaps letting him nibble her neck as she studied a Monet across the room, calculating its value and the solidity of the Ryder marriage.

On the drive home, I could only guess at the Mona Lisa-like smile Gloria offered to me. She was not about to say, nor was I to ask.

CHAPTER 4

DIVORCE IS PAINLESS

The papers were served the following Monday at my office on the university campus. No sheriff's deputy, no fanfare. Just a process server. I opened the envelope and unfolded the correspondence. *Incompatibility after twenty-two years of marriage.* Stuffing the entire package into a drawer, I went to my last class of the semester.

When I arrived home that evening, Rodney sat on the door stoop working a crossword puzzle. He glanced up as I stepped from the car.

"I told you so," Rodney said, not unkindly. "She packed all her belongings this afternoon."

"How are you feeling about it?" I asked. I leaned against the car door.

"Can I stay here with you?" Rodney asked.

"Of course."

"Then I feel fine."

"Are you upset? Or angry?"

"I can take it or leave it," Rodney said. "Want to play catch?"

"I should walk Homer."

"She took Homer."

"She took Homer? I thought she hated Homer."

"I think it was you she hated, Dad," Rodney said. "She actually likes Homer."

Rodney retrieved two baseball gloves from his room and we played catch for thirty minutes while he updated me on school, a myriad of would-be girlfriends, sports, a hierarchy of his best friends, and his summer employment option.

"You'll be seventeen in a month," I said.

"Eighteen. And the beach is a great place for an eighteen year old to spend the summer. George and Tally are going along. We'll room together. What do you say?"

"Did you ask your mother?"

"This could be your decision, Dad. I don't want to put you on the spot, but it's really up to you."

"You know how she can be."

"We can keep her out of the loop."

"I doubt that."

"There is no reason for me not to go. I'm responsible, I drive, I'll be a senior next year, I've vowed to always use a contraceptive, I don't drink, and I need the money. It's a perfect set-up."

"You're right. I'll miss you."

Rodney stepped forward and draped an arm around my shoulder. "I'll miss you too, Dad. But it's time I do this."

Rodney called for pizza. We ate watching re-runs of *The Big Bang Theory*. When Rodney went to his room, I wrestled clean sheets onto the bed and positioned myself in the middle of the mattress. I thought of the Lioness and her purple eyes, how she watched me as I touched her ankle, her skin. Then I thought of Gloria. Twenty-two years is a long time. Even for two incompatible people.

Three a.m. I was still awake. There seemed to be nothing to sleep for.

The following morning, I received a telephone reminder from the dean's secretary that a colleague, who had died over the weekend, was on display that afternoon at a local mortuary. The dean urged the faculty of the college to make a showing during viewing hours, two to four p.m.

"Also," the secretary said, "President Packer is organizing campus-wide discussion groups. You know, follow-up to the workshop at the Lorelei? As a senior faculty member, the dean requested that you attend a meeting to set a good example for our college."

With grave reluctance, I agreed to both.

I arrived at the funeral home at three-fifty to discover I was the fourth member of the college and the only member of the History Department to have checked in. Perhaps the others were waiting till the last minute, but more likely the poor turnout resulted from the fact that this colleague had not been very well liked. While I had never considered lack of like-ability a good reason for avoiding this sort of social obligation, I easily agreed that Professor Tight-Asses's obsessive-compulsive disorder could be very distracting. At faculty meetings, for example, he insisted on wiping down the conference table and each chair with a mixture of Lysol, bleach, and gunpowder. When exhibits or handouts were passed around, he donned his latex gloves and a cotton mask. He refused to touch the light switch and walked in strange patterns to reach his seat, avoiding certain sculpted designs in the carpet. This maneuver often required others to break off conversations, as he sometimes had to pass between them. His office was strewn with stacks of articles, journals, and books teetering at heights approaching the ceiling. Compounding the problem, once periodicals reached a certain maturity, Tight-Ass refused to touch them. Rightly or wrongly, he harbored the belief that inks grew toxic with age.

Standing at the brink of the casket and gazing at his waxen image, I was aware that the handful of family members present had slipped into an anteroom, presumably for refreshments. Tight-Ass and I were alone. Perhaps the family felt he should have company at all times and chose the occasion of my arrival as an opportunity to take their break.

I'm not sure how much my thoughts were on Tight-Ass as I stared at the cadaver. My mind drifted to the image of the attractive teenage daughter who had shown me to the mourning site and the enormous size of her boobs. *What had he been feeding his children?* I wondered.

That's when it happened. One eye popped open. I had heard of the phenomenon, but couldn't believe it would occur to a freshly prepared cadaver. The voice, however, shocked me considerably more than the eye-popping experience.

"It's not as clean in heaven as it could be," Tight-Ass said.

"I beg your pardon."

"Could you slip me a pair of latex gloves?" His lips never moved.

"Latex gloves? What will you do with latex gloves?" I asked.

"It's not as clean in heaven as it could be."

I turned to survey the empty room.

One of us is crazy, I thought. *It can't be you. You're dead.*

"Could you slip me a pair of latex gloves?"

"Hadn't they anticipated your arrival?" I asked.

The presence of the teenager at my side, her left boob brushing my arm, further startled me. "He's not going quietly, is he?" she said, snickering into her sleeve.

I turned to her, momentarily distracted. Then I looked into her hazel eyes and said, "You rigged this?"

"We loved him, but he was never much fun when he was alive. We were hoping his close friends and associates might get a laugh and forgive him his foibles. He wasn't really a bad sort. What do you think?"

Should I admonish her for bad taste? Or just scold her for scaring the crap out of a man with a lot on his mind? I went straight to a smile. "Good choice of lines," I said. "But how did you get his voice so perfect?"

"My brother does great imitations."

"And the eye? How did you get his eye to pop open on cue?"

She looked down at the corpse, aware of the exposed eyeball for the first time. Her shriek sent a shiver through me as she turned and ran from the room.

CHAPTER 5

MEETING DOCTOR "KNOW-IT-ALL"

My department chair suggested therapy, a recommendation she pushed on anyone going through a divorce. It had worked for her. "Why not?" she said. "Even though classes are out, you're obligated to be on campus till the fifteenth. That means you can't leave town. And you're covered by insurance for ten sessions. If nothing else, it's a good way to kill a couple of hours while you're here." She was right about having time to kill, now that Homer had found a new home.

I located Dr. Silverman's name in the yellow pages. Silverman had an opening that next day and I found myself lying on a couch, head propped on a comfortable pillow, telling the story of the past week, including the bank episode, my last walk with Homer, the ugly meal on Sycamore, and, of course, about the Lioness.

"And the woman didn't recognize you at first?" Silverman asked, more intrigued with the details of my tale than I had supposed he might be.

"The topic didn't come up until we were alone. I explained what a silly prank it was."

"But you think she watches you?"

"Yes, she watches me. She studies me as if she were trying to send me a message. And I watch her, too."

"Why do you watch her?"

"To see if she is watching me."

"Do you find her attractive?"

"She's very attractive."

"So you find her attractive."

"She *is* attractive." I looked over at the doctor. "She's attractive. Anyone would find her attractive."

"But *you* find her attractive, correct? That's the important thing."

"Yes, I do find her attractive."

"Do you have fantasies about her? Sexual fantasies?"

"I haven't had time, but I will."

Silverman finally got to the all-compelling question. "You have this strange encounter with a beautiful woman half your age, your wife leaves you, your son is roaming the beach for the summer, and you think you are a failure in your profession and at life in general." He folded his arms across his chest and sighed. "So what's the problem?"

I sat up and turned to the doctor. "What's the *problem*?"

He ignored my insinuation. "The only real problem you face is your belief in being a failure. However, you see, you actually are not a failure. You only think you are a failure. You have simply placed the bar too high."

"But the bar is where the bar is. It's there for all my colleagues. They are all successful."

"How do you know they are all successful?"

"I can see their work. They publish, go to conferences, and generate money for the university through grants. I could go on. They are successful and I am not. All I've ever done is teach."

"Are you willing to lower the bar?"

"Why should I lower it for myself when they haven't lowered it for themselves?"

"The bar can be anywhere you wish it to be."

"I wish it to be up there."

"No, you don't. If you did, you would work toward that goal. You have stuck the bar up there because you think *others* believe it should be there for you. But that's not where you wish it to be at all."

The doctor was on track; I didn't want the bar up there. I didn't want a bar to jump over at all. I just wanted to live my life and teach my students. "You're right," I conceded. "So what do I do?"

"Accept the fact that you are not a professor who gets grants and publishes and goes to conferences. You never wished to be such a professor. Your dreams of success lie in teaching, which unfortunately is considered a third-rate time killer on many university campuses."

"I love my teaching."

"But you are wondering, is there more to life?"

"I don't know."

"You must have some idea."

"I do have some idea."

"Tell."

"It's too absurd."

"What's absurd is that you are paying me money not to talk. That's absurd."

"You'll laugh."

"So? I have a right to laugh, too. I'm only human."

"Magic," I said.

His eyes lit up. "Magic? Then magic it shall be," the doctor said. "Where shall you begin?"

"I can't."

"And why can't you?"

"Because no one knows about the magic, no one but you."

"But that's the beauty of it. You are a professor. Suddenly you are a magician. That's real magic."

"People will laugh. They will lose respect for me."

"Now we are at the crux of the matter. Respect? You don't mean respect. You mean acceptance. Approval. People won't accept you as a magician."

"Yes. That's right."

"Acceptance is highly overrated. Many of the geniuses of the world were not accepted. The masses don't readily accept individuality. That's why they are the masses. You wish to be an individual. A very frightening prospect. Once you become an individual, you stand out. You become a target."

"I don't want to be a target."

"But you *do*. Otherwise, you wouldn't have pulled that ridiculous bank caper that could have gotten you thirty-years-to-life. Your unconscious was at work."

"I was being a fool."

"You were being who you wish to be. Despite yourself."

"I can't afford to step out of my mediocre life. What will happen to me?"

"An interesting prospect."

"You are not being of much help, doctor."

"Nor are you."

"But *you* are supposed to help *me*."

"And I *am* helping you. You have already revealed to me your desire to be a magician. That's something you've never done. See, I, too, can perform magic."

"Revealing my secret was *my* decision."

"So it was. Well, if I can't take credit, I shall take lunch instead."

"Where do I go from here?"

"Try the deli on Traymore Street. They have wonderful marble rye and fabulous kosher dills."

"Doctor, I think you are incompetent."

"You've had a breakthrough today, my boy. Be thankful for that. Now, go and wow the world with your magic."

CHAPTER 6

THE "GROUPON"

On the drive home, I reviewed my session with Dr. Silverman. Although his manner was obnoxious, I admitted to myself that his logic held. I loved my teaching and I didn't wish to have to jump over the bar. I just wanted to be me, whoever that was.

Suddenly, I remembered the dean's mandate to attend the self-development group that afternoon and turned the Nissan in the direction of campus. Because traffic had backed up at the drawbridge, I was ten minutes late for the meeting. I found the group in the dean's conference room, seven occupied chairs assembled in a circle. Creating some commotion, I managed to drag a chair from an adjacent waiting room and push it in place. All eyes turned to me as I sat. They waited.

"Sorry I'm late," I said, blushing.

"We're not waiting for excuses," Pollard from chemistry said.

"Then what?"

"Why you are here."

I shrugged. "I was asked to attend."

They looked at each other. Then Finbar, chair of the English department, spoke up, his Irish brogue still very evident after forty years in the States. "Me too. Someone thinks I need this. That's the worst."

"I'm suppose to be a model," I insisted.

"A model of what? I saw you sneak out of that workshop. And I didn't see you return," Finbar said. "What are you modeling?"

"I haven't been feeling well," I said.

"And now?"

"Must I feel a hundred percent to be here?" I asked.

"You're being defensive, man. Loosen up. There are rules about confidentiality. You can say anything you wish, for we're all sworn to secrecy. No one can talk about what's said here. That's a pledge we all have to take. Like a secret society."

I couldn't imagine anything being said by any of them bearing repeating, so I felt confident I could take the oath. Raising my hand, I said, "I promise. Mums the word."

"This isn't to be taken lightly, Simon," Pickering of business and accounting said. "You wouldn't be here if someone didn't think you needed to be."

Was that it? Did my chairperson think I needed to develop myself more? Was this supposed to be an adjunct to my individual therapy or something concocted purely to squeeze more work from us? All these years, no one had troubled himself with my devotion to teaching. I had made my contributions in the field of publishing and volunteered for enough committees to avoid appearing irksome. After all, no one liked serving on committees. Maybe Brody Fine was right. Maybe the president's decision to leave had opened the door for the Board of Directors to prepare the community of scholars for a change of direction. New leadership. High profile publishing. Fresh dedication to academic pursuits. Grants to underwrite our salaries. All the activities I despised, the reason I'd remained at State where those demands were minimal, where my teaching emphasis had been ignored.

They continued to focus on me. "So?" Finbar said.

"So what?" I countered.

"If you don't know why you're here, why do you *think* you're here? That's where we began. We've all done that. Now it's your turn."

"I don't have to be here," I said.

"None of us has to be here," Axelrod said. "Not technically. But it was suggested we come. And a suggestion here at State is like a mandate someplace else. We figure with the rules about tenure changing and the cutback on funding, we want to protect our jobs. None of us has enough money saved to hang it up."

"And you notice," said Pollard, "we're all old farts who've been around a while. So you can figure they'd like to get rid of us so they can hire some younger blood."

"And replace our staggering salaries," Finbar quipped. "If I make much more, I may have to pay income tax."

"Times are changing, gentlemen," Eagerman said. "And we have to adapt or die out."

"Spoken like a true evolutionist," Finbar said

"Listen to what Eagerman said. That's it. We're all gentlemen," Pickering said.

I glanced around. True, an all male ensemble. Old gray beards hanging on. Perhaps we were unwittingly preparing to be led through the desert to determine who had the resources to survive.

Axelrod said, "That's their problem. Frankly, I don't give a shit why they want us to be here. But since we're here, I do have something I want to get off my chest. It's been troubling me for weeks and I can't get any sleep."

Finbar gestured with a generous sweep of his arm. "Be our guest." He looked about the group. "No objections, I take it?"

Axelrod didn't wait for an acknowledgement, but jumped right in. "It's all confidential, right?" A few mumbled acknowledgments. "Okay, here goes. I had sex with the president's wife. That's why he's leaving. A dozen times, maybe two dozen. I lost track. I feel like a heel, but I couldn't help myself." His story poured out as he studied the carpet at his feet. "She came to me for instruction on computers. Individual tutoring, she'd ask for. As I stood behind her, coaching her along with one keystroke after another, her hair smelled so fine, I couldn't control myself. I reached down and stroked her breasts, both at once. I figured if I was going to get fired and live out my life as a sexual offender, I might as well go for the double header. It was one of those ridiculous impulses. Now it seems so crazy. I have no idea why I did it, but I did it. Maybe I wanted to get into trouble, I don't know.

"Imagine my surprise when she grabbed my hands and began rubbing them over her breasts. Before I could stop her, she tore open her blouse and my hands were on her naked skin. I freaked out, thinking, 'I could deny touching her breasts with her clothes on, but with the open blouse, all she would have to do is run out of the office screaming'. She didn't. She stood and turned to me and put her arms around me and kissed me.

"We went to my place and we had sex the rest of the day. By evening, I was exhausted. Before she left, she made me promise we'd do it every Tuesday afternoon. We did for the entire semester. Then in early April, she came to me and said she'd told her husband. She knew he would be embarrassed and want to leave and that's what she wanted, to go to a larger campus near a city where she could enjoy the nightlife. It turns out she is a real swinger. She'd had enough of small towns and knew telling him about me would get him to move."

Axelrod exhaled a great sigh, seemingly depleted. The group remained silent for several minutes, stunned by the revelation. Then Finbar said, "Well, did you enjoy yourself?"

Axelrod shook his head. "That's not the point. I was such a fool. My stupid impulsive behavior could have gotten me an even twenty years. I just don't know what got into me."

Wesley, also biology, stroked his bearded chin thoughtfully. "Are you afraid you'll do it again?" he asked.

Axelrod brightened. "Yes, that's exactly it. I'm afraid I can't be trusted alone with women. Oh, I'd never try it with just anyone. I mean I would never accost a student or a child or anything like that. It's only mature women, women who seem like they can handle themselves, who would punch me out or scream or report me immediately."

"Is that what you are looking for?" Wesley continued. "Someone to turn you in?"

"Perhaps it is," Axelrod said. "Perhaps I can't handle my own sexual impulses since I no longer have an outlet."

"Since your wife's death," Wesley said.

Axelrod nodded. "Yes, since that."

"Have you considered therapy?" Pickering asked.

"Do you think I need it?"

"I think you definitely need it," Wesley said. "Get yourself a therapist today. And don't leave yourself alone with women you deem vulnerable. Call one of us, if you must." He surveyed the group to confirm we'd all be available to Axelrod in his time of crisis, as if by being fraternal brothers of this new secret society we were committed to this task.

"If I'm around," Pollard said weakly. "I mean, I'd do what I could. I'm not the sort to wrestle a man to the ground to keep him from his impulses, if you know what I mean."

"No one is asking that," Wesley said. "But if Axelrod called you, you would lend him a hand, wouldn't you?"

Hearing no confirmations, Axelrod glanced anxiously about the group of faces. "Someone must have had this sort of thing happen to them. I mean, an impulse to do something completely unacceptable that could land you in trouble. It can't be that unusual." His soulful expression moved me. "At least it would help to know that I'm not the only screwball on this planet with sudden urges."

I fought the desire to speak out, but my hand shot up anyway. "Yes, I've had the urge."

"To feel a woman's breasts?" Finbar asked.

I shook my head. "To rob a bank."

"Do you have money problems?"

"No, I don't have money problems. Mine was just an impulse, similar to Axelrod's. In fact, it happened the day of the workshop. When I left, that's what I did."

"You robbed a bank?"

"Not exactly. I handed a teller a silly note, one saying I wanted to make a withdrawal. Then took it back. I was about to tell her I just wanted fifty dollars for lunch, when she reached for the telephone. I panicked, thinking she was calling the police. When I ran, a young man followed. He caught up with me and turned out to be a former student whose father owns the bank. No one seemed to take my note seriously. The young man actually invited me to lunch. We were joined by the teller I gave the note to, who happens to be this former student's fiancée. I spent the rest of the day trying to figure out why I did what I did. I mean, I really didn't intend it to be a holdup note, but it could have been construed that way."

"And did you? Figure it out?"

They were all looking at me. "I'd rather not say."

"Well, you've already told the worst of it," Eagerman said. "All we want to know is whether you've figured anything out." He paused and cocked his head. "Unless you haven't told us the worst of it. Is there more?"

"There's more," I said. "But I'm not ready." How strange it was that I would relate the bizarre tale of my silly, pointless escapade in the bank, but couldn't reveal my secret passion, magic. Not even after confiding to my therapist.

The group members looked away, all nodding sagely as if the process, now fully born, had its own life, one that must be respected, if not fully understood.

Time passed, then Sawyer said, "I'll go next. Most of you know I'm in foreign languages. What I'm about to tell you has been on my mind for a long time. I've just never had a forum like this in which to discuss it. Like most of you, I had comprehensive examinations to take before I got my Ph.D. A Ph.D. in languages includes a translation, a long, complex one I was to do on my own in forty-eight hours. Well, I hired someone. A Russian who spoke and wrote six different languages. He did a terrific job. That was eighteen years ago. Last year, the son of a bitch contacted me. He had gambling debts he couldn't pay, serious ones. The kind you rack up through bookies who break knees."

"How much did he want?" Eagerman asked.

"Ten thousand dollars."

"What did you do?" Finbar asked.

"I told him to meet me one evening by the abandoned railroad trestle out toward the by-pass, that I'd have the money. I knew he was desperate and wouldn't take any precautions. He would have to trust me."

"I don't understand," Finbar said. "The question would be, could you trust him, not the other way around. After all, most times blackmail isn't something that happens just once. Blackmailers always come back for more, if they can angle a way." He glanced about the room as if this were common knowledge about blackmailers that anyone of us could easily confirm. "Isn't that true?"

Before anyone responded, Sawyer said, "My thoughts, exactly. That's why I killed him."

Silence. Now all eyes were on an imaginary focal point in the center of the carpet. When I finally looked up, Sawyer was smiling. Finbar took the lead. "Is it funny?" he asked.

Sawyer said, "Of course it's funny. I'm only joking. I made the story up. I've been in groups like this before and it's bullshit. People concoct all kinds of yarns just to get attention. Or to shock. I don't care what they do to me, I'm not coming to this weekly sob party. This is the stupidest thing they've ever come up with. I just couldn't leave without making my point."

"Which is?" said Finbar, who seemed to have emerged as our leader for the day, clearly not afraid to take on a member who belittled the honest efforts of the others.

"That this group therapy or whatever you want to call it is a lot of crap. You people may need it, but I certainly don't." With that, Sawyer stood and grabbed his briefcase. "I'm out of here."

We waited for the door to close behind him. Then Axelrod said, "He won't tell, will he?"

"About your transgression?" Pollard said.

"About my impulse," Axelrod replied. "The business with Angela is over. I just don't want him spreading rumors about my impulse for fear someone will deliberately tempt me, put me in harm's way."

"We'll keep an eye on you," Finbar said reassuringly. "If need be, we'll buddy up with you, won't we boys. You know, take turns hanging out at your office, screening your visitors, things like that."

The response was totally unenthusiastic. Finbar surveyed the group. "Where's your loyalty, for God's sake? This man needs us."

"What worries me more is whether Sawyer was kidding or not," Wesley said. "Maybe he did kill the Russian."

"Why would he admit it, then deny it?" Finbar said. "That makes no sense."

"He could have admitted it to ease his conscience. Then deny it so he didn't have to deal with the consequences."

"Frankly, I'm glad he's gone," Pickering said. "I never liked him. And I don't even know him."

"I think it's best we forget him and his story," Finbar said. "We can all agree right now that we never believed him, not for a minute. And we can just put it from our minds. What do you say?"

"I agree," Pollard said. Heads nodded all around, including my own. I had no desire to believe Sawyer, even if it was true.

Finbar glanced at the wall clock. "Well, gents, we've been at this a while. What do you say we call it a day and save the rest for our next meeting."

Wesley said, "Before we stop, have we dealt with Axelrod's problem sufficiently? I mean, he still has to handle his impulses. Plus, what about his relationship to President Packer. Does he go and apologize? I guess I'm asking, how do we know when we're done with something?"

"A cogent inquiry indeed," Finbar said. "We certainly can't fix every problem that comes up in an hour or two. And none of us can afford to do this non-stop. We have other commitments. So we'll just have to learn to table matters until we can meet again. I therefore propose we meet weekly at this same time throughout the summer. Those who can't make it because of other demands are excused from those sessions. When they are able to come to meetings, the ones who have been here more regularly will fill them in. What do you say?"

There was general agreement on Finbar's proposal. On the way out, Pickering, of accounting, took my arm and whispered, "I've done pretty well in the market, Alec. I could give you a loan at very low interest."

I thanked Pickering, assuring him it wasn't the money that drove me to my silly prank. What I still couldn't bring myself to do was admit the truth. As I drove home, I realized I also had made no mention that my wife of twenty-two years had left and filed for divorce.

CHAPTER 7

A REUNION VS. A CRUISE

Rodney left for the shore that morning. I spent my first night alone in the house. Pouring several strong drinks, I poked through a lukewarm TV dinner, and then dozed in front of the television until three in the morning. The seven-thirty a.m. telephone call from young Ryder came as a surprise.

"Mom and Dad are inviting you and Mrs. Simon to the beach house for the weekend. Won't you please come?"

Mrs. Simon was now out of the loop. But what else did I have to do? "I'm delighted," I said. *De*-lighted. And the Lioness?

"Penny will be there, too."

I arrived in the old Nissan, the rear seat still smelling of Homer-piss. The Ryder beach house along the Atlantic coast was magnificent. Iron gates provided a dike, separating the Ryder compound from the ebb and flow of the surrounding flotsam and jetsam. I was shown to my quarters, a charming bungalow adjacent to the main house, red tile roof with a white stucco exterior. A private hot tub, sheltered by rows of potted gardenias, stood just off a covered terrace.

Inside, pale walls reflected the late afternoon sunshine and contrasted with the mahogany ceiling panels. Richly textured rugs, strewn generously beneath the dark leather upholstered furniture, graced the carefully matched blocks of marble tile. A bathroom the size of my favorite seminar room on campus sported a sunken tub. In every room, pale light filtered through diffusers strung artfully across skylights. A small lap pool was situated just outside a set of French doors.

My tour guide, Philip, handed me the key to the liquor cabinet and demonstrated the remote control operation of most every device in the place. Then he advised me of the evening's schedule, cocktails at seven-thirty with dinner at eight.

Alone, I stepped to the balcony that overlooked the ocean. Late afternoon sunlight thrust bold shadows across the sand dunes. Eastward, pink plumes reflected off banks of cumulous clouds drifting out to sea, a quiet, peaceful scene. I breathed in the salty air and never heard the padding of naked feet ascending the marble staircase behind me. As I turned to fix a drink, a stemmed glass appeared, held by a slender hand, fingers gilded with rings.

"I thought perhaps you would like this after your long drive." A martini, two olives.

"How did you know?" I asked. Somehow, I knew she knew. Always, from the very beginning.

The Lioness smiled, violet eyes holding me transfixed. "You are very transparent, professor," she said. A shiver ascended my spine and I prepared myself for the inevitable confrontation.

"You remembered me," I said.

"How could I forget you?"

"Were you amazed?"

"Very much so."

"I'm embarrassed," I said.

"Please don't be," the Lioness replied, but with little beseeching in the word, *please*. I saw her now more completely, a beautiful woman, tall, long hair, sensuous features. She wore a summer dress, yellow with splashes of orange flowers, thin straps arched across her delicate shoulders. "Would you be so kind as to do something for me?" she asked.

I sip the martini. "Yes." My heart fluttered. Anything, I thought. My life.

She placed one naked foot on the lower edge of the wrought iron railing, arching her instep. The hem of her dress rode across her rounded knee. "My ankle is tender. Where I twisted it the other night. Do you believe it's serious? I mean, should I be seen?"

"Well, I'm not a doctor," I said. "Not a physician, I mean." Not a *real* doctor, that is. I stared into her violet eyes and felt the compelling power of her request. Bending, I reached forward with my free hand, gently touching her skin. A tingling sensation coursed through me as I moved my fingertips against the pulsing heat of her flesh.

"What do you think, Professor? Is it warm? I mean, warmer than it should be?"

I stood, drank, felt the chilled liquid hot against my throat, smelled the fragrance of her skin on my fingers melded with the aroma of gin. Her eyes sought mine. I waited, dumbstruck, unable to speak.

Her smile broadened. "Perhaps it simply needs time to heal," she said. She lowered her foot and leaned on the railing, gazing out to sea. "I had to seek you out. You understand that the others don't take me seriously. Jeffrey thinks of me as his little princess and the parents believe I'm only interested in the family fortune." She paused. "I'm not. Not really." A moment of candor? Or a setup?

"I do understand," I said, uncertain as to my predicament. Was the Lioness merely grazing in a nearby pasture or was she ready to pounce? I hadn't long to wait for the answer.

"Somehow I knew that," she said. With my simple admission, I had conceded an invitation for her to exercise the advantage she held from the moment I had swallowed those flames. I felt her teeth grip my jugular as she turned her lovely face toward me. "Do you like living dangerously, professor?"

"That wasn't my intention," I said. My throat dried.

"I don't believe that," she replied. "You knew exactly what you were doing when you gave me that note. You liked the excitement. I could see it in your eyes. I could smell your excitement. You were venturing from the safety of your ho-hum life. Your life is boring you, Professor, isn't it?" She smiled, her tone throaty. Was this flash of sensuality intended to coax a confession? Apparently. "Tell me the truth."

I considered Axelrod's admission. Was it simple boredom that fed his impulse? And mine? I replied, "I'm very sorry about the note. I apologize. I never intended to frighten you. I only wanted to perform a magic trick. And I fully intended to withdraw fifty dollars from my account for purchasing lunch that day."

"It was quite a magic trick," she said. "Very impressive." She glanced at the setting sun, then at me, reflected light illuminating her prey; the gazelle, in her grasp. The law of the jungle had prevailed, even in that civilized setting. Her mastery now assured, she could go about other matters, returning later to feast upon me at her leisure. I shuddered in anticipation of the danger in which I had placed myself. Clearly my peril went far beyond the risk of a misunderstanding; I had surrendered to a sensual domination from which I saw no way out.

The Lioness offered her arm. "Shall we go to dinner, Professor?"

The Ryder's had invited a dozen guests in all, several neighbors and friends, myself and the Lioness. As we drifted through dinner, a menu of lobster and crab, I watched the Lioness charm the group, attending to me with barely a glance. Waiting anxiously for her to turn her focus in my direction, I shivered on the few occasions her violet eyes washed over me. Our conspiracy had been set in motion.

As the evening slid by, I found I had drunk too much wine. Making my way to the little cottage by the sea, I slipped alone between the cool sheets of the king-sized bed and quickly fell into a dreamless sleep.

Morning arrived and the schedule proved to be a rigorous one for a fifties-something professor; snorkeling on a reef several miles offshore after breakfast, then catamaran races following lunch. Deliberately missing the snorkeling boat, I managed to avoid round one, but following a noonday meal of cold seafood salads, young Ryder insisted I serve as his partner in the catamaran races. We rode the swells out to sea until we capsized and were swept onto the high breakers, finally washing ashore. The boy begged for another run at it, so we pushed the heavy craft back into the surf, catching an outgoing trough that carried us to the others. The race appeared to have no rules other than to stay in it and ride the surging swells without drowning.

Late afternoon came and I finally begged for mercy. A kayaking neighbor, who had joined the sport, offered me a ride. Caught in the roaring onshore tide, we crashed into the beach and ground to a halt atop a mound of shells. I rolled out onto the rough sand and dragged myself to the guesthouse where I climbed into the hot tub, grateful to be on firm soil once again.

By cocktail time, I had seen the Lioness but twice, for short periods and with barely a sign of recognition from her. I began to wonder whether our interaction the previous afternoon had been an illusion, a fanciful encounter brought about by my frustrations and the stress of my impending divorce. Because she had offered virtually no acknowledgement of my existence through mid-morning Sunday, I attempted to reconstruct our secret conversation with the hope that I would come to my senses and abandon speculation that it had been pure fantasy, a daydream concocted to stimulate my dull and mediocre life. However, when the Lioness paid no attention to me during the remainder of the afternoon, I could only conclude that our liaison had been pure delusion and vowed to request a restorative drug from Silverman.

Finally, the time to leave. I said my *thank yous* and my *goodbyes.* Senior Ryder appeared friendly, but brusque, as he prepared, with some ritual, for the last cocktail hour of the weekend. Martha flashed her choppers. Young Ryder bopped here and there, thanking me with sugary profuseness for attending that weekend. The Lioness, however, made no appearance. Throwing my bag onto the floor of the Nissan, I maneuvered a turn into the driveway of the bungalow. As I glanced toward the main building, there she stood on the balcony, facing west, eyes flashing in the fiery rays of the late afternoon sun. She placed a bare foot onto the iron railing and raised her skirt to the edge of her knee. A chill rattled through me in the heat of the old car. I could have sat there and watched unto eternity, but young Ryder's lyrical voice calling from along the sandy road broke my trance.

"Professor," the young boy sang, bare feet pounding along the ridges left by tire tracks. "Mother wants you to have this for your dinner." Cold lobster. "Do come back, Professor," Young Ryder said. "Soon." He smiled sweetly.

When I glanced back at the balcony, the Lioness was no longer to be seen.

I reclined on Dr. Silverman's couch, the formerly comfortable pillow now lumpy from the pummeling of the previous patient who had punched his way through fourteen years of sibling rivalry.

"You're smitten," the doctor said as I finished my narration.

"For lack of a better word, I suppose."

"There is no better word. And she is half your age."

"Nearly."

"And she is the fiancée of a former student. A student who apparently worships you."

"I'm a cad."

"I didn't say that."

"But I am."

"Only if you think you are."

I looked at the doctor, twisting my neck in the process. "Why are you shrinks always so relativistic?" I said, snottily.

"Why are you patients always such absolutists?" he countered. "If you had the answers, you wouldn't be coming to me. Capece?"

My Jewish psychiatrist was now speaking Italian. "So what next?" I asked with a glare.

"I was about to ask you that."

"I have the entire summer ahead of me. In June, there is a high school reunion in Buffalo. I'm thinking of going."

"Yours?"

"Of course it's mine. Why would I go to another person's reunion?"

"Don't be touchy. I'm just asking. And my advice is, don't go. Period."

"Maybe I'll see someone who has done worse in life than I have."

"Suppose a lot of them have done better?"

"But maybe I only need to see one who has done worse."

"You're taking a chance."

"You mean it's possible everyone in my graduating class has done better than me?"

"I'm only saying it's a risk. Why don't you take a cruise instead?"

"I've never taken a cruise, but I'm sure I'd hate it."

"Then fly. Go to Bermuda. France. Ireland. Spain. Anywhere."

"Alone?"

"You're alone here."

No, I thought, *I have the Lioness.* But I couldn't bring myself to say it. Silverman was right and I didn't want him to be right. His smugness about my dilemma had grown irritating. Besides, if I agreed with him, I would be acknowledging my new reality, that indeed the Lioness had smote me. I was now a cliché. A fifty-something paunchy mediocre professor falling for a beautiful woman engaged to a former student. Absurd.

More denial. "Somehow I would feel more alone traveling."

"Tell me about being alone."

"What do you mean?"

"Have you felt alone your entire life?"

"I have *been* alone my entire life," I said, further annoyed.

"Even as a child?"

I thought about that. My childhood. Mother, skirting the edge of success as a professional dancer, a ballerina for a short time, then a second-class showgirl. My father, a professional driver of semi-trucks and trailers, a driver who would sit in the *professional drivers only* section at stops along the interstates, smoking and telling stories to anyone who would listen about the youth he never had. Somewhere in my teenage years, I recalled, he had insisted I accompany him on a cross-country haul, a man-making road trip, day after day of CB chatter in the oily cab, and drinking, and women with no place to go. I hadn't thought of that experience in many years.

"Yes," my voice said, taking control for me.

"Did you hate your father?"

"Why would I hate my father?"

"Many lonely children do."

"I didn't hate him. He just wasn't very good at being a father."

"Because he drove a truck?"

"How do you know he drove a truck?"

"Or was he a failure as a father because you were lonely?"

"This is going nowhere."

"Is that a metaphorical comment?"

"I'd like to be done," I said.

"Yes, I'm sure you would," Silverman replied.

I failed to tell Silverman about the group that had formed, the post-self-development group on campus that I had pledged to attend. Why? I couldn't say. Perhaps I thought he'd be jealous. More likely, I feared he would malign them and their amateurish efforts to understand their lives. Strange how in that hour and a half in the dean's conference room I had formed an alliance with six people I hardly knew. Perhaps I hoped we would protect one another from ourselves.

CHAPTER 8
YOU CAN RARELY GO HOME AGAIN

I skipped the next group meeting and attended the reunion instead. From a class of two hundred ninety, one hundred and seventy graduates, most with spouses, showed up. With the exception of a few glamorous trophy wives, and three younger gay partners, all were nearing their mid-fifties.

The *Motoramas*, a local seventies group, had been reassembled in some machine shop for the occasion, playing an array of uninspiring classics. Beneath the whirling mirrored glass ball reflecting sad colors of red and blue, fat people shuffled across the old gym floor, barely able to leave their drinks unattended long enough to involve both hands in the process of dancing. A cloud of Viagra vapor drifted above the crowd like cigarette smoke might have some thirty years earlier.

I watched from a safe distance, carefully avoiding eye contact with all the women and the one apparently gay man who had taken a fancy to me. The long line to the men's room discouraged me from drinking much of anything. As I hugged the sidelines, a man approached, holding forth his labeled lapel; *Donny Frenzel.* "Al, baby, how they hanging?" He shook my hand vigorously.

"Donny, what a delight," I lied.

He sidled next to me. "So, how's it going?"

"Just wonderfully," I exclaimed. "And with you?"

"Fantastic. Couldn't be better. I own a string of car dealerships here in Western New York that run themselves. Bought one of those fancy old castles on Le Bruin Road. Got other homes in Vail, Geneva, Switzerland, Madrid, and La Jolla, California. Married my twenty-year-old secretary last year. Her twin sister joins us for sex twice a week. Inherited ten million dollars from my dead ex-wife. I'm debt free. No in-laws. Have a private box for the Bills games. Rescued a child from a burning building and received a special commendation from the President of the United States at a State dinner. Had cocktails with the Pope last week after he said High Mass in my honor. My children are attending Harvard Medical School, except for the lawyers who graduated from Harvard Law School and are working on Wall Street. My dog shits gold bricks; my new secretary sat on a grapevine and now pisses champagne. I own fourteen Rolls Royce's, all chauffeur driven. And my doctor says I'm going to live to at least a hundred and thirty-two." He took a swig of scotch and turned toward me. "So, no kidding, how about you?"

"I teach."

He nodded. "A teacher, huh." Silence. A chuckle. "Couldn't get out of the classroom, huh?" Snigger. "I had the urge to be a teacher, kind of a pressure right in the pit of my stomach. Then I took a crap and it went away." Snigger, snigger.

"I find it highly rewarding," I retorted.

He exchanged the empty scotch glass as a waiter passed. "Say, you remember the time we stuffed old man Miller into the cardboard box and tied it to the railroad track?" He turned toward me so that I could see into his puffy eyes. "You remember? They never found out we did it, did they? You ever think we might still get caught? Christ, I do. I can't sleep most nights. I break out in the sweats about three o'clock every damn morning thinking about that, about how it was when the train came and crushed the old man. I think about the cops banging on the door, breaking in, dragging my ass off. I think about losing everything, the house, the dealerships, the twins, my Roll's, everything. You ever think about that?"

I stood dumbfounded. "No, I never do," I said.

He scrutinized my face. "Jesus Christ, no you wouldn't. It wasn't you that done it with me. It was Freddie Krozmac. Sorry, bud." He studied my nametag for a moment. "Alec Simon. Christ. What a screw-up. I thought you was someone else." He walked off.

As I looked after him, I thought about Mr. Miller, then wondered about the extent of my obligation. Should I report our conversation to the police? Tell Mr. Dorsey, the school counselor? Write an anonymous letter to the local paper? Send a belated card to Mr. Miller's family? Before I could make a decision, a buxom woman, looking vaguely familiar, took her place along the sidelines. She wore a pink taffeta dress with a purple bow in her hair. "Al, don't you remember me? We dated for three years in high school. Sally Siskin. With the braces and the pigtails? And the glasses? No tits. Remember?"

Sally Siskin. I did remember. Sally had definitely found her tits. "How nice to see you," I said, unable to take my eyes from her chest.

"Big, aren't they? I had a lot of help getting them. Six kids, to be exact, all sucking and tugging on these mammillary like there was no tomorrow. Then, of course, there's Jake, who insists I hover over him while he does pull-ups." She smiled, I presumed at the imagery. "So how's it going?"

"I'm a teacher."

"A teacher? Like old Mrs. O'Malley?" She pointed to our decrepit history teacher, one of the survivors in our little time capsule.

"College."

"So, you went for the big time. Jeez, I'm impressed. I hear college professors make a lot of money." She looked at me expectantly and I tried to get a gander at her ring finger. Was her reference to Jake in the past tense? Was she looking for a new trapeze artist?

"Just a silly rumor," I said. "A handful makes big money, like sports stars who score a lot of points. Most work for actor's wages."

She seemed clearly disappointed that I wasn't a superstar on the lecture circuit. I thought she was about to crow, 'better luck next time', but, instead, she said, "So, you married?"

"Happily. My wife couldn't make it. Her collection of stew went on tour this week and she's been traveling from one can signing to another."

"Jake and I have been divorced and remarried three times. Can you believe it?"

Somehow, I could.

My attention drifted to Donny Frenzel, talking to another alum, someone I didn't recognize in profile. His new audience nodded vigorously and I overheard muffled exclamations. Then, a startled declaration: "Alec Simon did what?"

The entire ballroom spun in their direction. The music stopped.

I wanted to secret myself within Sally Siskin's boobs. Too late. The unknown alum marched in my direction and stood before me in a posture of confrontation. Before I could formulate my denial, he said, "Ladies and Gentlemen, Alec Simon got a commendation from the President of the United States for saving a child from a burning building. Let's hear it for Al."

I protested by gesture, which only stirred the frenzy. Groping hands pulled me to the stage where a chant of 'speech' drowns out any attempt on my part to disavow myself of the lie. "It's not true," I screamed. "There has been a terrible mistake. Donny Frenzel made that up." As I looked frantically about the gym, Donny Frenzel was nowhere to be seen.

"I told you so," Dr. Silverman said. "A cruise is always better than a reunion. I'm thinking of writing an article on that very subject."

"I had to satisfy my curiosity."

"You're happy now?"

"No. I'm not happy. No one is honest at reunions. I couldn't tell who was really successful and who was faking it."

"Let's assume, for the sake of an argument, that they were all successful. All more successful than you."

"I would feel terrible."

"So then let's assume they are all failures, much worse than you. Terrible people. Bottom of the barrel. How do you feel?"

"I shouldn't, but I would feel good. Actually, I would feel great."

"Our conclusion is that you are willing to gauge your self-esteem totally through the eyes of people you went to school with over thirty years ago. This is the oversight board you have selected to determine whether you are a winner or a loser in life?"

"I don't think of it that way."

"How else can you think of it? My advice? Get rid of the gauge. Don't think in terms of winner or loser. Don't measure yourself at all. You just are. You exist. Just like other people exist. Everybody exists. And you choose to spend your time doing certain things. That's it."

"That's it?"

"That's it. People are neither better nor worse than you when it comes to self-esteem. They just are. *You* just are. It doesn't matter what you are doing. There is no formula for living. No one right way to do it."

"You're not saying there is no right and wrong, are you?"

"Of course not. Did you hear me say that? I'm saying there is no one way to live life that makes you a success or a failure. You just *are*. And you spend your time doing certain things and not others. Some things work out the way you want, and some don't. The judging part is all artificial."

"I don't buy it."

"Of course you don't, because you have to gauge yourself against someone else to feel like you are worthwhile. Let's take it down a notch. You think of yourself as a failure as a professor. There are people who would think they are a success just *becoming* a professor. I can picture someone completing his or her studies, taking a job as a professor, then retiring a year later and collecting shells along the beach. That person feels successful merely achieving a professorship. He or she goes around with a sack of shells introducing himself or herself as *professor*. It's not so crazy."

My shrink was a liberal philosopher, a sociologist and a demographer all wrapped into one screwball. At this rate, I would never feel better.

"I am not yet retired," I said, offering my best non sequitur for the occasion.

"Tell me about your mother," Silverman said, matching my non sequitur.

"What do you want to know?"

"She's deceased?"

"A year before my father."

"You loved her very much?"

"She was kind to me."

"Yet you felt lonely."

"She had a world of her own." I glanced at him. "The life span of a ballerina is short. You've got to make the most of those years." I could hear my mother speaking to my father.

"Your father was on the road and your mother was caught up with her career. And you were an only child."

"Did I tell you that? That I am an only child?" I became suddenly mystified at what I had told the doctor. Was he guessing? Was I forgetting?

"I am correct, am I not?" he said, more kindly than he had spoken to me since our sessions began.

"Yes," I said. "No brothers, no sisters."

"And so you felt alone and isolated from the world at a very early age."

"Yes," I agreed.

"Have you ever considered the pursuit of the study of history as a statement of your search for an identity?"

"I am a presumed expert in the study of European cultures, specifically the world wars. How does that compute?"

"What was the atmosphere like in your family growing up?"

"Warlike? Is that what you want me to say? That they were shooting at each other all the time?"

"From the mouths of *only* children comes the recognition of the truth. But, for now, my boy, our time is up."

CHAPTER 9

MY SEDUCTION

The Lioness left a message on my answering machine and a return telephone number directly to her lair. After downing two martinis, I placed the call.

"I missed you," she said.

Missed you, as in, 'I really missed you'? Or *missed you,* as in, 'I aimed the knife blade and you flinched'? Most likely, missed you, in that *I had to leave a message.* I nearly passed out at the first two possibilities. The hair on the back of my neck prickled.

Composure. "How thoughtful," I said. Thoughtful? What did I mean by that?

"Jeffrey and I are flying to Madrid on Thursday, the beginning of our two month holiday in Europe. I want to spend tomorrow with you."

Not, 'do you have plans?' Or, 'would you be available?' Of course, even if I had had plans, I would have cancelled them. Suppose I had a twin who needed a kidney transplant? I'd use a can opener on myself and send the organ by overnight delivery. Or a scheduled Pulitzer Prize award ceremony for my book, *Generating Historical Rumors: a working journal.* I'd telegram my regrets along with a copy of my acceptance speech and the kidney. Anything for a day with the Lioness.

"May I ask why?"

"One, because you're bored. Two, because you like me."

"Is it obvious?"

"Three, I have the tape."

"The tape?" The lump in my pants vanished, the one in my throat swelled, nearly choking me.

"The surveillance tape from the bank. I slipped it from the machine just after you left."

"But why?" *My god, man, why? So she can enslave you for the rest of your life before sending you to prison.*

"Why? Because you are insane, falsely modest, cute, and unhappy. You are also a bit of a snob, but I think that's because you are insecure. Most of all, you are on the verge."

"Of what?"

"I don't know. Perhaps unraveling. But I find those characteristics charming, and, I must admit, a little attractive."

"But I am a middle-aged, out of shape, lothario twice your age. Don't you find that disgusting? At least annoying?"

"Would you be happier if I were exactly your age?"

"Yes."

"Well, I'm not. And I have the tape."

"I'm a stereotype. We could never be seen together. You'd be the laughing stock."

"Being seen together is not in my plan. We'll drive to a friend's cabin north of the city." Pause. All I had to offer was my labored breathing. "I'll pick you up at ten a.m. Don't keep me waiting."

I could tell, she wasn't kidding about keeping her waiting.

That night, the temperature fell into the forties. I threw off the covers, turned down the heat, rolled and tossed, got up, read, watched the *Weather Channel*. Two a.m. Three a.m. Four a.m. Finally, I dozed.

Morning. Standing in front of the mirror, I studied myself. When I sucked in my paunch, I could conceal most of the flab beneath my flannel shirt, one Rodney had given me as a Christmas present several years earlier. I'd never worn it. After fussing with my clothing more than I could ever remember, I sat in the sunroom window, waiting, panting. The Lioness pulled up on time, dressed in jeans and a denim shirt, her blond hair pulled back. Her car was red.

"Did you drive by my house one night several weeks ago?" I asked, buckling up.

"I sometimes have trouble sleeping, but I generally don't go to such lengths."

"So you didn't."

"Are you disappointed?"

"Then it was my wife's new lover."

"Does that bother you?"

"Not as long as he walks Homer regularly."

"Because you like Homer?"

"I don't want Homer to give up in frustration and find his way back."

She laughed. First time. "You intrigue me."

"Why?"

"It's not what you want, that intrigues me. It's what you don't want. I know what you want."

"You think I want to have sex with you."

"Don't you?"

"I'm not sure."

"Are you afraid?"

"Yes."

"Of what?"

"Breaking the rule."

"What rule can there be for us?"

"The pleasure rule. If it feels good, it must be bad."

"Perhaps you should see a therapist."

"Great idea," I said. "I'll find one in the morning."

"Are you deeply disturbed?"

"I want to know what it is I *don't* want?"

"You don't want to get caught at life. So you hide. Except every now and then, something inside wishes to get out, on stage. That's why you came into my bank."

My bank. She was further along in her acquisition than I had thought. "Are you and Ryder Senior having an affair?" I asked.

"An affair? Let's say we have a partnership arrangement."

"With Jeffrey as the key?"

"I will sign a prenuptial agreement and treat young Jeffrey well and he won't stand in our way."

"But you *are* having sex with Ryder Senior?"

"That's a very possessive question. I don't like possessive questions."

"I have no reason to care if you are. I simply don't want to inadvertently let on to young Ryder."

"You are a very poor liar, Professor."

"Can we come to an agreement? I'll do anything you wish. You'll give me the tape. That's it."

"You'll do *anything* I wish?"

I swallowed hard. "Perhaps that's an overstatement of my earnestness."

"Do you like to please?"

Dr. Silverman: Acceptance is highly overrated. "Don't you?"

"Not particularly."

I thought of the tape in her clutches. Was there a statute of limitations on idiocy? Our society of the Twenty-First century sends errant children and screwballs to prison for two lifetimes. Pleading insanity for committing magic would get me sixty years in a tin can with a slop bucket. I'd be nearly a hundred and twenty when I got out. What would the job market for professors be by then? A tenure contract would be out of the question.

"Do you negotiate?" I asked.

"If the terms are to my liking."

"If you get what you want?" I said.

"I generally get what I want."

Clearly I was no match for the Lioness. So I shut up and let her lead the way.

We arrived at the cabin, a royal palace in cedar and redwood tucked above a gurgling brook. The Lioness knew her way around. She opened a bottle of Champagne and found cold chicken and fruit in the refrigerator. With Mozart playing in the background, we made our way down a set of granite steps to the brook, food and drink on trays. Once settled in, she slipped out of her clothing with ease and sat naked on an expansive rock in the sunshine. Holding her glass, I poured Champagne, averting my eyes from her nakedness.

"You may examine me," she said. "That's why I undressed. And it is more comfortable. I like the feel of the warm sun on my body and the cool granite next to my skin." She paused to sip. "Try it."

I fumbled awkwardly with my clothing, feeling all the joy of having to strip in the woods to take a dump. Forming a neat pile, I sat out of her direct line of vision and drank the fuzzy wine in two gulps. "Do you come here often?" My line.

"When I want to think, to get away. Or to seduce someone. I want to seduce you, Professor." She held her glass for me and I poured without getting up.

"Suppose I don't want to be seduced?" *Listen to me.*

"But you do. What you don't want is to take responsibility."

"I am truly sorry about the note, about the magic trick. I don't know what came over me." The stone was chilling my behind. I worried about my hemorrhoids.

"You said you would do anything?"

"Within reason."

"I have the tape."

"Anything."

"I liked Ryan's proposal."

"Ryan?"

"Ryan Ryder. Jeffrey's father. I have chosen ten of your former students and prepared dossiers. You are to seek each out and learn about them, about their lives, what they have or have not become. You have the summer in which to complete your assignment. Pace yourself. By the end of August, you are to be finished. Not sooner. Not later." She studied me.

"But how could you have found out all this information in such a short period of time?"

"Computers, Professor. I'm somewhat of a computer genius. One of several skills Mr. Ryder appreciates." She reached for my hand. "Intriguing, isn't it?"

"My seduction?"

"Exactly. And if you perform to my satisfaction, you may have the tape."

"If I'm thwarted? If I can't find them all or they don't cooperate?"

"Do your best, Professor. Just don't lose your focus and blow it. I can be very disagreeable when I'm frustrated in my intentions. And I have absolutely no qualms about handing that tape over to the authorities. It will be my word against yours. Attempted bank robbery is a very serious offense."

I decided on a bold move. "You know you would have a very hard time proving robbery was my intention. After all, I do have an account there."

"It's not unheard of. Besides, without your note, I can tell the authorities pretty much anything. And your behavior on that video says the rest." She smiled and stroked my hand. "Professor, you must know my real motive is to save you from yourself. You are bored with your life. You have hit a mid-life crisis. You need a life experience that has the potential to rejuvenate your thinking. After all, why not discover what has become of a few former students? Granted, it's a small sample. But it may open your eyes to the wonderful gift you have."

I was about to climb on the horns of a dilemma: Terrified, with a ten-week erection. The source of my anxiety had suddenly shifted; it became less about the Lioness accusing me of engineering a bank robbery. My new and very real fear, I realized, was facing myself and my own history.

⊷ ⊶

We finished lunch. The Lioness dressed as effortlessly as she had disrobed, while I lumbered about the rock, putting my legs in the wrong openings, tripping on my laces, missing a belt loop. Finally clothed, she led me along the path through the woods and to the car. As I climbed in, I spotted a stack of envelopes on the rear seat. We rode in silence to my little house. The Lioness pulled up, waited, engine running, while I scooped up the envelopes. My seduction now complete, I stood obediently at the driver's side window gazing into those opal eyes. "Where do I begin?" I asked, awkwardly, helplessly, childlike.

She flashed her cranberry smile. "What do you tell your students, Professor, when they ask that very question about an assignment?" She leaned forward and kissed me softly on the lips, then drove off.

CHAPTER 10

GENIUS OR WITCH?

S ilverman: "She's a genius."
"She's a witch. She already had my heart and soul, but that wasn't enough."

"You're complaining because she knows you better than you know yourself?"

"I'm complaining because of the price I'm paying for a very slight indiscretion," I said.

"You call holding up a bank *a slight indiscretion?* My boy, you are not an actor playing a part in *Going in Style.* It was fine for George Burns to lead a gang of over-the-hill bank robbers, but our justice system has tightened up on you professors. They have you in their sights, you bank-robbing professors, you workshop-skipping professors, you foreign film attending tree-huggers. They have your names and numbers."

"I rarely go to films of any kind. And I've only seen three foreign films in my entire lifetime," I said, defensively. "Furthermore, I don't hug trees."

"That's no excuse."

"You're of no help."

"What should I do?"

65

"That's my line."

"Accept your assignment like a man. Stop whimpering. Your Lioness has your best interests at heart. Just do her bidding. And, by the way, she very likely has no intention of turning that tape over to the authorities."

"So you say."

That was it. My shrink's best shot at unraveling the mystery of my life was a line from a shoe ad: *Just Do it!*

When I was nearly out the door, he called, "Do you hate your father?"

"I hadn't thought about it one way or the other."

"Well, think about it. Now go. And don't forget to call. I expect that much at the very least."

I borrowed against my retirement fund, sent half to Gloria as part of our divorce settlement, and emptied the balance of the savings account. The tired little house got rented to a visiting professor from Sri Lanka who had come to teach a ten-week course on *Semi-Conductors and the Railway Industry*. I never bothered to ask for details.

My chairperson released me from a promise I had made to survey our library's holdings on the U.S. Civil War. And I traded the Nissan for a two-year-old Taurus with a full spare tire. With my clothes packed, I decided to attend another group meeting before hitting the road.

"You skipped last week," Finbar said. "Is everything alright?"

Only Axelrod was missing and, of course, Sawyer. "I've been caught," I said.

"Caught? The police?"

"The teller. She has the security tape and has given me an assignment to complete over the summer."

"What on earth could it be?" Finbar asked, still clearly setting the pace for the group.

"I'd rather not say," I replied.

Pollard said, "Why not? What can be so terrible about it? Unless it's something sexual. Is it?" He hovered expectantly.

I thought, *What could I possibly fear in revealing the assignment?* My answer: *The obvious.* What do professors dread the most? Not getting grants? A disappointment, but we live through it. No raises? So, what else is new. What professors dread the most and are as reluctant to discuss as erectile dysfunction, is a poor student rating. By announcing my assignment, I would be raising concerns for all of us.

"Let's say it's a survey she wants me to do," I said coyly.

"A survey? Like market research?"

"Close, but not exactly."

Finbar took the lead again. "Simon, we don't have all day here. There are too many problems to discuss and not nearly enough time. If you are coming to our group, you are obliged to speak up. It's not fair to sit here and listen to the rest of us when you have matters that you throw out, and then refuse to discuss. You challenge our trust."

I gulped. "She wants me to survey former students to see what they thought of my classes."

Stunned silence. Finally, Eagerman said, "Good God. You'd be better off going to prison. The worst that could happen is getting beaten to death by a cellmate."

"This woman really hates you," Pollard said. "Did you do something to her besides try to rob the bank?"

"Hold on," Finbar said. "It's something we've all had to face at one time or another. Alec actually has a pretty decent reputation as a teacher. How bad can it be?"

"But those evaluations," Eagerman said, "are collected before the grades are given out. You have to be a real shit of a teacher to do poorly. These are *former* students no longer on campus. They can say what they damn well please with impunity."

If this discussion was intended to help me feel better, it failed miserably. "Please," I said, holding up my hand. "I have no choice but to carry it out. If I don't, she'll turn the tape over to the authorities. Even though I had no intention of robbing the bank, revealing my silly caper would shame me. My life would never be the same. I've got to go through with her assignment." I failed to add that the Lioness thought she was doing me a favor.

More silence accompanied by hangdog looks. Finally, Pollard said, "We wish you the best, Alec. If you need a hand, you can always call on us."

The others nodded in agreement. After an appropriate period of silence, a pause I interpreted as grieving my assignment, the group moved on and covered the death of Pickering's son in a kayaking accident some years earlier, Wesley's sixtieth birthday, and the dark day Finbar left Ireland with his parents, never to return. As the group disbanded for the day, each member stood by the door and somberly shook my hand. Evidently, my summer task loomed far more daunting emotionally than anything they could imagine.

When I returned to the house to pack the Taurus, Brody Fine was rocking in his bentwood chair, waiting. "So she finally ups and leaves you," he said, "and takes the mutt with her, I see."

"She's in love with another man," I said, standing dumbly by the open trunk.

"Can't blame her for that," he said. "Woman like Gloria has fine tastes. Not exactly what a man can provide for on a professor's salary, eh?"

I resisted the temptation to cross the lawn and punch Brody Fine in the face. Where did he get off assessing my capacity as a provider? Yet, my inner self admitted he was right. His greatest sin in the matter was his astute assessment of Gloria. She needed more than merely a man and a relationship. She needed 4,500 to 6,000 square feet of living space with a pool and cabana and a waterfall and a gardener and enough furniture for the interior to feel crowded. And who was I to get in her way? If life is one time around, then it was her right to have all that and more. Perhaps I admired her courage to go for what she really wanted from life.

"No offense intended," Brody Fine said, apparently correctly interpreting my silence as a sign of peevishness.

I couldn't take offense at the truth. I shook my head, as if intending to distract a pesky fly. "I should have seen it coming," I said, revealing my inadequacies to my neighbor in a way I could never do with my shrink. "Perhaps it's for the best." Two nice clichés. Maybe that will shut him up.

"You don't seem too broken up about it," Brody Fine suggested. "Looks like you're off for your summer vacation."

I fought the resurging urge to punch Brody Fine and settled for an alternative that I prayed would keep him up nights. "Your new neighbor is a person of another culture," I said. "From Sri Lanka. Rumor is, he's a cannibal. So I'd keep your doors and windows locked this summer. And be especially careful when you see him firing up the grill." I truly believed I was doing my renter a tremendous favor by spreading this rumor. Assessing the expression on my neighbor's face convinced me he would keep his distance.

As I pulled away from the little house on Brian Avenue, I acknowledged to myself that my life had altered dramatically in a matter of weeks. My wife had left me, my son was off seeking his fortune, and I had managed to indenture myself to a woman whose integrity was yet to be tested. If I had wanted novelty in my life, I was certainly getting it.

CHAPTER 11

WHO'S CRAZY, DOCTOR?

I drove westward toward the first stop on my summer travel schedule, Chicago-land. A day and a half later, I checked into a motel near a neighborhood of vintage brownstones.

Fulmer Hasbach had taken two history courses from me some fifteen years earlier, *Perspectives on World War II*, and *Post War Soviet Politics*. Hasbach stood out. He was tall, angular, sporting a distended belly that made him look very much like a bent lamppost with a balloon tied around its middle. Hasbach had a habit of conversing audibly with himself during class, correcting his interpretations of the material as I lectured, reassuring himself that he could learn all the facts necessary to complete a study unit, and occasionally formulating political observations and offering them as astute commentary.

At first I had found the rumbling and mumbling a distraction. He and I spoke several times about his obsession, but to no avail. After a while, I noticed the other students were not only unruffled by his idiosyncratic babble, they seemed to remain more focused, as if his monologue served as counterpoint to my lecturing.

Listening more carefully, I realized that his utterances traced my thoughts like a sketch on paper. Hasbach served as a barometer.

When he got lost, the others were not far behind. I'd stop, back up and re-route them until we were all literally on the same page.

History, however, was not Hasbach's forte. He wanted to be a writer more than anything else in life. That afternoon, I located him in a brownstone attic atop a row house not far from the motel. "Professor Simon?" he said, incredulous as I stood in his doorway. Standing before him unannounced, it occurred to me that my former students might consider me a stalker at best; and at worst, a maniac recently escaped from the State University Asylum.

"Fulmer. Surprised, aren't you?"

"How did you find me?"

"Computers," I said. "Amazing, aren't they?"

"I read your e-mail just yesterday. But I never expected you would show up so soon."

"My e-mail?" *The Lioness, of course.* "Is this a bad time?"

"Not at all. Let me clear a place."

Six computer screens glowed in the sprawling one room attic studio strewn with papers. A corner of the room served as a kitchen, barely discernible beneath piles of dishes and a collection of outdated fruit, complete with orbiting flies.

"Living here long?" I asked.

"Most of my life. I was born in this room. My parents were poor and just starting out. That's why I came back here to write. I thought this place would offer inspiration."

"And has it?"

"I have some wonderful plots. Come sit. I was actually just getting them organized. Of course, some are further along than others. You would like to hear them, wouldn't you?"

"Absolutely." Did I have a choice?

He thumbed through pages of a dog-eared journal. "These are a few of my short plots, not too well developed yet, but with real potential. Let's see what you think. I'm a little nervous, Professor, so bear with me."

He began. "A doctor came home and checked the refrigerator only to find that the liver he had intended to transplant that morning was still in its original paper carton, but a bunch of radishes was missing. He called the hospital and discovered that the patient was doing well but had taken a nurse hostage and was demanding a quart of ranch dressing." Hasbach looked at me, large brown eyes, like two plums, staring. "Not bad, eh?"

"Original," I said. I watched for a playful smile to contour his thin, rubber band lips. Just the large, plum eyes. No grin. "Are there more?" I asked, holding my breath.

"Of course." He turned a page.

I couldn't handle the plum-eyed look. Glancing down, I inspected my fingernails as if there were tiny messages scrolling across them.

He cleared his throat. "A neurosurgeon plans to transplant the brain of a chimp into the skull of a human being." He paused and glanced up from his notebook. "I went through a medical phase when I had my appendix out." Back to his scribbles. "The human being had been dead and frozen for six months, but the surgeon, Dr. Marcus Farkas, had overcome challenges before. He has all in readiness when he realizes for the first time that he has forgotten the formula for pi*r squared. His staff search high and low, finally locating the r-squared, but are unable to find pi. Dr. Farkas is not about to take, 'We can't find pi', for an answer. He is not sure what he *is* willing to take for an answer and contacts the producers of *Jeopardy*. His call is delayed by heavy volume and arrives at the studio twenty-two minutes later, during the introductions to *Wheel of Fortune*. He watches as Helen, from Topeka, spins the wheel, which stops on an E. He decides to add the E to the pi and accepts that as pie." He paused and glanced up. "My timelines here may be off. Perhaps *Wheel of Fortune* comes before *Jeopardy*."

Continuing, he said, "The operation is a success, although the chimp dies. The entire medical community hails Dr. Farkas as behind his time, someone not razzle-dazzled by the trappings of modern medical technology. Dr. Farkas applies for the Nobel Peace Prize on the grounds that, other than the death of the chimp, he has made no trouble at all. He is turned down, however, because his application has insufficient postage.

"Now an embittered old man, Dr. Farkas wills his liver to medical science. After Farkas's death, the chief surgeon is amazed when, upon cutting open the Farkas carcass, she finds a bunch of radishes where his liver should be. The radishes are placed in a pickling jar and delivered to the Medical Academy luncheon three weeks later. Some diners complained; but most thought the pickling time was just about right."

I glanced about the kitchen for a bottle of medication. Perhaps he hadn't the money to keep his prescription filled. I wanted to ask, but I also didn't wish to offend Hasbach by my inquiry, not at least until I was closer to the door.

"There are more," he said. "May I fix you a cup of tea?"

Relief. "That would be great, just great," I said, trying to sound collegial, as if we were two college chums taking a break from a tough cram session. Perhaps I'd prowl through the cupboards looking for his medications or maybe even coax the name of his psychiatrist from him. "So, have you explored other career options, Fulmer, since leaving school?" I shadowed him to one corner of the kitchen as he searched for clean china. He settled on two coffee-stained Styrofoam cups. The teabags were to be recycled as well.

Water heated in a rusty kettle as Fulmer leaned against the counter, a balding straw with a bulge. "Funny you should ask, Professor. I've never wanted to do anything but write. And that's what I'm doing. Isn't that splendid?"

"Splendid," I said. No meds. "Have you submitted any of these pieces for review?"

"As you can hear, these particular plots are not quite ready. But I'm getting there. How about one more." Another page flipped.

I was at a loss. The kettle boiled and I rose and poured hot water over two stained teabags. Handing him a cup, I said, "You must have given a great deal of thought to these plots."

Fulmer reached for a fresh notebook and found a marker. "I have, Professor, I have." The teabag levitated in the Styrofoam cup like a floater in the river.

I placed my cup on the edge of the sink. "Have you ever thought of therapy?"

"I have. But I was very disappointed with the plot I came up with, so I canned it."

I walked to a window and looked down onto the street, surveying the row of neat townhouses, each graced with a tree in the early stages of a late Chicago spring bloom. "Certain people are cut out to be writers," I said, not looking back. A cat, hanging tightly to a tree branch just outside the window, glared at me. "Some may find, however, it's best to go on to other vocations."

"Yes," Fulmer said. "How sad."

After a few moments of silence, I decided that sharing my current dilemma with Hasbach could do little harm. "Fulmer," I began, "I'd like to tell you my story. My wife left me. A teller at a bank I tried to rob back home is blackmailing me. The teller retrieved the security camera tape and has threatened to expose me if I don't visit ten of my former students." I turned to him and flashed a smile. "That's really why I'm here."

"Professor, you may have plots of your own, but please don't pilfer mine, if that's why you've come. What I don't like is competition. I can be very insecure about my writing."

"Fulmer, please. It's nothing like that. This is my real story. Why I'm here. I just got a divorce. My son is all grown up and about to leave home. The Lioness has given me ten weeks. I'm doing the best I can with this."

"My parents got a divorce. My mother ran off with a dwarf." His plum eyes rolled around the room. "I cried for days."

I sighed. "Do you have more plots?"

"Will you promise not to steal them from me?"

"How could I not promise?"

"Very well." He shuffled to the middle of his journal.

I looked the cup of saggy water straight in the eye and sipped. The brew tasted like old socks.

Suddenly I felt overwhelmed and blurted out, "Fulmer, this is crazy." Fulmer looked alarmed. "Not your story plots. I mean, that I'm here." Insanity is not supposed to be catching, but as I heard my own voice, and watched Fulmer's jaw tighten and his plum eyes rotate, I wasn't so sure.

"Maybe you *are* here because of my stories," he said. "You are the first person I've shared these plots with. Now you know more about my true life than anyone in the world."

That wouldn't be difficult, I decided. "I think I'm suppose to figure this out on my own. May I ask; what did you think of my courses?"

"English?"

"History."

"Yes, history. They were fine, very fine."

"Did anything I say or do influence your life?"

"I chose English. Is that the sort of thing you mean?"

"Exactly." Thank God. English. You are an ambulatory schizophrenic and are safely tucked away writing word salad. "Of course. English."

The telephone rang. Fulmer looked bewildered. "It's here somewhere." He went on a frantic search, finally locating his remote phone hidden in the cupboard beneath the sink. "Yes?" he said into the receiver.

I could hear an occasional muffled exclamation at the other end. Hopefully it was his deceased mother giving him instructions for the day. I eyed the door, aware that Fulmer stood between safe-ty and me. Glancing at a carving knife laying within his reach on the countertop, I considered taking a chance and making a swift, silent exit. In retrospect, I felt fortunate I had never insisted that he quit mumbling in class all together. My comments to him to cease and desist had merely been recommendations.

Fulmer hung up. "My publisher." He shuffled to one corner of the room and pried open a warped closet door. From within, he retrieved a manuscript box, neatly taped and addressed. "I was two weeks early on this one. I'll take it to the post office in the morning."

"You have a publisher? What on earth for? What are they publishing?"

"The Tabby Gunrattle Mysteries. Ever heard of them?"

"They are on best seller lists every six months. You write those?"

Fulmer nodded. "Number thirty-four." He held the box forth with one hand, as if it were an offering. "But I can't tell you the plot, not until it's published. That's an agreement I have with my editor. I can never talk about the plots to anyone, not until the books hit the bookstores."

"But the Gunrattle Mysteries are written by Zack Henley. You're not Zack Henley."

"In the flesh." He loosened his grip on the manuscript and placed it on the table. "How about one more plot before you go, Professor? Now this one will definitely grab your imagination." This one he apparently knew from memory. No shuffling through the journal.

Stunned by Fulmer's revelation, I barely listened to him mum-bling about a high wire artist who missed his footing. He rambled for several minutes, and then brushed a tear from his eye.

"It's very touching, isn't it? Vetch and Vang. How often I think of them."

"How is it possible?" I asked aloud.

"Yes. It is incredible, isn't it? And to think, they are lovers and the best of friends," he said. "That says it all."

CHAPTER 12
ADORATION BECOMES ME

I sat stunned behind the wheel of the Taurus as a patrol car pulled up behind me, lights flashing. The uniformed officer stepped to the window. "You forget to pay your rent, or something, buddy? No sleeping in your vehicle."

I glanced at my watch. "Is it really five o'clock?"

"From time to time, we have to chase stalkers from Zack Henley's place. Someone reported you coming out of there and sitting for a long time, so we thought maybe you were one. Are you?"

"A stalker? No, I have no intention of stalking Fulmer. I mean, Zack. I was just paying a visit to a former student. You see, officer, I've been assigned…." I stopped. Go ahead; mention the attempted bank robbery, even though it was only a prank. Describe meeting the Lioness and falling totally out of your mind. Blurt out your therapist's pessimistic view of your future. Detail an account of your countrywide tour to interview formers students for no known purpose other than self-humiliation.

I gazed at the policeman's tough, unrelenting expression.

"You been assigned what, mister?"

"Actually, I'm a university professor looking for historical markers. I may have found one."

"Just get it moving. And if I catch you here again, you're going downtown."

As I drove away, I asked the inevitable question: *What* was *I doing?* What grand wisdom did the Lioness think she could expect me to arrive at by completing this absurd assignment? What precious lesson was I to learn? That life didn't have to be boring? That I'd *chosen* my lifestyle, and I could choose something different? Okay, I had fallen into a twenty-some year rut like millions of other people and have made no concerted effort to extricate myself. What was wrong with that? They were *my* years.

Then, again, why not crisscross the country? I had nothing better to do with my summer. It might be entertaining to discover what former students were doing, Fulmer Hasbach aside. They couldn't all be like him. And, although I resented the grip the Lioness had on me, she *was* beautiful and I had been *smitten.* Seduced, and at a terrible price. She wanted to snatch me from my rut and, like a stubborn child, I didn't wish to give it up. On the other hand, would prison be an acceptable alternative? Quiet days and nights reading all the books I'd promised myself to read. Expanding my magic repertory, perfecting my disappearing rabbit trick. Perhaps I'd even teach someone to read so that, if he ever got out, he could find the men's room without having to divine whether the modernistic design etched on the door was wearing a skirt or just baggy culottes. I might find solace in the solitary routine, alone with my thoughts and my fantasies.

A horn blast shook me. Crime of the Century: I had sat immobilized through an entire rotation of traffic lights. I checked the door locks. What I'd prefer was to not be dragged into the street by a group of angry motorists and pummeled into semi-consciousness.

The schedule that the Lioness set forth had me backtracking from Chicago to Cincinnati. I could discern no reason for the abrupt about face and considered poking through the carefully sequenced envelops to arrange my own itinerary. How could she know if I followed her schedule? She probably couldn't. That was, unless she was in touch with all the subjects on the list. She *had* e-mailed Hasbach, impersonating me. What would prevent her from checking in with each and every former student, foreshadowing my visit, even conducting a follow-up query? That was well within her powers, even as she traveled throughout Europe: A great method of monitoring my behavior, insuring that I didn't blow-off the project.

I was taking no chances. If I were to please the Lioness, whatever the rewards, I'd stick to the plan. Cincinnati it was.

I arrived in Cincinnati the next evening and checked into a Motel 6. Finding Sara McCovey on the large main campus of the University of Cincinnati was no small feat. Impersonating a visiting professor, I finally convinced a student working in the scheduling office on the evening shift to let me glimpse the assignment calendar for the week. Sara clerked at the library from 8 a.m. till 10 a.m. each weekday morning.

Barely twenty-four years old, Sara graduated from State U. and, after a short stint teaching senior high history, enrolled for graduate work at UC. I remembered Sara well. A slightly built brown-haired young woman with a shy smile. And smart, all 'A's'.

Rolling out of bed late after a restless night, I grabbed a cup of coffee in the motel lobby and arrived at the campus visitor's center where I signed for a pass. I circled the parking area for nearly twenty minutes before finally edging out a car driven by a young man intimidated by my overbearing glare. The library was across campus and, even as I hustled, it was after ten a.m. when I arrived.

As I approached the desk, I saw Sara on the job, advising a young woman, apparently confused about her library assignment. It occurred to me, as I motorized my smile that, once again, I had absolutely no rationale for my sudden appearance. In the seconds I had to consider my approach, I conceived of a grand story about a nationwide contest for middle-aged college professors. That was it. I had won a spot at the top, Level One of the Big Pyramid, and now I was going for broke, doing a survey of select former students to be eligible for the grand prize, a set of gold-embossed encyclopedias. Encyclopedias? Who owned encyclopedias? Too mundane, even for a mediocre professor. How about a trip? Southeastern Russia? The Arctic? Madagascar? A Colombian drug ranch?

But watching Sara's enthusiasm as she advised this young student about selections on her reading list, I saw in those eyes a trust that had never been betrayed. I'd be the first. Her former history professor having driven hundreds of miles only to deliver a lie.

Sara directed her protégé to the stacks, and as she looked up, recognition glowed in her expression. Circling her desk, she strode toward me with the confidence of the young adult never wounded in battle, her slender hand extended. "What a marvelous surprise, Professor Simon," she said, her voice more mature than I had remembered. "What brings you here?"

Our hands met. I smiled. We pumped twice, a third time, and I hung on, because once I let go, I would have to answer her question. "How nice to see you again, Sara." *Let go*, I admonished myself. *Damn it, let go!*

Sara looked deep into my eyes and I could see her formulate her own version of the story. Stalker! *State U. professor stalking former students*. Banner headline. What would Gloria think? What I suspect she had always thought. I was a nut about to pop my shell. She would tell Ackerman Fink, her paramour (I discovered his identity when a copy of an email to him inadvertently was sent to my email address), in the presence of Homer, the fat-assed dog, that she had escaped my clutches *just in the nick of time* (a phrase she loved). She'd tell Ackerman how she had suspected for years that I had been on the verge of a nervous breakdown, how I slipped out to the garage in the middle of the night and performed rituals with rabbits and pigeons, how I read voraciously, unnecessarily. Those would be my ultimate crimes. Not attempted bank robbery. But stalking, conspiracy to make animals disappear, and unnecessary reading.

"I'm off duty now. Would you join me for coffee, Professor?"

"Yes, coffee," I said, as if the drink has just been removed from the list of controlled substances. "What a wonderful idea." Creative, original, deserving of an 'A'.

We crossed campus, Sara nodding and smiling at younger students and an occasional professor whom she addressed by name. When we arrived at the student union, she directed me to a table in a quiet dining area and went for coffee.

A moment later, my time was up. We sat across from one another, steaming coffee vapors swirling, she smiling, me bobbing and weaving.

"So," she said. The ball was in my court.

"I suppose you are wondering how I just happened to pop in, aren't you?"

"I presume you're teaching a summer course here? How wonderful. I'll have to enroll."

"No," I said. "I mean, no course. Actually, I came to see *you*." Oh, boy. Now what? I came to see *you*. That's great.

You see, I have a collection of your striped cotton panties in my briefcase, ones I stole from your laundry basket while you were at State, and I want to return them. Clear my conscience, negotiate a surrender. The panties for an absolved conscience.

I looked across the table at this bewildered young woman. "I'm doing a follow up on certain students, Sara. Strange as it may seem, I have reached a point in my life where I want to find out if I've made a difference." *See, that wasn't too difficult, was it?* "After you teach so many classes, it's easy to lose track of your own effectiveness." *Please tell me you are not going to call the police. I wouldn't blame you, but don't. Just tell me to bug off and that will be enough for the Lioness.*

"How wonderful, Professor Simon. You can't imagine how wonderful. I'm a history major, all thanks to you, and one of your biggest fans. And to think you came all this way to see whether you had an impact on my life. Of course you did, silly." She stood, came around the table and threw her arms around my neck. "This is truly wonderful."

I thought of the effusive young Jeffrey Ryder and suddenly imagined the two of them teamed up, forming a network of Simon groupies, establishing a web page, annual hootenannies, badges, contests, tee-shirts, hand-painted silk ties with my silhouette, regional picnics, children called Simon, grandchildren, candlelight vigils, memorial services, renaming of streets across the nation, *Simon Way.* "How is this truly wonderful?" I asked.

"Because I want to be a professor just like you. And it is your teaching that inspired me."

Places of worship are renamed, St. Simon Church of the Vital Professor, Simon Methodist Council, Temple Beth Simon, Church of the Good Simon, The Universal Center for Thought and Meditation ala Simon.

"Me?"

"Don't be modest, Professor. You know you have had a great deal of impact on all your students. You were one of the few professors who put teaching first. But tell me, how did you decide to do this survey now? I mean, I'm about to propose my dissertation topic and am looking for an outside committee member. You will be perfect, if you will only do it. Please?" Sara jumped up and down like a twelve year old, pleading her case, her shallow breasts scarcely rippling the front of her peasant blouse.

"Serve on your committee? Yes, of course. Why not?"

As long as they pull the staples and paperclips, I'll be able to read your proposal in prison.

"Super," she squealed. "I can't tell you how pleased this makes me. Wait till I tell Professor Warren, my chair. She'll be elated. She's read your books and quotes frequently from your papers.

Once she told the class that, while you were not prolific in your writing, you produced such quality that it more than made up for your lack of quantity."

"Really." *How many streets could be named* Simon *in one community?* Simon Way *was taken.* Simon Boulevard. Simon Avenue. Simon Street. Simon Court. Simon Circle. *Perhaps,* Interstate Alec Simon. *Would that run north and south, or east and west?*

"I'll get you a copy of my proposal before you leave. But you can't leave yet. You came to see *me*." She paused, mind churning. "I've got class at two. But I'm free after that and all evening." She smiled coquettishly. "We could have dinner at my place. How would you like that, Professor?" Her intonation was all too obvious.

"Sara," I said, "thank you. But I don't think that would be possible. You see I'm on a timetable of sorts. Actually, I'm really following an agenda that has been set up for me. I must stick to it."

"I thought you were visiting former students to study the impact of your teaching on our lives. If you leave now, how can you hear all I have to say?"

"That's true. But I've enlisted the help of someone to organize my travels," I said, sidestepping her logical query. "Someone objective who chose the particular students I will visit. I thought that would be more scientific. Don't you agree?"

The young and inexperienced are often without guile. Her expression turned from disappointment to thoughtfulness. "I suppose. Yes, that would make more sense. Otherwise, you might unconsciously only visit students you believed would have nice things to say about you." Pause. "Like me." Wide grin.

"You're very sweet, Sara. If I had a daughter, I'd want her to be just like you." *Except for the potential of incest.*

"Really, Professor. Oh, can't you stay even for a little while?"

"Sadly, I must move on. But have your committee chair write me a letter about serving. I'll run it by my department head and give you an answer as soon as I can."

I stood, extending my hand. We pumped once. I left her there, a bobbysoxer with a crush and hoped to make it to the exit before she came to her senses and realized the absurdity of my abrupt entrance and exit.

CHAPTER 13

DESPERATION

Silverman sounded surprised by my call, but rearranged his schedule to see me the following afternoon.

"Let me get this straight. You bought an airline ticket, left your car at the Cincinnati airport, and flew back here just to see me?"

"I am desperate," I said.

"Not very flattering."

"You know what I mean." I told him about my first two encounters with former students, crazy Fulmer Hasbach, aka Zack Henley, and Sara McCovey, co-president of my fan club.

"Three for three."

"Meaning?"

"You obviously have influenced at least three students, albeit in different ways."

"That counts?"

"It all counts. What doesn't count is your *dis*-count. You can't brush under the table twenty-some years of influencing developing minds."

"Twenty-two. I'm responsible?"

"If not you, who?"

"I have a tiger by the tail."

"A Lioness. Unfortunately, you have approached this assignment begrudgingly. Take matters in stride. Be curious. Instead of viewing this as a penance to pay for your redemption, go forth truly interested in the fate of your flock. Though your influence may have been slight for some, profound for others, you are a part of each of their lives like a grain of sand in an oyster. Whether they know it or not, you are a trace element in all that they do, perhaps an irritation in all that they are or will become. Even your mediocre and boring lectures, your pointless assignments, your lazy, indolent grading habits, have guided them to who they are today. Rejoice…."

I thought: *What you will never become, Dr. Silverman, is a spiritual leader in a Simon community of fans.* "In other words," I said, "I should stop whining. Whining has become a common theme in my life."

"I am but the messenger," he said with a shrug of innocence.

In some societies, they shoot the messenger. I wish I could remember exactly where. "Doctor, I must say, you have expanded my faith in the value of positive thinking," I said with sarcasm.

"That's the least I can do, my boy. Now, we must have a plan. Who is next on your list?"

I had anticipated the question and jotted down a name. "Dr. Cecil Worksworth."

"A doctor? See? By your own formula, your stock rises."

"Evaluating my self worth in terms of my progeny?"

"Your call, not mine. I tried to tell you, but who listens to me?"

I wondered that myself.

"Okay, so you're saying maybe I can approach this visit with less trepidation."

"I didn't say that. Who knows what the good doctor thinks of you. Maybe he remembers you as a squalid, dirty old man."

"But I've never been a squalid, dirty old man."

"No one thinks they are a squalid, dirty old man."

"Besides, what's wrong with a squalid, dirty old man? We all get old, and some people can't care for themselves as well as they might wish." I felt indignant, suddenly defensive of the old, the dirty, but especially the squalid.

"If I had known you were such a liberal, I would have referred your case to someone else. I have too many liberals on my client list. They confuse my thinking with all their claptrap about the poor and underprivileged of the world. I say, let them eat *Twinkies*."

"Doctor, I have studied virtually no psychology. But I have read about paradoxical intention. Could it be that your therapeutic strategy with me is just that, to set me up?"

Silverman smiled; not a smile I could see, but one to be heard in his tone. "Remember, my boy, a good magician never reveals his tricks."

Dr. Cecil Worksworth practiced medicine at a trauma center in San Diego. After the flight to pick up the Taurus, and the three-day drive west, I took a full day to rest and recover. I had never been to San Diego in my mediocre life and was pleasantly surprised by the wonderful climate and the mesmerizing coastline.

A tourist map hyped the delights of La Jolla, an up-up-scale community north of the city. I paid a visit. What beauty. What charm. Winding streets with elegant shops and galleries. Expensive, yet unpretentious. Unlike Los Angeles, where people were busy making it and making the most of showing it, those in La Jolla had arrived. Lots of expensive blue jeans and gold filigree jackets and jewelry. Women in embroidered vests and high-end walking shoes. Understated vehicles in the form of twenty-year-old Mercedes that purred along the road like jeweled watch movements. A community that worked for everyone who could afford to live there.

I discovered quickly that, while the streets and avenues of La Jolla and the hills beyond were inviting, sooner or later everyone was drawn to the sea. A small, unpretentious park nestled along the Pacific Ocean, stretching from a seal refuge aptly named *Seal Beach*, to a current-strewn mile-wide bite in the coastline called

The Cove, a favorite swimming hole for the courageous and strong of heart.

Watching rugged octogenarians swim a mile across *The Cove* in goggles and wetsuits stirred my parallel dreads; exercise and water. In talking to locals, I discovered the swim was at least a thrice-weekly ritual for many. They gathered in small groups to make the crossing, balding pates, kinky white curls, death defying in attitude. Swim buddies coated one another in sunscreen, adjusted goggle straps, and cued their readiness with thumbs-up signs. Even in mid-summer, some donned wetsuits to ward off cool waters of the Pacific.

As I stood by the railing watching the gathering of swimmers on the shallow sand beach below, a woman glanced in my direction, apparently aware of the intrigue the scene held for me. She introduced herself and invited me to join in the sport the following morning. While claiming to be eighty-eight, she had the appearance of a young sixty year old. I thanked her profusely, and then explained my plan to be in the trauma center interviewing a former student. She smiled slyly and said, "You youngsters have so little mettle. That's the poorest excuse I've heard in decades. When I was your age, I had both my kidneys removed. Donated them to twins who were about to be separated at the spine. I've been on dialysis ever since. Swam San Francisco Bay two weeks after the surgery." She padded soft-soled in her wet suit to the edge of the cove and, like a curvaceous little otter, slipped into the briny water to begin the swim. The others were a dozen strokes ahead of her, but she quickly caught up, and then passed. I watched as she reached the half-mile marker. She clung to the float for a moment or two, and then began the return trip. Before she hit the shoreline, I scampered to my car. The irony of our interaction was that I suddenly preferred my inadequacies to glare in a world I understood rather than one into which she might have drawn me. My cowardice apparently knew no bounds.

CHAPTER 14
I'M NOT A *REAL* DOCTOR

My nights on the road had become restless, perhaps from the lack of a normal routine, or the consumption of more comfort foods than I would ordinarily take in. As a result, I was consuming more coffee in the morning and had developed an artificial hyper-vigilance that verged on hysteria. As I pulled into the parking lot at the trauma center, I took several deep breaths to calm myself before the electronic entry doors opened. Swept into a massive lobby filled with frenetic activity, I dodged a foray of carts passing at breakneck speed, pushed along by surgical scrubs of every conceivable color. For a moment, I imagined myself on a television set where the director was about to give the order to *take one*, but somehow the blood appeared more real and the clatter of voices more strident than even the most talented director could elicit from the most skilled actors. I stood in the center of the real thing, feeling alive, vibrant, and about to be caught up.

A stocky woman in white dragged me out of the pathway of an oncoming crash cart. Flung against the edge of a desk, I waited while the fingers of a skinny woman in blue skittered across a keyboard. Finally, her eyes flicked in my direction, locking me in an impatient glare.

"What is it, Mister? I don't have all day."

"Dr. Worksworth," I said.

"What about him?"

"Is he in?"

"Station Eleven. Straight, left, then right."

I skipped a thank you, fearing any two syllables might put her on overload.

Folding into the flow of foot traffic, I stumbled along with the jumble of humanity until I reach the designated station, then spun out. The door to Eleven stood ajar. I knocked timidly, then pushed into a room blazing with light and dazzling stainless steel.

"Nurse?" a man swaddled in white shouted. He turned to me. "You're not a nurse."

"I'm Professor Simon."

"From CDC?" He held a tube to the throat of a prone patient on a cart and looked around frantically. "Where is the damn tape?"

"No. State University."

"Get a gown and mask on, for Christ's sake. Over there. Quick. And gloves. Then hold this trach tube while I get an I-V started."

His strident demand shocked me into action and my adrenaline took over. I slipped quickly into a pale blue gown, tied the laces in front, then snapped a white mask over my face. Gulping for air, I made an adjustment in order to breathe, then yanked a pair of latex gloves from the dispenser and fought to pull them on. My respect for Tight-Asse's devotion to his neurosis raised a full notch as I struggled to slide the tight gloves over my knuckles. Rubbing the palms of the gloves against the sides of the gown, I watched the fingertips swell with air.

Dr. Worksworth inspected my getup. "You've never done this before, have you?"

"Sorry," I replied weakly.

"Well, hold this." He wrapped my hand around the flexible tube. The patient gasped at my appearance and struggled to climb off the gurney. "Don't pay any attention to him. We're saving the moron's life. He should be grateful." Dr. Worksworth reached for a wall phone, punched three numbers, and cursed, I presumed his trademark in desperate situations. Apparently in response to the tremors that had set into both my hands, the patient's eyes grew wider, if that were possible. My smile beneath the mask did little to reassure him as I struggled to control the shaking.

Dr. Worksworth ransacked several drawers until he found the equipment he sought, a needle, tubing, and clear tape. He grabbed the patient's arm, swabbed a patch of skin with alcohol, and jabbed. The patient flinched. I flinched in response. The patient gasped and grabbed my arm with his free hand. Forcing a wider smile, I prayed someone would arrive momentarily to relieve me. With the I-V needle in place, the doctor hung a bottle from a chrome rack and connected the tubing. After a period of gazing and tapping, the fluid flowed.

At that moment, the door flew open and white gowns, like angels, swept into the room. A sturdy nurse nudged me aside and sliced the patient's clothing from his body. Another gowned figure assembled surgical instruments on a tray and refocused the lighting. Finally, my hand was pried loose and the tube stabilized with a strap. A masked face turned to me. "Who the hell are you?"

"Professor Simon," I said, and was about to explain how I happened to stumble into the room, thinking I was entering Dr. Worksworth's office.

"He's from CDC," Worksworth says. "He stays."

"He's got his gown on backward."

"I've got a grant pending, for Christ's sake. Shut up and disinfect this clown so I can get the surgery going. My kid's soccer meet is at one." Worksworth plunged the scalpel into the now unconscious patient's abdomen just one side of a small hole. "I wouldn't swear to it, but I'd say it's a thirty-two slug. Someone get on suction."

The angry woman in white shoved another plastic tube in my hand, this one smaller and roaring like a vacuum. She looked over the edge of her mask. "You ever do this before? No, I didn't think so. Suck the blood out of the way so doctor can see what he's doing. It's like vacuuming the trunk of your car. Think you can do that?" She held my bewildered expression for a split second. "And don't say *no*."

Ordinarily, the sight of blood made me queasy. However, I felt so intimidated by my surroundings that the thought of passing out didn't occur to me. Somehow, they needed me and I realized, as I held the blood-sucking machine in place, I hadn't felt needed in some time.

Worksworth located the bullet, a mangled piece of metal that apparently had been stopped by sheer muscle density. His assistant held open a plastic bag as a repository. The bag was sealed and labeled, presumably for a police lab examination.

"You're not with CDC?" Worksworth said from the shower stall. Scrubbed clean, he dried off and dressed. "You certainly don't know your way around an operating room. So what, then?"

"I'm your former history professor."

"I never took history."

"Not very flattering."

"Look, are you some kind of kook? Or a plant? I've never had a serious lawsuit in my life. If you think you're going to get me talking about my practice, you're nuts."

"May I go with you to your youngster's soccer meet?"

"Forget about it. I've got a busy schedule. Now if you can't find your way out, security will help."

"Honestly, I'm not here to cause trouble. You really did have me for a history class. I'd only been teaching for a couple of years and I'm sure my class was not memorable. I know it wasn't for me."

Worksworth studied me for a moment, apparently weakened, and said, "Any questions about my surgical practice, and I boot you out onto the street. Understood?"

"Of course."

We climbed into his Mercedes and took off down the road. Worksworth was an aggressive driver, cutting in and out, pushing the lights. I checked my seatbelt, then looked over at him. He had a large head, a receding chin, and a full mustache. His hair was dark and full-bodied, with streaks of gray.

He said, "My junior year, I was a wreck. My parents got a divorce; I was drinking up a storm, playing with drugs. I almost flunked out. If I'd gotten one more D, I would have. But some softy gave me a C, and that kept me in for the year. In my senior year, I met this girl." He shot me a glance. "And now look at me." Was he genuinely proud or simply arrogant? I guessed it didn't matter. "How the hell did you find me? And more to the point, why?"

The Lioness had included a copy of his junior year grade sheet for me. I was the softy to whom he referred.

"I'm kind of on a mission," I said. Skip it. Why not offer up the truth? "Well, that's not exactly correct. I tried to rob a bank. At least one of the tellers thought that's what I was trying to do. She later recognized me and threatened to turn over the security camera tape if I didn't go on this grail hunt. She thinks I think my career has been mediocre and is trying to prove otherwise by sending me out to interview former students."

"History professor? For life? Christ, I'd say that's pretty mediocre. How'd the robbery go?"

"Not well. That's why I'm on the hunt."

"Too bad. If you'd come away with a million or two, that might have redeemed all those years. As it is, a guy your age doesn't have much time to make it up. Reminds me of my old man. He was a gardener, cut grass, dug culverts, shit like that all his life. Can you imagine being on your death bed and thinking that's what you did?"

"Is this the same dad who put you through school?"

"I borrowed two hundred grand and paid back every nickel."

"He didn't contribute anything to your getting where you are today?" Perhaps I was out of line, but I didn't care.

"He walked around breathing, that's what he did. Do you know what it takes to become what I've become? Ambition. Do you know what I've done without? The hours I've put in at the books, in the lab, as a resident, working seventy and eighty hours a week for years for peanuts. What have *you* done? Probably scratched out some piece of trash they call a dissertation. What do you teach, three or four courses a week? That's not even half time in an office. Then you go home to your dingy house and your little flea-bitten lawn, just what you deserve. You academics make me sick, with all your supposed standards. I apply for research money to do real things, and I have to jump through your hoops. Most of those jerks holding the purse strings earned Ph.D.'s just like you and have never been inside an operating room or in a real research lab. You all make me sick."

We were at the soccer field. Worksworth threw his door open and ran onto the field without a parting word. I heard him call, "Hey, Marcie, over here." His daughter, a girl about twelve, jogged toward him. They hugged, then he began instruction on ball handling, demonstrating a bent leg kick. I eased the Mercedes' door open and slunk away.

Walking through the adjacent park, I found a small waterfall where I sat on a rock to watch the sparkling flow pass over a glistening ledge of shale. The sunshine felt warm against my back and my thoughts turned to my last day with the Lioness. While she continued to serve as my nemesis, prodding me into what was unfolding as a mindless search, there was something comforting in my memory of her. Perhaps it was the image of her loveliness. More likely her unseemly attention to me. Although our meeting had been chance, she had taken such pains to research my life that, in a moment of reflection, I was truly moved. I couldn't recall a recent time when I had been the object of such interest.

What confounded me the most was why she had chosen the former students she had? Hasbach, a successful literary screwball. Little Sara McCovey, an adolescent searching out the frogs of the world for her first true kiss. And now Worksworth. Was he on the list because my 'C' enabled him to remain in school? And to what end? He seemed a selfish, self-serving arrogant dolt. Okay, no one is perfect. And perhaps his life-saving skills as a surgeon more than compensated for his attitude. But if her selections were intended to highlight the crowning successes of my teaching career, I was doomed.

A wet nose nuzzled my hand and I looked up to see a yellow Lab puppy staring into my face, an innocent glow in her brown eyes. At the far end of the leash stood barely a whisper of a woman, a red scarf wrapped about her tufts of gray hair, an aged plaid coat buttoned up against the cool on-shore ocean breeze.

"I'm too old to have her," the woman said. "Too old." The puppy continued to look at me as if she were about to burst open with a secret, then bounded across the rocks down to the edge of the stream on a leash that seemed to have no end.

I struggled to my feet, realizing the stiffness of my age against the cold stone. "Your puppy is cute," I said, ignoring the woman's comment.

"She is, isn't she? I rescued her from the pound. But what will become of her when I die?"

The question was not an idle one. She looked at me, as if expecting an answer. "Do you plan to die?" I asked.

"Are you daft in the head? Of course I'm going to die."

"Very soon?"

"How should I know."?

"Then why shouldn't you have your puppy?"

"That's what my daughter told me. 'You're too old to have a puppy, because you are going to die soon.' That's what she said."

"Your daughter, the soothsayer?"

The woman broke into a chuckle. "That's the one."

"Does she play the lottery?"

"She doesn't have to. She's a big shot accountant with a lot of money."

"If she's so good at predicting the future, she should play the lottery."

"I understand." The woman looked down at the pup, which had befriended a butterfly, letting it dart from ear to ear. "Pretty pup, don't you think?" the woman said.

"She's very pretty. I can see you love her very much," I said.

"I do. I love her very much," she said. A tear, perhaps generated by a puff of wind, formed on her lower eyelid and ran down her cheek. She studied me, pale eyes keen and wise. "I used to be very beautiful."

She leaned forward and the puppy ran playfully into her arms, the butterfly flitting off and settling on a nearby branch. Standing, the woman let the puppy lick her face. They turned, and as the woman shuffled down the trail, the puppy settled quietly into the crook of her arm. I watched after them, the tail of the colorful scarf fluttering across the woman's narrow shoulder and lacing through puffs of silver hair.

CHAPTER 15

A FULL TANK OF GAS

Enthusiasm for my assignment, such as it was, had dwindled. What small amount of pride I had possessed regarding my work had pretty much dissolved. Other than two post-pubescent former students who were apparently enamored by the modest degree of respect I afforded them in class, I had made less than a lasting impression on a famous, albeit screwball, writer and a high testosterone surgeon. Now I had little choice but to forge ahead with or without a sense of personal esteem.

My next mission was to track down Andrew Winforth, an African-American student who graduated from State U. twelve years earlier. He lived in a small town in Montana. The Lioness included a photograph she had apparently found on the internet. As I drove through the Montana countryside, I wondered why a young Black man would choose to live in a rural community where he was likely the only minority in town.

Cisco had a population of twelve hundred plus. The Winforth residence, a small white clapboard house set back from the main highway, was a mile north of the town square. Knocking at the front door and getting no answer, I decided to lunch and drop back later in the afternoon when Andrew might return from wherever he spent his days.

Near the town's center, I found a rustic diner with a handful of pickup trucks parked in the lot. Inside, I walked past the counter of chrome-trimmed stools, feeling the eyes of the locals on me as I slipped into a booth. A teenager followed me with water, coffee, and a menu.

"What's your favorite item on the menu?" I asked.

She popped her gum. "A burger, fries, and a chocolate shake."

"Everything but the shake," I said.

"You're not from around here," she said, tucking the menu beneath one arm as if it were a schoolbook.

"Back east."

"You passing through?"

"Looking for someone. Maybe you know him, Andrew Winforth."

She stared off through the large plate glass window, popped her gum, and shook her head. "Nope, don't know anybody by that name. Maybe it's his sister. There's an *Andrea* Winforth just up the road. Little white house on the right." She whirled and bopped behind the counter.

It wasn't long before a sheriff's deputy sauntered in, sat at the counter, and ordered coffee. He was big, with a handlebar moustache and raw, weathered cheeks. When he removed his hat, I saw his head had been shaved to the scalp. He sipped hot coffee two or three times, glancing periodically in my direction. Finally, the inevitable happened. He rose to his full height, readjusted his paraphernalia-laden belt with one beefy hand, and ambled in my direction.

Well, it's finally over, I decided. The Lioness, having tired of the game, had turned the tape over to the FBI. There was an all-points bulletin out and this deputy was about to make the collar. I placed my hands on the table, palms flat, fingers spread. *No need to pull out the big forty-five, sir. No rough stuff required. I'll go quietly.*

Rodney, my skate-boarding youngster, would understand. Perhaps he'd agree to stay with his mother for his last year of high school. I've got enough put away to fund two years of college. Maybe Ackerman Fink, the paramour, could see his way clear to kicking in the rest. The house would bring a little cash. My colleagues could cover fall classes while the department recruited my replacement. Of course, my photograph in the row of faculty mug shots strung along the hallway would come down.

The magic collection I kept secreted in the garage could be donated to a local kid's organization. Much of it was self-instructional. My collection of rare books at the office would provide a little income, maybe enough to cover my legal fees; maybe not. If I pled guilty on all counts, I might get by without a lawyer. At my age, the difference between thirty years and sixty years didn't seem that great anyway. By cooperating fully, perhaps the judge would send me to a prison close to home so Rodney could visit once in a while. I'd like to stay in touch with him, see how his career was going ten or fifteen years down the road.

Towering above me like the giant in Jack and the Beanstalk, the deputy said, "You a stranger in these parts." Not a question; a statement. His booming voice startled me and garnered the attention of the half-dozen patrons.

"Yes sir," I replied, my voice quivering in spite of my efforts to remain calm. "Professor Simon. I'm doing field research." I extended my hand, but my gesture went ignored.

"Exactly which field you researching, Pro-fessor?" he asked with what I hoped, for the sake of the good people of Cisco, was a touch of sarcasm in his voice.

"I just meant that as an expression," I said, knowing there was absolutely no way to amend my opening. "I'm doing a follow-up on my former students. Kind of a special project on my summer vacation."

"You *did* see the sign coming into town," he said, bending forward slightly, far enough for me to feel his hot breath on my face. "No soliciting."

I swallowed hard. "Yes, sir."

"Doing research on our residents, that's a kind of soliciting, ain't it?"

"No, sir. I'm not doing research on the residents. I'm just visiting one resident, a former student of mine. Andrew Winforth."

"I know everybody in town, Professor. There ain't no Andrew Winforth here."

"The young woman behind the counter told me there is an An*drea* Winforth. I was hoping they might be related."

"Ms. Winforth never told me she had kin in these parts. I expect you just got in the wrong town. There might be an An*drew* Winforth over the mountain, over in Claiborne, but not here. No sir, I never heard that name around here."

"Well, if you don't mind, I'd like to stop by and speak with Ms. Winforth, just to ask if she knows Andrew."

"But I do mind. The judge is a busy woman and I don't think she'd want her time taken up with somebody doing no door-to-door research."

"But this isn't just a random stop," I said, feeling slightly more confident now that I wasn't about to be arrested for bank robbery. I hoped unlicensed soliciting would only get me a night or two in the local jail. "If I may reach into my coat pocket, I have a piece of paper that explains everything." A note from the Lioness with a name and address and the photo. He nodded. I moved with great caution, keeping one hand visible as I pulled the paper free with the other. Spreading the document out on the table, I pointed. "See? I didn't just select Andrew Winforth at random. He was one of my students at the university and I would like to interview him. It's a follow up program I was assigned to do on my former students." I hoped to get through by repetition, if not logic.

The deputy studied the paper, scrutinizing the photo in particular. "Sure does resemble the judge," he said musing, stroking one end of his moustache. He looked down at me with cool blue eyes. "Alright, I'll tell you what. The judge gets home about five-thirty this evening. I'll stop by the courthouse this afternoon, tell her you're in town. You come by the house at five-forty. If she wants to see you, I'll show you in. If she don't, I'll escort you out of town." The offer was unequivocal.

"Thank you," I said, relieved.

The deputy's expression was as impassive as when he first approached me. It was as if I'd asked him for directions and he had obliged.

Optimistically, I checked into a motel, hoping to get an audience with Andrea Winforth and be able to spend the night in Cisco. Time dragged as I flipped through the four television channels. I settled on a cooking program, figuring I'd better learn to prepare a dish or two in case I was forced to eventually augment my diet of pizza and takeout.

Shortly before five-thirty, I climbed into the car and drove to the little white house down the road. I spotted the sheriff's SUV in the driveway and hoped that was a positive indication. As I stepped from the car and approached the house, the door swung open and the deputy loomed in the doorframe, appearing larger than he had at the diner. He held the outer storm door for me and I entered the small, but comfortable living room. Sitting before me in a wing-backed chair was the person in my photograph, except he was a she.

"Ms. Winforth," I said deferentially, "I'm Professor Alec Simon. I had a student in my class by the name of Andrew Winforth. I was given this address. I wonder if you can help me?"

The deputy intervened. "You're to address Ms. Winforth as Judge Winforth, stranger."

Judge Winforth waved her hand. "Oliver, be still. Now what do you want with Andrew, Professor?" she asked.

"I'm doing a follow up on a select group of former students on whom I've made a so-called lasting impression. Kind of a summer project. Very subjective, no particular agenda other than to find out how these students are doing and what, if anything, they might have taken away from my classes." Somehow I'd managed to adopt a touch of Oliver's syntax in my response, softening the edges of my vowels, saying 'vera subjective' and 'doin'.

"I don't remember, that is, Andrew never spoke of his under-graduate work, so I can't help you with your study, Professor."

"So you do know Andrew?" I said.

"I haven't seen Andrew for several years. He kind of disap-peared and I don't think he'll be back anytime soon. Sorry."

I turned to Oliver and decided to go the distance. "Deputy, if I don't find Andrew, I might end up in jail. As someone associated with law enforcement, you know how undesirable that can be."

"Come again?"

Looking back at the judge, I said, "May we speak privately?"

"Oliver, wait outside."

"But...."

"Outside, Oliver."

Reluctantly, Oliver stepped onto the concrete stoop, but left the door slightly ajar. Judge Winforth motioned me to a chair.

"Settle in there, Professor, and explain to me what the hell you are talking about?"

"I played a practical joke on a friend, a teller at a bank. I gave her a robbery note, all in good fun, but the scene got caught on the se-curity camera. She lifted the tape and is blackmailing me. She wants me to interview ten former students all over the country. It's driving me nuts. But if I don't do it, she'll give the tape to the police."

"Professor, that's the craziest story I've ever heard."

I reached for my wallet and brought forth a photo ID issued by State U. "See, I am a professor at State U."

"This is a sorry-ass picture, Professor. Okay, I'm convinced you are who you say you are. What the hell have you been smoking? Your story makes no sense at all."

"Do you know where I can find Andrew?"

"Professor, I have a mentally challenged older brother and sadly, in the days when he was growing up, they actually rated him on a moron scale. If they rated you, you'd be right at the bottom of that scale. Who do you think *I* am, Sleeping Beauty?"

"I thought maybe a twin?"

"A twin? A twin name of *Andrea* with a brother, Andrew? You seemed a lot smarter in the classroom, Professor. I was afraid you were here to screw things up for me. Of course I remember your classes. In fact, I remember them real well. The eight a.m. class I slept through, but I have to admit that afternoon class on great women in history was pretty darn important to me. Yes sir. It's because of you that I'm Andrea, not Andrew."

"That's terrible," I said, registering a surge of guilt.

"No, it's terrific. Professor, I knew I was different since I was a kid, just not how I was different. When I got aware of my sexuality, I began to feel I was a woman in a man's body. But I wanted to *be* somebody, and in my family I was taught women couldn't achieve what men could achieve. In your class, you pointed out how many bold and powerful women there are in the history of the world. That's when I thought, screw it, no matter how I feel inside, I can still do anything I want. So I did. I enrolled in law school and decided to become the best damn civil lawyer in San Francisco. When I finished school, I took a job with a law firm that specialized in challenges to the federal government on environmental issues. As I won case after case, I grew more confident and decided I had the courage to begin the sex change process.

"I was riding high when one day I got a phone call from the chairman of the town council of Cisco saying the federal government was going to flood their valley, and all twelve hundred and some residents were going to be displaced. They'd heard about my winning record fighting the government and begged that I come out here. Of course, they were shocked to see they had hired a black female, because by then I was pretty far along in my sexual transformation. I dressed like a woman, talked in a woman's voice, was taking hormones, had breast implants, and it was only months before I was scheduled to have the actual sex change surgery. When I won the case, the people in this community were so enthralled, they put me on a pedestal and asked me to hang around. I got appointed judge, met Oliver, and, five years later, here I am."

"You and Oliver?" I said.

"Ain't he cute? He worships the feet I walk on, believe me"

"He knows?"

"He knows what there is to know. I never completed the operation, Professor. I got these big tits, which Oliver loves, and I still sport a sizable you-know-what, which he loves even more."

"So you are an African-American transsexual living in an all white community, dating a white sheriff's deputy and serving as the judge."

"Close. I'm a Black transgendered woman living in an all white community, embroiled in a torrid love affair with a white sheriff's deputy, who soon will be the sheriff, and serving as judge for life. And I owe it all to you, Professor. I couldn't be happier. I'm welcomed everywhere I go. White men hold doors open for me; white women of all ages are deferential. When they say, 'here come the judge', they say it with good humor, but respectfully. Each year, the elementary school children are paraded into my courtroom and get to interview me. And they are taught racial respect, even though I'm the only person of color most have ever seen. Granted, I don't make as much money as I would practicing in San Francisco, but I also don't have the rat race to contend with. And believe it or not," Judge Winforth said, nodding toward the deputy leaning contentedly against the outside doorframe, "I don't miss the variety. That boy loves me with all his heart and soul. He'd do anything for me, including shoot your white ass full of holes if you breathe a word of any of this to anyone, anywhere, anytime."

I sat stunned. Not because I was sitting in front of a Black transgendered woman having sex with a white deputy in an all-white community while sitting as judge, but because I had been the prime mover, the *sine qua non*. How could I have known? Sure, maybe I promoted the notion of women's rights, but I had no idea anything I had said could evoke such a dramatic change in another human being. Looking at Andrea, I saw happiness, success, and, above all, contentment.

"If they ever find out about, you know, and have a change of attitude?" I asked.

"What the fair citizens of Cisco don't know is that in my private safe deposit box is a paper that could send the waters of yonder river onto their heads with the filing of a single brief. I came to a settlement with the Department of the Interior. They were afraid of outright defeat if we went to trial, so we agreed they would hold off on the dam, but the community has the right to change their minds at anytime. Part of the deal is that the locals get to sell their property to the government at double the appraised value. I figure, as the younger people eventually leave town and the economy goes south, there won't be much for the old folks here. So why not provide them with a financial backdoor, in a manner of speaking. Someday I'll reveal the details of the settlement and let them vote. But, of course, if they give me any b-s in the meantime, like cross burning or n-word-talk behind my back, I'll call Interior and tell them we're ready to go. The good citizens of the community will barely have time to take down their laundry before the river is rolling down the main drag." Andrea smiled. "No pun intended, Professor."

"I'm amazed," I said.

"Me too. And, in truth, I never thought I would have a chance to thank you in person. So thank you, Professor. You were the only man, white or black, the only person, to inspire me to find myself. And here I am. I am a black woman, defiant, powerful, relatively wealthy, and actually, if I say so myself, a pretty darn good judge. I mix a little touch of Solomon, a sprinkling of Malcolm X, and a lot of Will Rogers in my decisions and for the most part, the citizens are happy. I'm tough on violent criminals, abusers, swindlers, and drunk drivers and facilitative in cases of divorce and child custody. The worse they can say about me is that I spent ten thousand dollars of county money to have my own little bathroom built next to my chambers and nobody, I mean nobody, goes in there but me. What I wasn't going to do is get caught with my package hanging out while peeing next to Elvira Perkins, the county clerk."

The judge stood. "Now be a good Professor and give me a hug like we came to some cozy understanding about this misunderstanding. That'll appease Oliver so he lets you get out of town alive. Not too close, please. No pelvic contact. We don't want him jealous, neither."

Judge Andrea gave me an auntie-type hug, pressing her ample breasts into my chest for effect, then, with two powerful arms, held me in front of her. "My oh my, Professor. They sure aren't feeding you well on this research project of yours. Except for that pouch, you all bony. Tell you what. Rather than running off, you hang around here for dinner. Oliver has a pot roast in the oven. I'll tell him I told you Andrew was a cousin now living back in San Francisco. That way, he won't be trying to put a bomb under the front seat of your car tonight while you are sleeping."

The pot roast was delicious and the conversation dominated by Judge Andrea as she extolled the splendors of Cisco and the wonders of Oliver, the want-to-be sheriff. After a time, she turned the focus to her alma mater and quizzed me about life on campus. Fortunately, she didn't ask how my research was going or what I knew of other former students.

I thanked them both shortly after my second piece of Oliver's apple pie, headed for my motel room, and slept easily knowing that somewhere in the dark, Deputy Oliver sat protectively with his shotgun by his side, waiting for me to rise in the morning and take to the road.

CHAPTER 16
DON'T FENCE ME IN

I made an advanced cellphone call to the Federal prison in Leavenworth, Kansas, to set up a meeting with former student Jonathan Stiles. A successful visit to the prison would put me halfway through my cross-country pilgrimage.

As I dialed the number for administration, I feared penetrating the gates of this fortress might prove to be challenging beyond the charms of the Lioness. But, once again, I was wrong in my estimate of her capacity to surprise.

"Professor Simon?" an administrative voice at the other end of the line said. "You bet we're expecting you. Yes sir, once you're in town, just give us a holler. There's a bit of paperwork for folks who are not related or working in a legal capacity, but we'll take good care of you. Now don't be shy, Professor, if you need anything. Don't hesitate, you hear?"

As I hung up, paranoia flooded me. *You bet we're expecting you.* What did *that* mean? Maybe I'd been tried in absentia and this entire project had been designed as a ruse to get me to a federal prison at my own expense. What did the voice mean, ...*a bit of paperwork...*? Incarceration documents? *We'll take* good *care of you.* Translation, we'll have you processed and in your cell before sundown.

STOP, I shouted to my addled brain. *You are driving me nuts.* And it was at that moment that I *knew* I had lost my sanity. Not because of talking to myself; that I did with regularity. But because I felt there really were two of me. There was the *me* who was whining and complaining. And the *me* who was tired of hearing it. Which was the *real* me? That was the most disturbing question.

I found a motel district along the interstate not far from the prison and stopped for the night. After locating a liquor store and buying a fifth of scotch, I dropped by a chicken place and got the whole meal, beans, rolls, salad, the works. Returning to the motel room, I poured a tumbler of booze and sat dumbly in front of the television thumbing through one hundred and eighty-two satellite channels.

After downing half a glass of scotch, I decided to call Silverman. It was ten-thirty p.m. his time, but I didn't care. The doctor wanted me to take the Lioness's challenge in stride, and I was doing my best. But I definitely needed a pep talk to work my way through the remainder of the schedule.

Silverman answered on the first ring. "My boy," he said, before I had identified myself, "I'd been hoping to hear from you. So how is your Don Quixote quest?"

"More adventure than insight, I'd say, Doctor." As I spoke, I realized the booze had my brain spinning.

"Not surprising," he replied jauntily. "You called to get gassed up, I take it."

I snickered. "I *am* getting gassed up," I said.

"I mean motivationally, my boy. Have you lost your drive? Hankering to come home?"

"I've totally lost my drive, Doctor. And I want to come home in the worst way. How do traveling salespeople do it? I want my own bed in my own little house. I want to sit and vegetate in front of my small screen TV. I want to walk on my block of understated houses. I even miss my old pal, Homer, the fat-assed dog."

"The dog that farts?" Silverman asked.

"That dog." I giggled and rolled across the mattress, gasping for air. "Sorry, Doctor, but I seem to have lost control here." After several deep breaths, I said, "Okay, I'll try again." Unfortunately, I couldn't and went off into a series of spasmodic gasps, spilling scotch every which way.

Silverman waited patiently. Several minutes passed, then he said, "If you can hear me my boy, let me say this. Your reaction is very normal under the circumstances. We need to refocus your journey. You must remember you are doing this, in part, because you don't wish to spend the balance of your active life in a federal prison. *Entender?*"

"Nintendo?"

"*Entender.* That's Spanish for *understand.* Do you?"

"I do." I calmed my visceral spasms momentarily, but could sense another bout of the giggles squirming in my abdomen, timing its rise to the surface. Focusing on the surge of guilt that flooded me for having roused the doctor at such a late hour only to foist my adolescent shenanigans on him, I fought to keep the roiling chortle suppressed. "Doctor," I said, "I think I'm losing my mind." That was it. I couldn't hang on any longer. I rolled across the bed doubled up, the near empty glass of scotch fending for itself as I let out great bellows of laughter. I waved the phone before my face, hoping its sight would bring me to my senses, but I only guffawed harder. With one final gasp, I said, "Sorry, Doctor," and ended the call. Then I fell onto the floor and shook and shuddered with laughter until my sides hurt nearly beyond endurance.

The summer morning in Leavenworth, Kansas, was warm and humid. I arrived at the United States Penitentiary just past nine a.m., was processed quickly and courteously, and then shown to the visiting area. After a ten-minute wait, a guard summoned me to the room where I was to meet with Jonathan Stiles, a twenty-five year old former student who was unmemorable. If the Lioness had truly made conscious choices in developing my itinerary, I had to believe she threw in Stiles to refocus me; *Let's take a closer look, Professor, at life in the federal correctional system.* Oh, the Lioness was shrewd. She had second-guessed I'd be running out of steam about now, wondering why I was going through with this. Considering my breakdown the previous evening, she'd calculated well.

Perhaps it was the bright sunshine, the good nights sleep, or my emotional release, but I didn't find the surroundings as intimidating as I had imagined. And my reaction was buoyed further by the glowing expression on Jonathan Stiles' young face as he was led into the room and seated opposite me. I could tell he had no idea who I was, but he seemed overjoyed that I was there. Perhaps my visit provided an opportunity to break the daily routine. Or perhaps he imagined I had plans to spring him.

"Fifteen minutes," the guard said.

"Jonathan," I said, "I'm one of your former professors. Alec Simon."

He nodded and smiled. "Yes, of course. Psychology."

"History."

"Of course. History. Do I owe you an assignment, Professor? Is that why you are here?"

I liked his sense of humor.

"Nothing like that," I replied. "I'm doing a survey on a select group of former students, wondering how they are doing and what they remember from their history courses."

Jonathan's blank expression spoke louder than any critical assessment he might have offered. But what could I expect? Not everybody loves history. Or even likes it. Or really understands it. "I don't remember much, Professor. Sorry."

At that moment, I felt an urge to deliver a speech to Jonathan, one I'd given at the commencement exercises of the graduating class of Rushford High, some years earlier.

"The trouble is, most people think history is something only to mem-orize; places, dates, battles. History is anything but that. To study history is to seize a slice of time in the traveling universe, to look into the lives and emotions of those who have laid down the foundations of who we are...."

I smiled. Jonathan Stiles returned the smile, unaware that I had just lectured him on a subject so dear to me.

He said, "I wish I hadn't been perpetually high in your class. But you know, it was a time in my life when I was learning my craft, trying every drug I could get my hands on. Can you imagine how much money I have put away? In four short years of being in the marketplace, it's damn near mind-boggling. I've got twenty-five million dollars spread all around the world, in secure banks. That's about a million dollars for every year I'll spend here. How many jobs give you that kind of retirement plan? When I get out, at age fifty, I'll never have to work another day in my life. I'll live like a king. What'd you say to that, Professor?"

"Remarkable," I replied.

"It is. Remarkable." He paused and sucked in a breath. I sensed I was about to hear a rebuttal to my imaginary lecture on the val-ues of studying history. His eyes sparkled. "I marvel that it all came from a market of people who want to blot out the past and change the present. You were trying to take people into the past; I was helping them forget about it. They don't want to know what hap-pened back then, not in their own lives or anyone else's.

"Think of the typical conversation when people greet each other.

'Hey, how's it going?'
'Okay. How about you?'
'Yeah, okay.'"

"We know they are lying through their teeth. They don't really want to know how it's been going with the other one. Cause it's painful. There's stupidity, there's treachery, there's loss. They don't want to be reminded what a crappy job they are doing with their lives. They cheat, they lie. They screw up at work. How many times have they forgotten birthdays and anniversaries? They are behind on their car payments, their mortgages, projects at work, visiting their kids, their child support. A toke on a joint or a snort of a little white powder changes everything. Suddenly their reality changes. Now they tolerate it. In fact, they feel good about it. Snort a little coke, and all of a sudden you've got a thousand great ideas about that project at work. You think of dozens of things to do with your kids. You work out an entire budget in your head, how to get out of debt. Nothing in the outside world has changed, but your inner reality is altered totally. And that's what counts, Professor. Inner reality. Let's face it, outer reality sucks. It's never going to change. We're always going to have wars as long as there are greedy politicians and executives of big companies willing to sacrifice the lives and well being of others for their own selfish little interests. We're always going to have droughts and starvation in the world, because Mother Nature couldn't give a crap. People will always go to bed hungry and sick, with no hope for the future. But, with a little chemical adjustment, the half empty glass becomes half full. Life's not so bad. In fact, for a few minutes, life becomes beautiful. Because it is always in the eyes of the beholder. That's what my shrink says. Adjust your thoughts and a change in your feelings will follow. He's right. In fact, my shrink makes the greatest argument for mind altering chemicals." Jonathan sat back. "Do I love this place, or what?"

"You seem to have adjusted very well," I said.

"I got twenty-four and a half years to go, and I can do it standing on one hand. Every day I count up to twenty-seven hundred and thirty-nine? You know why? Cause that's how much money I earned of my twenty-five million that day. Every day I'm in here, I earn twenty-seven thirty-nine. And the greatest part is, I have no expenses. I get three squares, television, and a bed to myself, strolls in the yard, an exercise program, movies, and the potential of becoming a trustee and someday venturing out. And I'll be the greatest trustee in the world, you can bet on that. They can send me anywhere and I'll come right back to them, like a boomerang. Because when my time is done, I want to walk out of here free and clear."

"You sound as if you have your program pretty well figured out," I said, thinking about doing thirty years, having nothing to show for it, and coming out a decrepit old man, if I even lived that long.

"You say those platitudes, Professor, but you're not kidding me. You don't for one minute think being in here is a good idea. You're thinking of all the years I'll have to do without. No women during my most virile period of life. No booze. Scrounging drugs for favors. No travel. No close friends. Well, you can think all that, you don't have to say it. But you're wrong. I can do without. Because when I get out of here, I'll have it all."

"My quick calculation suggests your twenty-five million, at three percent inflation a year, should be worth about six and a quarter million in actual buying power. Which, let's face it, isn't bad," I said. "You probably won't be renting any corporate jets, but if you are prudent with your spending, you'll still be able to have a nice house and car, pay your medical bills, buy food, and have enough on which to travel."

Jonathan Stiles looked stunned. "Why did you really come here, Professor? Who sent you? Amos? Jolene? They want a bigger cut, is that it? Well, they're never going to see a nickel more. They got theirs. I took the rap. I'm doing the hard time. Tell them to go stick it. I don't need them. I don't need you. I've got all I ever want right here."

Jonathan Stiles leapt from his chair and stormed from the room.

When I emerge into the hot mid-summer Kansas sunshine, I wanted to kiss the ground. The Lioness had accomplished her goal, definitely refocusing me. Regardless of the toll, the next five interviews would feel like a breeze. The thought of having Jonathan Stiles as a cellmate served as a long, cold shower.

CHAPTER 17
LOSING FAITH; A CONSTITUTIONAL RIGHT

The drive from Leavenworth to Washington, D. C., took me three and a half days. I enjoyed the cross-country trip, content with the sunshine and the rain, the small diners sprinkled along the back roads, and the people, even when they treated me with the coolness often bestowed upon strangers. Jonathan Stiles proved right about inner reality. The prison visit changed my perspective. I found myself happier than I'd been in some time. I was free and dedicated to staying that way.

In a small town in Ohio, I stopped to buy several CDs, one of Chopin piano pieces and a Karen Carpenter collection. The music helped pass the time. When I finally arrived in Washington, I discovered the office that employed Deter Crouch (formerly known as Peter, who chose to substitute a 'D' for a 'P') was located downtown. According to the brief description provided by the printout in his envelop, Deter served as a strategist for 'The Agency'; I presumed that meant the CIA. Everything he said and did was highly confidential. Strictly top secret. How the Lioness managed to get a pass to the office building was totally beyond my comprehension.

After several turns about the Washington Monument Mall, I located an upscale hotel, secure parking, room service, and genuinely clean linens that apparently were changed between occupants. The thought of treating myself to these sumptuous surroundings lifted my spirits even further, as did an afternoon visit to a traveling Edvard Munch exhibition at the National Gallery. As I moved from drawing to drawing, thoughts of my mission in the city receded and I immersed myself in the quiet beauty of the world of art. Even the moody subjects of the Munch exhibit couldn't quell my renewed enthusiasm for life.

Deter Crouch's office was within walking distance of my hotel. I called ahead and spoke with his assistant. If I appeared with my authorization document and proper identification *and* if I passed their initial screening, I was told there was a good chance I'd get an audience with Strategist Crouch.

When I showed up, I offered the document provided by the Lioness along with my driver's license. I was fingerprinted, photographed, eye-scanned, voice-imprinted, and searched. Strangely, the briefcase I carried throughout the process was ignored. Sufficiently sanitized, I was led to the inner sanctum.

Peter Crouch, as I had known him in class, was a memorable student. He was one of those bright shining lights any professor loves to have; that is, at first. Enthralled with every word spoken, every concept offered up, he hung on each and every syllable I uttered. After class, we stood in the doorway reviewing the lesson, dissecting statements, observations, historic facts. With time, we eventually gravitated to my office where he systematically delved into the intent of my lectures, challenging my premises, offering alternative observations, revisiting interpretations of facts as no one I'd ever met. He suggested my liberal bias drove my selection of texts, the content on my reading lists, and the thrust of my courses. His alternative explanations for historic events stretched the minds of even his most conservative associates. For example, the Nazi Holocaust, he proposed, was an illusion manufactured by the British to justify establishing a Zionist state and a withdrawal from the Middle East. Communism had actually been imported to the USSR by left-wing radicals from Hollywood for the purpose of colonization. Deep beneath the polar icecaps, he contended, live a race of aliens intent upon consuming the earth by the year 2030; thus the extensive government-supported research, especially at the South Pole.

While I always enjoyed a healthy exchange of ideas with my students, in time, Peter's somewhat radical perspective on the history of the world grew difficult to field, even tedious. Not wishing to curtail our discussions, thus lending credence to his assertion that I was a narrow-minded liberal bigot, I let him rant while I graded papers, prepared assignments, searched for earwax, polished my shoes, rotated the tires on my car, and even mowed the lawn. Finally, it occurred to me that I'd allowed his intrusion to go too far. Even the restraining order issued by a local judge would not dissuade him from pursuing his strategic arguments.

Fortunately, Peter graduated. Shortly afterward, I heard from a fellow faculty member and admirer of Peter's that the government showed considerable interest in his uncommon viewpoint. At the time, I presumed the government worried about Peter's radical concepts. Subsequently I learned, to the contrary, several top policymakers were entranced with what they considered his refreshing, 'out-of-the-box' thinking.

Apparently Deter, formerly Peter, wasn't one to hold grudges. He welcomed me, albeit with a somber demeanor, into the expansive conference room that served as his office. The rectangular room, painted entirely black, housed a narrow conference table surrounded by a dozen high back chairs dressed in black fabric. Indirect lighting scattered oblique shadows across the scene. At the far end of the room stood a large glass screen, backlighted, on which was projected, in black, a box-like design. Outside the box were x's and o's and scribbles. Within the box, nothing.

"I'm most pleased to see you, Herr Professor," Deter said.

"It has been a long time," I replied, slightly overwhelmed by the setting and the appearance of my former student, dressed in black. Black shirt, black tie, black coat, black-rimmed spectacles and, strangely enough, black onyx earrings the size of rabbit turds.

"As you once said, Herr Professor, time is but an illusion created by the powerful to become more powerful. Einstein, although a Jew, had it right when he identified *time* as the forth dimension. As such, time has no beginning and no end. We can roll it backward or forward. However, by creating the misapprehension that time is progressing, we generate the delusion that there is someplace to *get*. There is no place to *get*, is there, Herr Professor?"

He scrutinized me with an intensity I now remembered from our campus discussions. However, in this new setting, I found his ghostly countenance most unnerving. "Obviously, I can't take credit for that observation, Peter, but I certainly can't disagree." Won't disagree, was more like it. Let's do this interview, keep it brief, and let me out of here.

"Deter, Herr Professor. I sought the change for obvious reasons."

"Yes," I said. "And, if I may say so, a distinctive choice."

Deter motioned me toward the head of the table where we sat across from one another, adjacent to the illuminated glass wall.

"So, mine Herr Professor, to what do I owe this unexpected, if agreeable, visit. No one is simply passing through this office. You have a particular objective. As I recall your political leanings, I can only surmise that you are bringing me some new insight about the weak and cunning of the world. Or perhaps I have misread your intentions. Perhaps you've come to offer up the names of those at your place of work who have committed treachery against our country by promoting their seditious views."

"Neither, Deter," I said. "I have come on an assignment. I'm spending the summer traveling across the country interviewing former students to determine their views of my classes, what they might remember, my impact on their thinking, as it were." I said this with a boldness that had the potential to invite a torrent of abuse.

"Alas, Herr Professor, I embraced your classes and our discussions with much sentiment. You provided me with an opportunity to freely express my views, to hone my vision for the world. Ironically, your left-wing liberal openness allowed me a forum in which to develop a reputation that has led me to this position where I can begin to systematically regulate freedom of thought, word and deed. Our very future depends on this. This great country is teetering on the brink of a cataclysmic implosion driven by excessive freedom. Even the populous, when asked, believe we have too many freedoms.

"Flag burning, for example. People of this culture detest the act of burning their flag. They would tear the flag-burning monsters limb from limb in the name of freedom. Although I find viewing their fanatical raging against this most fundamental principle of freedom peculiar, I accept this response as an index of our progress.

"Our country has made great strides in the past several decades in narrowing these freedoms. Take another example, the systematic self-regulation of the news. Large media corporations do not wish to suffer the wrath of their government nor, more importantly, of their advertisers. Therefore, they have learned to control freedom of the press. How frequently do you hear a genuine debate of ideas presented on network and cable news programs? More controversy occurs on the *Jerry Springer Show*. As you know, Karl Marks once said that religion is the 'opiate of the people'. Today, we have created a new hypnotic. The news. We control the news, in form and substance. It is delivered with, if I may fall back on common vulgarity, the razzle-dazzle of the sideshow barker. To quote a great poet whose works will eventually be banned, it is '... full of sound and fury, signifying nothing.' And the masses can't get enough of it."

"You must be proud of your work, Deter," I said.

"Now, Professor, sycophancy does not become you. I am not proud of anything I do. I act for the good of the country, the good of the people. As an historian, you realize that the human race, in whatever form, must survive within this universe. Yet, you are aware that the entire world is headed for doom. It is diversity that is causing our breakdown. Too many different people interacting. Too many different ideas in the marketplace. What is the root of terrorism? Diversity. If we were all of one religion or one ideological belief system, would we have bombings in the streets of America? I think not."

"So by honing our thought process, by narrowing the field, we will achieve true understanding and peace?" I asked.

"Exactly. And to do this, some things will have to change. Think of this process as analogous to carving a beautiful work of art from a piece of wood. The ordinary piece of wood, while perhaps picturesque in its own primitive way, has no real form to its beauty. However, in the hands of an artist, a craftsperson, the wood will eventually take shape and become a work of art. To accomplish our goal, can we use all the wood? Of course not. It is what is *not* there, what is removed, that creates our beauty. Of necessity, some of the wood will be whittled away, swept up, and discarded. But what remains, that is the object of the artist, a new creation, a lasting beauty. This is our intent, a singular masterpiece."

I was listening to an esthetically grounded fascist. Although I wished to discard Deter as a fruitcake, as I viewed the trappings of his world, it was apparent he had sponsors, perhaps even a following.

I asked about the box. "There is nothing inside the rectangle," I observed.

"Yes. A reminder, Herr Professor. Think *outside* the box. Always think outside the box. When I, or my colleagues, generate ideas, we determine whether each idea fits inside or outside the box. If it fits inside the box, it is out. If it fits outside the box, it is in. Simple."

"And what determines its location?" I asked.

"Our criteria? You wish examples? Well, let's see. Has it been tried before? *Out.* Will it create controversy? *In.* Does it maintain the status quo? *Out.* Will the left attack it? *In.* Does it require the expenditure of money for their programs? *Out.* For our programs? *In.* Will it promote an exchange of ideas? *Out.* Will it promote a converging of beliefs, a narrowing of thought, a winnowing of options? *In.* Definitely in."

"Your criteria seem very *them* vs. *us* oriented," I suggested.

"An illusion, Herr Professor. These criteria are *we* oriented. Our objective? To create a new *we.* This is our goal."

"Can you give me a concrete example of what you have tried?"

Deter declined. "Confidential and top secret," he replied. "But look around you, Herr Professor. See what is happening under your very nose. You cannot help but observe the changes in daily life. For example, aside from so-called traffic-cams on every corner, the government can photograph fifty thousand faces at a sporting event or a public rally. Some detractors mistakenly believe the government is using these panoramic photos to single out certain individuals for persecution. Farthest from the truth. We have many more sophisticated means for dealing with that sort of trivia. Delinquent child support payments? Rubbish.

"The true purpose of wide-angle monitoring is to determine how rapidly the faces in the crowd are changing. Gender, race, color, size, build. The way environmentalists photograph erosion, we photograph the sea of humanity. Of course, photos of this type are taken continuously all over the country from government satellites." He paused. "But I have said too much already."

"And this is all done under the auspices of the Central Intelligence Agency?" I asked.

Deter smiled for the first time. "A trick question, Herr Professor? Shame on you. CIA stands for Center for Independent Analysis. The extensive screening process you endured is our own concoction." He stroked his virtually hairless chin. "We are a privately funded think tank. Do we have a connection with the Central Intelligence Agency? Or any governmental agency?" He waved a finger ceremoniously before my face. "Only her hairdresser knows."

"Her hairdresser?" I asked.

"That is a joke, Herr Professor. You have undoubtedly seen the advertisement." Again, the finger waving. "Only her hairdresser...."

I have seen the ad, Herr Crouch; only about a gazillion years ago.

Making a beeline for the door would be rude. Engineering a graceful exit seemed a more prudent alternative. "Deter, I must say, we haven't had such an elucidating visit in quite some time. But I should leave you to your work. Perhaps you'll join us on campus to share the evolution of your thinking." Asking this of a lunatic fascist was another sign of losing my mind.

"If you *have* a future on campus, Herr Professor, I would be most honored."

On cue, the door opened and a blond woman, dressed in black, ushered me into the blinding light of the foyer. Moments later, I stood on the street, attaché case by my side.

CHAPTER 18
SKIRTING THE EDGE OF INSANITY

Whether it was the ideas of Deter Crouch, the sudden switch to dazzling daylight, or a lack of food, I wasn't certain, but my brain reeled. Staggering into a corner tavern, I ordered a draft beer and a turkey club. After a quiet meal, I felt somewhat better. As I wandered past the Air and Space museum, I continued to process my time with Deter. Beyond the glass doors hung the *Spirit of St. Louis.* Were he by my side, would Deter point out that this first noble endeavor, human flight, shrank our globe, making virtual neighbors of residents in cultures whose ancient customs, forged centuries before, still guided their daily lives. Had the speed of modern travel compressed time so greatly that the ancient Afghans were now at the head of the cultural parade? Had we lapped ourselves? Was progress blocked by a past that we had caught up with? Can Deter's assertions regarding diversity have merit? Is promoting the melting pot an oxymoron, a misdirected goal never to be effected for the human species?

As I trudged along in the Washington, D. C. heat, I wondered if Deter Crouch had infected me with a hallucinogen. Was this

Deter's attempt to spread his philosophy? Was I to become one of his drones in my classroom, preaching the gospel of universal sameness? A whittler of minds? A *Manchurian Candidate* set to go off at the critical moment, spewing Deter's nonsense?

Searching for a place of refuge from the scalding heat, I spotted a park bench set among shade trees and trundled toward it. A traveling vendor thrust a cold drink in my hand in exchange for several dollars and I succumbed to the heat-soaked air as I replenished my fluid level. After a time, I made my way back to the hotel, fell onto the bed, and dropped off to sleep.

When I finally regained my senses, it was late afternoon. I called Doctor Silverman at his office.

"Moving right along," he observed when I told him of my whereabouts.

"I just interviewed a neo-Nazi who is one step from recommending that all dissenters be rounded up and processed through the local sports arenas."

"A former student?"

"Must I claim him?"

"Only for the record."

"He was a wacko in class, too."

"Don't be so disparaging, my boy. Neo-Nazis bring diversity to our political landscape."

"When you are hanging from a goalpost by your feet, Doctor *Silverman*, you may not feel so glib about the neo-Nazis."

"Perhaps when we are together once again, I shall introduce you to the philosophy of Zen and the universality of humankind. We are all but molecules that have taken discriminate shapes. We are they; they are we. When you hate them, you hate yourself. When you love the ones you wish to hate, ah, then you have achieved the first level of enlightenment." The doctor paused. "But perhaps you are not in a frame of mind for such contemplation.

Suffice it to say, my boy, your road trip seems to be having its desired result."

"Which is?"

"An assessment of your impact on the world, I believe. And a concomitant determination of your real value as a human being. Putting it in the vernacular, you remain caught up in the process of deciding whether your life amounts to anything at all. Am I correct?"

He had me. Like it or not, I continued to assess the value of my life's work with each interview. Was this the intent of the Lioness? Had this young, erotically inspiring sociopath taken me by the scruff of the neck, like a cub pup, to rub my nose in my own droppings? Was she demonstrating wisdom beyond her earthly years? Or merely extinguishing the egoism of a burned-out, over-the-hill professor?

"My boy," Silverman intruded, "have you made your discovery? Has the trip been worth it?"

I liked my therapist less and less. Perhaps it had been a mistake to call him. "Are you sure that's what I'm doing?" I asked.

"Looking for validation? What else? My boy, your patron, the Lioness, as you refer to her, wittingly or not, has sent you on a search for the Holy Grail. You have obviously come to *that* conclusion, I trust."

Can you hate your therapist and still expect to get help? Is that like asking the god you've scorned since childhood for salvation in a foxhole? Can a skeptic enter the confessional and gain absolution as an atheist? I was forming a trauma bond with Silverman. I would be better off throwing myself on the mercy of the court. Or in front of a taxi. This entire fiasco had gotten out of hand.

Finally, I spoke. "The only conclusion I have come to, Doctor," I said, with a degree of sarcasm, "is that I am not getting any better. While I realize that getting better is *my* responsibility, I wouldn't mind a little help from you."

"Tsk, tsk, my boy. Although whining does not become you, pouting becomes you even less. Take the high road in these matters. Accept the reality that you are a difficult patient. And, above all, remember, *you* came to *me*, not the other way around."

"I thought that was the way it was supposed to work in these matters," I said.

"This is a two-way street," Silverman replied. "There should be something in it for me."

Although I somehow continued to cling to the hope my doctor could someday provide help to my addled brain, I was losing faith. Perhaps a kind word? A gesture? An opportune moment of silence? Was that too much to ask?

"Perhaps you are right, Doctor," I said with as much congeniality as I could muster. "It's time to lower the bar."

"You see, my son, good things come to those who wait."

"Do you mind that I call you on a whim?"

"Do I not seem good natured?" he replied. "Have I not given freely of my time? Have you not been getting my bills?"

"My life is on auto-pay," I said. "Perhaps if I gave you a raise to cover the inconvenience."

"I have given myself a raise for that very reason. Quite a sizable one, I might say. Generous, by most standards."

"Then I guess, it's goodbye."

"Adieu, for now, my son." He hung up.

CHAPTER 19

ON THE STREETS OF MANHATTAN

After two days of recuperation, wandering through art galleries and several private historic libraries, I placed the Taurus in temporary storage and took the train from Union Station in D.C. to Penn Station in New York City. The trip was not unpleasant. Most fellow traveler's sat with notebook computers or tablets on their laps, some apparently working, others playing computer games, or perhaps composing e-mails to secret pen pals. I glanced occasionally at the *Zen Practice* book laying open on my knee, a book I'd picked up at a kiosk in Union Station while waiting for the departure of my train, a book I hoped might help with my mental health by teaching techniques to quiet my mind. Unfortunately, as I struggled to focus on the text, I was constantly distracted by thoughts of the Lioness. Where was she at that moment? What were she and young Ryder doing? Was he kissing her shyly on one cheek or had he advanced to a more arduous medium of demonstrating his affection? That thought generated a spear of jealousy as I pictured the boy affixed somehow between her thighs, one or another body part flailing away in bliss as she scrutinized her nails, gauging the interval to her next manicure.

When I exited the cool tomb of Penn Station, the mid-summer heat sucked the air from my lungs. After several minutes of struggling to become orientated to my surroundings, I flagged a taxi and asked to be taken to my hotel. The driver and I seemed to have a communication problem and I arrived at my destination twenty minutes later and thirty dollars poorer. The cost of a room for two nights would surely deplete my travel budget, so I cut it to one night, hoping to conclude my business by the following morning.

The former student I sought was Ambrose Archer. When I asked the concierge at the hotel for directions to the address the Lioness has provided, he scowled, recommended the subway, and suggested I divest myself of any valuables.

My destination turned out to be a mission in lower Manhattan, two blocks from the waterfront. When I knocked on the massive steel entrance door, a small panel slid open and an eye glared out at me. "Do you got any baggage?" the voice hidden beneath the eye asked.

"I'm not here to stay," I replied. "I'm looking for Ambrose Archer."

"This ain't the missing persons bureau," the voice replied.

"I was given this address. Is there any way to find out if he is here?"

"Indeed there is."

The panel closed with a bang. Then silence. I waited, five, then ten minutes. Finally, I knocked again. The panel slid open.

"Yeah? What'd ya want?"

"I'm looking for Ambrose Archer," I said.

Same eye. "I know that."

"Well?"

"Well?"

"Is he here?"

"How the bloody hell should I know?"

"Can I talk to someone who might know?"

The panel shut again. I heard a mumbled exchange from within, then the entire door opened and I was greeted by a smiling nun in a long flowing robe. "Come in, my son. Come in. You look tired from your long journey." She pulled me by the arm and closed the heavy door behind me. The cavernous room in which I stood, apparently once a warehouse, was filled with cots and sinks and tables and curtains that could be drawn to create amorphous divisions of space. "I see you are traveling light. Well, no matter. We shall take care of that. But first we must feed you." She escorted me to a table and signaled a nun standing at a caldron to bring on the porridge.

"Please," I said. "I'm only here to find someone."

The nun placed a kindly hand on my shoulder. "My son, we are all looking for Him. He is here among us. You will find Him in your own time and in your own way. But we must nourish the body first."

"Ambrose Archer," I said. "I'm his former history teacher."

"History?" the nun exclaimed. "That was my subject at St. Joseph's. I taught history for thirty-two years. Do you miss it? I do, terribly. But I'm now doing God's work in a different way."

"I was given this address for Ambrose Archer. By any chance, is he here?"

"Not by chance. Oh, no. By Divine Providence. All our children come to this place by Divine Providence." She glanced knowingly around the room, obviously her domain. "Yes, right over there. In the corner. I believe he's napping at the moment." She looked at me full in the face. "Your name again?"

"I'm Professor Alec Simon. Ambrose was a student of mine at the university back in 2010."

She smiled wistfully. "Twenty-ten. Who would have thought we'd all have lived into this new millennium? Past the turn of the century of 2000." She sighed as she moved away from me. "Ambrose, you have company. Time to rise and shine." She motioned for me to follow in her wake.

A convoluted pile of fabric stirred, and a face appeared from beneath an old army blanket. Two eyes blinked, then Ambrose sat up, a broad smile on his bearded face. "I was stargazing last night, Sister Angelica, and I must have stayed out too late." He looked around. "What a beautiful morning."

I glanced about the room, wondering where he found the instant beauty. Having decided to make my interview with Ambrose as brief as possible, I said, "Hi, Ambrose, you probably don't remember me at all, but I'm Professor Alec Simon from your undergraduate days at State. You are wondering why I've looked you up after all these years, aren't you? Well, I'm conducting a follow-up on a select group of former students. How are you?" I stepped forward and extended my hand.

Ambrose jumped from the bed and grabbed me for a fierce hug. "Professor, of course I remember you. How kind of you to visit. Has Sister Angelica wined and dined you?"

"I'm really fine," I said. "If you have five minutes to spare, I'd like to ask you just a few questions. About my teaching. If class had any impact on your life. Would you be willing?"

"Of course, Professor. Why don't we step into the garden. We'll have privacy there"

Ambrose took my arm and guided me down a dark, musty corridor to a door marked with a red exit sign. We stepped into a garden blooming with brilliantly colored flowers. The garden's centerpiece was a three foot high stone statue of St. Francis holding a pitcher above a copper birdbath with the potential to spew water were it not for the severed copper pipe leading underground. A ten-foot high wall, draped in flowering vines, surrounded the perimeter.

"Nice spot," I said.

"Thank you, Professor. These plants are mostly donated, dregs from area florists that have grown a little shabby and can't be sold. Some must be discarded, but many are nursed back to their healthy radiance. Like the nuns do with the souls of our residents."

"So do you live here full time?" I asked.

"In winter, I make my way to a warmer climate. But all spring, summer, and fall, this is my home. And gardening is how I earn my keep."

"You're not, you know, a street person then?"

"I'm a person of the streets, Professor, but not a street person in the conventional sense."

"But with this kind of talent," I said, with a sweep of my arm, "you could earn a living on the outside."

Ambrose cocked his head. "This is the outside, Professor. No one keeps me here. I relish this life." He motioned to a stone bench near the fountain. "I have never been happier than in the years I've been living among such splendor."

"Have you tried holding a job? You could have your own apartment and buy the kind of food you want to eat. You would have money to go to the movies, to travel."

"I already do a great deal of traveling, Professor. And I don't much care for movies or television. Of course, I read a lot. Such a wonderful way to expand one's imagination. And I talk with people from all over the country who pass through the mission. And I have this wonderful garden to create each spring and to nourish during the long summer and autumn."

"Don't you miss a family?"

"I have a family. My intentional family. These people love me more than any blood relatives ever could." He extended his arms and glanced down at the worn clothing draped shapelessly about his narrow frame. "And they don't want me to change. Isn't that the best part?"

"Don't you ever get lonely or afraid?" I asked.

"Yes. Isn't it wonderful? I love those emotions. I feel so alive when I am lonely. Then I seek out someone and we have a wonderful reunion, even if we've only been separated for a few hours. If I'm here in the garden and I grow lonely, I step inside and find a stranger who needs my love. We embrace and I'm no longer lonely. They have given me what I need and I have given them what they need. And no one had to buy a ticket or pay a monthly fee."

Ambrose seemed annoyingly joyful with this existence. "Do you mean to say you would rather be living in this mission than in a house in Queens with a lawn and a garden of your own? Where you could invite any friend you wished. Where you would have a complete sense of freedom."

Ambrose took my hand. "Professor, let me ask you, are you ever afraid?"

"Everyone is afraid."

"And lonely?"

"Of course."

"Do you sometimes worry?"

"I do."

"Are you ever anxious?"

"My psychiatrist has asked me those very questions. Where is this going?"

"We share the same human emotions. Now, do you have a hundred or more people loving you at the same time?"

"Not usually," I said.

"Are you free to pick up and travel anytime, anywhere?"

"During breaks and holidays from the university."

"Do you ever worry about getting all your bills paid?"

"I have from time to time?"

"Do you ever wake up at night in a cold sweat wondering if you've done something or not done something?"

"Doesn't everyone?"

"Do you have a dog, Professor?"

"Now, that's a good example. You could have your own place with a dog."

"I have hundreds of dogs in my life," Ambrose said. "Walk the streets for a day or two. You'll encounter such a range of wonderful animals. Large. Small. Beautiful colors. Expensive dogs. Even dogs that are free to come here for a night or two to cheer up the residents before going on their way."

He dropped my hand and gently grasped the leaf of a thriving rhododendron. "I am not on drugs, Professor. And the nuns have not indoctrinated me into some strange cult. On the contrary, my mind is free and clear, my body healthy. I could do many things with my life and I am consciously choosing to do this. There are few people in the world as fortunate as I. And, by a strange coincidence, I can say that I owe much of my philosophy to you and your classes.

"The study of history demonstrates the downside of conventional living. The lives of those who follow the yellow brick road, that's how I phrase it. I doubt very much if the lives of the thousands of souls who pass through this mission each month will ever make it into the history books. They can't be discovered in your classroom, only from firsthand encounter. And I recall vividly that firsthand encounter is your recommended strategy for understanding the past. Primary sources. First editions. Well, inside these walls are primary sources and, believe me, first editions. Knowing and understanding these people is to know the history of humankind in a way that kings and politicians and generals will never know, can never know, the people they serve. These people live within the vessel of their own design.

"Generals create wars so soldiers may fight battles. Politicians legislate so presidents may rule. My friends within live in a world that is of no ones making. It is a world that has evolved from the beginning of time, a world to which they react, with which they must cope. One in which all emotions are free to roam. Love, hate, devotion, fear, happiness, sadness. No one puts on their best face here, Professor. Their faces are real. Their faces are honest, responsive to what they are feeling and thinking."

"You clearly don't lack sanity," I said.

"Thank you."

"But, there is more to life."

"Yes, there is," he replied.

We sat for a few moments, then he said, "Do you hear it?"

"Hear what?"

"The traffic."

I listened. Suddenly, for the first time since our presence in the garden, I heard the whoosh of street sounds. "Yes, I hear traffic."

"Isn't it a beautiful sound?"

"It's noisy," I replied.

"That is because you know but one element of it. People rushing around, impatient with themselves and one another. Have you ever lain in bed on a sultry summer night with the window open and listened to the sounds of traffic? The ever-present whirring of moving wheels, rubber on asphalt? The melodic ebb and flow? The sound of a siren gaining and losing intensity as it moves through space? The bark of a dog. A voice calling. And the strident punctuation of automobile horns, the sound of emotion, anger, frustration, panic. Many wish to block these sounds out. As you say, this cacophony represents noise to them. Yet, these sounds are as much a part of our reality as a breeze stirring the leaves, birds chirping, breakers pounding on the shore. It is not the sound that counts, but our associations put to the sound. When we use the street only as a medium, when we are in a hurry, pent-up by not being able to get someplace, or by the crowds of people blocking our way, frustrating our objectives, we associate those sounds negatively. However, if you observe tourists who come to the city merely to experience it, they rarely complain, except at being overcharged. They meander, in no hurry, enjoying the window displays, actually liking the hustle and bustle."

The rattle of the steel door through which we came galvanized Ambrose's attention. "Mr. Archer?" Sister Angelica called in a lyrical voice. "Is all well out in the garden?"

"Yes, Sister," he replied. "All is well."

The door closed. Ambrose stroked the leaf with a delicate motion, then dropped it and looked at me with sad eyes. He cleared his throat and sat upright, dropping the rhythmic swaying of his torso. His tone hardened.

"Professor," he said, "I'm such a bull-shitter. Alec, isn't it?" He glanced at the sky as a jet flew overhead. "Everything I've said is a crock. I hate the city. I'm not here because I love this place." He pulled on his right pant leg to reveal a leather collar with a metal lock. "House arrest. This garden is all the outdoors I have right now. The nuns bailed my ass out on a possession-with-intent-to-sell charge a month ago. My trial date is sometime later this month, that's how backed up the system is. They were glad to get me out of there. This could be my last shot. If I screw this up, I'm looking at three to ten years upstate."

I studied his gaunt face. "So this isn't your garden?"

He broke into laughter. "Cut the crap, Professor. If I had my way, these would all be marijuana plants."

"And my classes?"

He shrugged. "Sorry, Professor. I don't remember you from Adam. Mainly because I never went to class. Of course, I never graduated either. My folks stopped funding me midway through my junior year. They'd never seen a grade report." He continued gazing at me. "You don't remember me, either, do you?"

I shook my head. "No. I have no idea who you are."

Ambrose grinned. "And you have no idea why you're here to see me."

"Not really."

"That's what I thought." His eyes cast skyward as a flock of pigeons beat the air and swooped beyond the edge of the stone wall. "Well, since you are here, Professor, can you loan me a twenty?"

I dug into my wallet and withdrew a twenty dollar bill. Ambrose scrutinized my cash reserves as if he were considering asking for more, but apparently thought better of it. "It's not much," I said awkwardly.

"No, it's not." He extended his hand. "But at least it's nice to meet you." We stood. "You know, even though you don't know why you came to see *me* in particular, the fact that you did makes it kind of special. You don't really want anything from me. You're not here to hassle me. You're just doing your job, but in a kindly way. I like that. I'm going to look you up when I get on my feet. In fact, I'll make a point of looking you up. We'll spend time together, maybe plant a garden or something." He dropped my hand and folded the twenty into a pocket.

"So who does tend the garden?" I asked.

"Sister Angelica. She actually does grow a little pot over there under that banana tree. About once a month, we make a small harvest and she shares it with the residents who have AIDS or are on heavy-duty meds for Hepatitis C. There's a lot of Hep-C here. You know, needle sharing. Some days those dudes can hardly make it out of bed. The pot gives them a few hours of feeling near normal. And you know what? I never touch the stuff. I see those poor bastards suffering and it does something to my insides. I'd feel like shit if I took a cut."

We stood in that awkward moment of silence that descends when it's clear the conversation has run its course and neither person knows how to break and run. Ambrose took the lead. "Sister Angelica will show you to the door. I'm going to check the crop while I'm here. I think we're about a week from taking a few fresh clippings."

CHAPTER 20

YOU CAN TAKE THE BOY OUT OF THE COUNTRY...

I dozed on the train to D.C., grabbed a sandwich in Union Station, and then headed west in the Taurus. By ten p.m. that evening, I'd checked into a motel and was working on the remains of the scotch before falling into a restless sleep.

The following morning, as I walked into the restaurant adjacent to the motel, I felt uplifted by views of the rolling countryside, with lush green hills and fruit trees pregnant with an early harvest. After breakfast, I slipped once again behind the wheel of the Taurus and continued westward, my destination a farm in south central Pennsylvania where I hoped to locate Lana Prescott, a 1995 graduate of State. With no GPS in the Taurus, I relied on the map enclosed in the Prescott envelope, one sufficiently detailed that I had no need to ask for directions. Two hours into the drive, I turned onto a dirt lane and passed beneath a gated entrance that read, 'Easy Hour'. The brand mark was a circle with an arrow running from top to bottom, a symbol for a clock face, I presumed. Continuing along the drive, I came to a large house. Cattle milled about on either side of the road. As I pulled into a parking area, a man on horseback rode from an adjacent pasture and waited for me to climb out of the car.

"I'm looking for Lana Prescott," I said.

"She's working. Better come back some other time."

"May I ask who you are?"

"I'm Nelson. Dirk Nelson. Foreman. Ms. Prescott doesn't need any more hands just now, if that's what you're thinking. And she's not in the market to buy no insurance."

"I'm her former professor. Alec Simon." I extended a hand, but Foreman Dirk Nelson remained solidly in the saddle.

"Didn't know she was a college girl. Anyway, she's busy. You can leave a message, if you like."

"I'm on a pretty tight schedule," I said. "This won't take much of her time."

I measured his hesitation. Finally he tossed his head toward a large barn several hundred feet from the house. "She's in there, delivering a calf. You better announce yourself, cause she packs a six gun and is likely to take a shot at you if you spook her."

Nodding my thanks, I crossed the lawn, climbed a fence, and stepped into a field that led to the barn. Somewhere on the road, I'd bought a pair of comfortable white athletic shoes. Halfway across the field, I begin squishing through animal dung. There seemed to be no going back, so I continued, picking my way through the thick grass so as to avoid, as much as possible, more exposure than my shoes could handle. By the time I stood at the entrance to the barn, my white shoes were moist and brown like two oblong cow pies.

Inside, I saw the back end of a woman with a long brown braid of hair. She bent forward, talking and whispering as a mother cow struggled and kicked. A pair of scrawny legs protruded from the underside of the cow. "Is that you, Dirk? Give me a hand here."

"It's me. Professor Alec Simon," I said.

Lana Prescott glanced across one shoulder. "Who? Well, I don't care, just get over here and give me a hand." I moved timidly across the barn floor. "Hold onto these legs so the baby doesn't move around while I reach inside." She shoved two wet legs firmly into my arms, and then reached inside the cow. "I'm going to pull, so you be ready to move. On three." She counted and we both catapulted onto our backs as the calf came through the opening and landed on its feet. It teetered for a moment, then let out a wale. Lana Prescott prepared the cord, then stepped back as the mother cow turned her rump away from her baby and began licking.

Grabbing my arm, Lana Prescott pulled me into the daylight. As we stood outside the barn, she said, "Well, look at you. You are a sight."

My shirt was covered with afterbirth, my shoes soaked in cow dung. "You do this for a living?" I asked.

She laughed. "I can tell you don't. You sure do look familiar. Who'd you say you were?"

"I'm a former professor of yours. Alec Simon."

"Alec Simon." She considered this information. "History, right? I remember. My, that goes way back. What on earth are you doing here? You've got to be lost."

"No, I actually came to see you. I want to find out if my classes had any impact on your life."

She laughed. "Alec Simon, do you have any idea how silly you look standing there and asking that question? Come inside and we'll get you cleaned up and fed." She led the way to the farmhouse. "Do you realize that was twenty-some years ago? You're here to interview me after all these years?" She shook her head. "There is more to your story, Professor Simon, and I want to here it all." Walking in step behind her, I noticed Lana Prescott's left arm prosthesis for the first time.

We climbed the steps to the porch and entered a mudroom where there were three shower stalls, several laundry tubs, and two washer and dryer sets.

"Get in there and strip off those grungy clothes," she said, pointing to the showers. "I'll get you a robe to wear while they're getting washed."

I did as told. When I finished showering, I slipped on the over-sized robe she had tossed across the shower partition and made my way through the house. Lana Prescott was in the kitchen slicing beef into slabs for sandwiches, her metal prosthesis holding the chunk of meat firmly against the cutting board. She looked up. "That's Daddy's robe. He's not going to be using it I don't believe. Hope you're not a vegetarian."

"No, meat is fine. Where is your father?"

"Upstairs. You'll hear him hollering soon. He's got Alzheimer's. Every now and then he gets lucid. I don't honestly know which way I like him better. But he's going back to the nursing home near my brother's place in a few days. We brought him here just so he could say goodbye to the old place. Yesterday, we rode horseback up into the hills. He was actually doing pretty well, remembering a lot of things. Last night, though, he took a bad turn. I was up with him quite a bit. The good news is he's tuckered out and sleeping in today." She turned to me. "You like mustard on your sandwich?"

"Mustard is fine," I said.

"Are you just being agreeable? You don't have to be, you know."

"I would speak up." She was working on her fifth sandwich. "You know, I'm really not that hungry," I added.

She laughed. "These are for the boys. Dirk will come around pretty soon and take lunch out to them. You met Dirk, I presume."

"I did."

"My self-appointed guardian. He's nearly half my age but has kind of a little brother crush on me. Nobody gets on the farm without passing through Dirk."

She worked quickly and within a short time, had the sandwiches wrapped and into a cooler along with drinks. As predicted, Dirk knocked on the screen door and stepped inside for the cooler. He looked me over, then removed a leather glove and extended his hand. We shook. "Didn't mean to seem rude out there," he said, "but we have occasional drifters coming by for a couple days work."

"I'm not a drifter," I said, "and I won't be staying long."

He nodded his satisfaction, hoisted the cooler, and headed out the door.

Lana made two more sandwiches, dished out potato salad, and set two places at the kitchen table. "Iced tea okay?" she asked. I nodded. She poured two glasses, then motioned to a chair. "Sit. We'll get reacquainted."

I had grown hungry and wolfed down the food without saying much other than that it was good. When we finished, I helped clear the few dishes and followed Lana into the large family room. Sunlight filtered through two cut glass windows projecting rainbows across the wood floor. She sat on a high-backed sofa while I dropped into a comfortable lounge chair, wrapping the robe tightly around my hips. "Thank you for lunch," I said.

"Thanks for your help in the barn," she replied. "Okay, now what is this about? The university doesn't just send professors out to interview former students without some agenda. I know because I'm on the board of one of the local community colleges. They always want something. Mostly, it's collecting money for a building project."

"It's one of those long stories," I said. I was not about to tell Lana Prescott about my prank and its consequences. Instead, I trotted out the myth I had created, now sounding like gospel truth, even to me.

"I have reached a point in my career where I've become curious about former students. Who are they? Where are they? How might they have been impacted by my teaching, if at all? That sort of thing. Anyway, a friend did a computer search and identified a sample of ten. You were on the list, so here I am."

"And what are your conclusions so far?" she asked.

I briefly considered whether details of my travels were at all confidential and concluded that, as long as I didn't mention names, I was free to narrate my experiences. "I've interviewed a successful, seemingly nutty writer, a young doctoral student with a residual crush, a cynical physician, a transgender judge, a drug pusher with twenty-four and a half years on his sentence, a fascist global policy strategist, and a street person with a yarn about the virtues of poverty."

"All influenced by your courses, were they?"

"As a matter of fact, several were."

"So where does that leave you?"

"I'm not sure what you mean."

"Professor, I may just be a farm girl, but I can tell when a person is having a crisis of confidence. Cause I've had my own." She gestured with her prosthesis. "And I've found that you have to forge ahead, despite the odds, despite what your public thinks of you, and most importantly, despite what you think of yourself. You look like a man who has lost his way."

"It's that obvious?"

"I am right about the crisis of confidence?"

"In a matter of speaking."

"And while you hoped your interviews might lead you out of the wilderness, that hasn't happened."

"It's really a long story."

"One you're not ready to tell me."

"It's embarrassing."

"Well, at least I remember you. I hope that helps."

"If I told you immensely, would you be surprised?"

"Since you seem a little dispirited by your research, I'd say no. I hope you're not making any life and death decisions based on your findings."

"I'd like to avoid that."

"So how can I help you feel better?"

I liked Lana Prescott more than I had anticipated. She was sane, intelligent, and mature and most of all, seemed genuinely interested in me. How could she help me feel better? I had no idea. Certainly not by regaling me about my influence on her life and career. But, given her openness and sincerity, I decided to reverse my original decision and tell her the truth about my predicament.

"I played a silly trick, pretending to hold up a bank. It was a stupid prank. Anyway, the teller got the security tape and decided on a form of blackmail. She chose ten former students for me to visit to ask about my impact on their lives. If I don't follow through, she threatens to turn the tape over to the authorities."

"What's in it for her?"

"I don't know, unless it's the sadistic pleasure in sending an over-the-hill professor on this cross-country marathon."

"Tell me about the prank."

"I performed a simple magic trick. I wrote a message, then made it disappear."

"Something like, 'this is a holdup'?"

"Close enough."

"How wonderful that you do magic!"

"My secret passion."

"In three days, we're putting on a program for the children at the county orphanage. They'll come here to spend the day playing games, riding horses, and generally having the run of the place. Your magic tricks would add so much."

"I should really be on my way."

"Will a couple of days make a difference to you? I know it will to these kids. It's likely none have seen magic. Are you any good?"

"I'm terrific."

"Then you've got to stay. Please. I'll even pay you if it's a matter of money."

"No, I'd never take money. Magic is too much fun."

Staying a day or two would not make much difference in my schedule. But to be on the safe side, I decided to contact the Ryders for the purpose of sending a message to the Lioness on her European vacation. I wasn't taking any chances on incurring her wrath. I wanted her to know I was taking her assignment seriously and I expected to be handed that tape on my return. If she knew my delay was for a good cause, I trusted she would relent on the schedule.

"I'll do it," I said. "But I've got to get a message to the young woman who has the tape hanging over my head."

"Use the house phone, if you need to. This afternoon, I've got to ride out with Dirk to mend some fences. Unless you would care to take his place?"

I looked down at the oversized robe draped around me. "If I could trouble you for something else to wear," I said.

"There is a set of coveralls in the washroom and a couple of shirts. Get dressed. I'll meet you out back by the pickup in ten minutes."

The coveralls were baggy, but fit comfortably. As I climbed into the cab of the truck, Lana Prescott threw barbwire and an array of tools into the bed. She slipped behind the wheel, cranked up the engine, and swung the truck toward the hillside. We traveled along a rocky dirt road to the top of the hill, passing what seemed to me hundreds of animals all chewing on tender summer grass. Our destination was a back field where the wire fence appeared to have been trampled. Lana stopped, hopped out, and tossed me a pair of leather gloves.

"These will save those tender hands of yours," she said. She donned a glove, then pulled a large roll of wire from the truck bed and headed into the field.

"So, what's the rest of your story, Professor," she said, as we worked, she cutting the downed wire and handing the salvage to me for disposal. "I mean the personal stuff. Are you married?"

"My wife just divorced me," I said. "I think she found someone she likes better."

"That's usually how it happens. Any kids?"

"My son, Rodney. He's at the beach working his way into emerging adulthood as a cook."

"Sounds like my kind of kid." She snipped more wire and slung it in my direction.

I found myself surrounded by snarling barbs encircling my ankles, snapping at the fringe of the wide-bottomed outfit I'd borrowed. As I worked on the rebellious strands, stray ends popped out and struck at me like provoked vipers. "Is there a trick to this?" I asked.

"If you find one, we'll patent it. Best not to corral too many strands at a time. They get temperamental if they feel crowded."

I smiled. "And how about you," I asked. "Do you have a family?"

"Just the ones I grew up with. No boyfriend, girlfriend, or husband, if that's what you mean."

"I suppose the farm keeps you busy."

"It does. But I have a health condition that limits my activity. That's the reason for the large crew." She saw me glance at her prosthesis and held it forward. "Not this. This is the result of a tractor accident first year out of college. Something else. I'd rather not discuss it just now."

We worked for an hour, Lana telling me about her life on the farm, her relationship with her two brothers, and her sadness at seeing her father succumb to his illness. She seemed content to talk about herself, and I enjoyed listening, feeling a semblance of normality in my routine for the first time since my encounter with Fulmer Hasback.

As we drove back to the house, she said, "I have a few more chores to finish in the barn. Cook will show up about four to make dinner for the whole clan. You can get out of those duds and back into the robe for now. I'll find something more suitable for you to wear when I get in and should have your clothes scrubbed up and dry by tonight."

Before going into the house, I decided to search out the address book in which I had scribbled several telephone numbers, including one for the Ryders. I hoped to find it buried somewhere under maps, food wrappers, and discarded coffee cups on the rear seat of the Taurus. Shoveling junk from side to side, I made a mental note to clean the car before getting on the road again. I finally located the book wedged beneath the rear seat cushion.

CHAPTER 21
LOVE AND DEATH

When I placed the call, I got Martha Ryder on the other end of the line. At the mention of Jeffrey's name, she burst into tears. "Professor Simon, the news is terrible. They were in Italy." Martha paused to gasp and sob. "A volcano, I can't recall the name, erupted. Apparently they were too close to the edge. They shouldn't have been where they were, but you know *that* woman. Anything for a thrill." More sobs. "We've not heard a thing, but it's possible they have perished."

I stood in shock, the telephone receiver frozen in my hand. Was it possible the Lioness was dead? If so, where was the tape? When I recovered my senses, I said a few consoling remarks to Martha Ryder, then pressed my question: "Did the authorities find anything, Mrs. Ryder? Personal belongings, that sort of thing?"

She gasped for air. "I don't really know." Again, a sob.

I waited, feelings split, sorry for Martha Ryder and terrified that a search party sent to the Lioness's lair led to the discovery of the tape. Once identified as a security tape from the bank, it would be turned over to Ryder Senior and then it was *sayonara* for the nutty professor. I imagined Senior Ryder piecing together a conspiracy theory and hammering me to the wall in his therapeutic quest for relief from his grief. *The Lioness and Me*. Perhaps it would become a musical play, like *Chicago*.

Then again, she could have put the tape in a safe place in case I had any ideas of circling back to search her residence while she was out of the country.

"Mrs. Ryder," I said soothingly, "I'm sure young Jeffrey's personal belongings will be handled by you and his father. However, what of poor Armand? Has she family to care for her things?"

"Ryan, that is, Mr. Ryder, took care of that. In fact, he seemed to know quite a bit about her affairs, Professor Simon. I was so relieved that he could be of help. Without Ryan's intervention, I don't know what would become of her estate."

"Isn't that nice of Mr. Ryder to be so thoughtful," I said.

Senior Ryder apparently lost no time combing through their lair to retrieve remnants of his liaison with the Lioness. If he found the tape, he might have already turned it over to the authorities. Worse, he would surely connect the Lioness and me. But what would he surmise? Perhaps he would credit her with foiling a robbery plot. But would he be so gracious as to let it slide? Doubtfully. By now there would be an APB out. It was only a matter of time. The FBI has likely searched my house, probably tossed the renter out on his ass.

"I almost forgot. Among Armand's belongings, Ryan found a package addressed to you, Professor. Perhaps it is a gift she had intended to give you but hadn't the opportunity before leaving the country. In that respect, she was such a thoughtful young lady, always doing the proper thing. I do have to acknowledge that about her."

"Yes," I said. "Very thoughtful." An overnight delivery service could get the package to the farm by the next day. "Let me express my sincere regrets, Mrs. Ryder. Jeffrey is a very fine young man, someone of whom you can be most proud and I hope for the very best. Do you suppose there is any chance you could have the package sent to me? Perhaps by overnight mail, since I'm on the road this summer. I'd be more than glad to reimburse you."

"Oh, I'd like to, Professor, but there isn't time. I am just on my way to the airport to meet Ryan. We're traveling to Italy to confer with the authorities and to actually determine...." She paused and sobbed. "I'm sorry, but I can't control myself. If we've lost Jeffrey, I don't know what I'll do with myself."

"It would only take you five minutes on the way to the airport," I said.

"I'm terribly sorry, Professor, but there simply isn't time. Besides how much more enjoyable it will be to convey the package to you personally. We'd love to have you to dinner and ask you about Jeffrey as a student. I think it would help with my grieving."

"When are you returning from Italy, Mrs. Ryder?"

"In ten days, Professor. And when will you return from your travels?"

Good question. I'd have to think about that. "I'll call you as soon as I'm back. I hope you have a safe trip."

"Thank you, Professor. It may be our last for a while."

"Really?"

"The bank is in financial trouble. As if we didn't have problems enough, someone embezzled millions of dollars. Can you believe that? A computer hacker, they say. The FBI has been investigating now for weeks, but they have had no luck. It looks as if the culprit got away clean." She sniffled. "Well, I must be off." She hung up.

Culprit, indeed. I smelled Channel No. 5, Armani, silk skin, hot, damp sex, all rolled into one hot trollop. The question was, had I unwittingly played a role in her scheme, or was I simply a diversion. Perhaps she intended to return the tape to me all along regardless of my success on the road.

Now I was faced with a new dilemma. Did I continue my trek, complete the remaining two student visits, or make a dash home and break into the Ryder's place to retrieve that tape? Adding a B

& E to my dossier seemed sensible enough. I was in for the proverbial penny, no pun intended, so why not go the distance, especially since something could happen to the Ryders en route resulting in the package, a.k.a. the security tape, being unveiled by the benevolently curious.

On the other hand, suppose the Lioness continued to have her eye on me in spite of her possible demise? Perhaps the package in the Ryders' possession was not the security tape at all, but a recorded message from the Lioness dictating my next hoop to jump through. And suppose she wasn't layered in the inert landscape of a volcano. Perhaps she had engineered a ruse and at that very moment lay lounging on silk sheets, ready to spend millions of Ryan Ryder's assets?

I seriously suspected that the Lioness had not risked her life to undertake the personal reconnaissance of a volcano. What I didn't know was whether she and Young Ryder had pulled off the scheme together or with the help of Ryder Senior. More disquieting was the thought that Jeffrey had fallen victim to a ruthless scheme at the hands of his lover. Embezzling millions was one thing; murder something else. Despite his maudlin, fawning ways, I liked the boy, probably more than the Lioness did.

A rattle at the outside entry door. A full-bodied young woman with a brilliant smile entered. "*Buenas tardes, Senior,*" she said. "I'm the cook."

I reached to shake her hand. "I'm the professor. Alec Simon. And your name?"

"Maria. Howdy Professor. I know my way to the kitchen." With that exchange, she was off.

I got to my designated room, a large comfortable space on the second floor with an expansive view of the rolling hills behind the house. Sitting by the window, I considered my predicament. So many things about which to conjecture: Was the Lioness alive or dead? And Young Ryder? Were they all in on the embezzlement?

Was that the reason the Ryders Senior were headed to Italy, to join Jeffrey and the Lioness in their secret tryst? Or was Ryan Ryder enticing his bride eastward to be ensconced in a top layer of volcanic ash so that he might consummate the liaison with the Lioness and the millions? *What a cynic I had become.*

I stretched out on the bed to doze. Ten minutes passed before a booming voice in the hallway shouted, "Who stole my robe?" The door flew open and a giant of a man, grizzled, in his underwear, filled the doorway. "You the son of a bitch stole my robe? Take the goddam thing off." He came at me, wrenching the cloth from my body in two pieces. Fortunately I retained my briefs. "You got a tongue?"

"Professor Alec Simon," I stammered. "I taught Lana's history classes."

"You come for my property, did you, you son of a bitch? Wanting to marry Lana, and steal every goddam cent I ever made? I fought for this place. Water rights. You got to have water. I fought when nobody was willing to fight." His fierce dark eyes stared at me. "You a lawyer?"

"No, sir. I'm a professor. I teach history." I could only feel sorry for the old man, Alzheimer's having taken his mind.

"Got no use for professors. Blood suckers. Sitting around finding fault with every dang blasted thing, making no contribution to nothing. Ought to hang every goddam one of you. Professors and lawyers. Hang the bunch of you." He looked at the two pieces he held. "Ain't no good to me now."

"Are you Lana's father?"

He ignored my question. "You smell like you walked in shit. You walk in shit?"

"I went to the barn to help Lana with a calf."

"You didn't have to walk in shit, did you? Christ, I won't be able to get no rest tonight if you sleep inside. You're going to have to sleep in the barn. Professors and lawyers. Bullshit."

"Don't you think you should get back to your room?" I said, trying to project a note of authority in my tone.

"Who you talking to, Professor? I'll go to my room when I goddam well feel like it."

"But your condition," I said. "Lana said you had to rest, that you were traveling back to the Home in the next few days."

"Who you think I am, some crazy old man?"

"No, I don't think so."

"See, that's just what I mean. You don't *think* so. It's that mealy mouth talk, comes from lawyers and professors. Communists. Fancy words, all them qualifiers." His glare intensified. "You think I don't know that word, qualifiers? You think I'm some dumb shit-faced peasant farmer? You want to step outside while I beat the crap out of you?"

"I'd rather not argue," I said, attempting to sound a conciliatory tone.

"Chickens. Professors and chickens. Ought to raise you together. And lawyers. Whole bunch of you. Chickens. You ever fight?"

"Not a lot."

"Armed forces? You ever serve your country?"

"No, sir. I never did."

"Me neither. Farmers, lawyers, professors, all chicken." He looked around as if suddenly aware that he stood in his underwear. "You seen my shirt? I had a shirt. You take that too? Took my robe, now you take my shirt." He continued searching, as if his clothing might be just over the rim of an imaginary horizon. "How's a man suppose to die in peace with all this racket. There's all this bellowing going on right in this room. How's a fellow suppose to think?"

A voice down the hallway came to my rescue. "Daddy, are you up and feeling better?"

It was Lana, my savior.

She appeared in the doorway and took her father gently by the arm. "This is Alec. He's staying for a few days, Daddy. And he didn't come to steal the farm. He's a magician. He does magic tricks. I'll bet he'll do one for you now." She looked at me. "Alec?"

I was on, there in my shorts. I rummaged through my bag of tricks and pulled out a rope. I made it longer, shorter, cut it in two, reassembled it as one continuous piece, plucked it from my ear, swallowed it and drew it out through my nose. Lana applauded as I took an exaggerated bow.

"How'd he do that, Lana?" her father asked.

"He's a magician, Daddy. Now let's get you back to bed and we'll have you take your meds."

She smiled at me as she turned to leave. "I'm glad you're feeling like your old self, today, Daddy," she said, as they made their way down the hallway.

There I stood in boxer shorts, my soft belly hanging over the elastic. I absolutely had to begin exercising, I decided.

═╪╪═

I found a pair of clean blue jeans in my bag. After scrubbing my tennis shoes for nearly thirty minutes and tossing them in the dryer, I tried them on. Because I'd been in their company so long, I could no longer smell the odor. However, I decided I was not the best judge, and donned a pair of slippers while leaving the tennis shoes to air by an open window.

Dinner was at six o'clock. Dirk and five young cowboys sat around the long dining table passing enormous serving dishes of potatoes, broccoli, pork chops, and applesauce. Lana sat at the head of the table. I saw that I was privy to an important daily ritual. Dirk reviewed the work of each of the hands, tossing in comments on the status of specific projects. Lana asked pointed questions in a kindly manner, often of the worker directly. The atmosphere was very business-like. I could have been sitting in on a board meeting of any company in America, except for the generous bowls of food, the contents of which were rapidly disappearing.

Before dessert was served, Lana laid out her wishes for the following day, asking Dirk to assign responsibilities, which he did in his own cryptic way. Then there was a brief discussion between Lana and Dirk about the calendar for the balance of the month, cattle to be culled from the herd for auction, a routine visit from the vet, the status of the water supply, and rising beef prices. As the business meeting wound down, one of the men spoke spontaneously for the first time.

"Ms. Lana," he said, "Bart here must'a walked in shit today. He sure does stink."

Ms. Lana nodded, then smiled. "No, Amos, it was the professor who walked in shit today. We're still getting him cleaned up."

My face flushed as young Amos looked quickly in my direction, grinning from ear to ear. I felt the need to come to my own defense. "I was on the way to the barn to see Ms. Lana," I said lamely.

Amos nodded and stared at his empty plate, the smile lingering.

"And I wasn't used to being on a farm and didn't realize my mistake until it was too late," I continued.

Amos burst out laughing. Bart nudged him, then laughed. Then everyone began laughing, Dirk the least. I liked Dirk for that. Walking through shit on a ranch seemed a mistake anyone could make.

"Alright, gents," Lana said, "the professor has learned his lesson. Dirk, if you'll see that the professor gets a pair of rubber boots while he's with us." She leaned forward. "Guess what's for dessert?"

"Strawberry shortcake," one of the other boys said.

"Whose turn to clear the table?"

Bart stood and deftly removed plates and serving bowls, returning with individual portions of dessert, each carefully cut and measured. Dessert was wolfed down in less than three minutes.

Then the young men excused themselves, rose, and marched out in single file. Dirk followed. Lana and I remained at the table.

She glanced at my dessert plate. "Don't care for strawberries?" she asked.

"Trying to trim down," I said.

"Why don't we go into the library?" I followed Lana to a large room on the north side of the house. "Care for a brandy?" she asked. I accepted. We sat on either side of the dark fireplace.

I continued to like Lana Prescott. Maybe it was just that I'd been on the move for weeks, interviewing former students, a number of whom had an array of moral, psychological, or social afflictions. Lana Prescott seemed to be a real person, apparently content with her life, managing a complex business while taking care of family matters. In the short time I'd been with her, she had not whined or complained about a thing, had made no statements about how things could or should be better for her, nor offered negative observations about anyone else or life in general. As we sat in silence, I felt accepted in her home like an old friend.

I asked, "How long have you been running the farm?"

"Nearly ten years. Daddy first showed signs of forgetfulness in small ways. When he missed an auction that cost nearly a quarter of a million dollars, I convinced him I should step in. For a while, he continued to play a part in management, teaching me a great deal I didn't know. About five years ago, however, we recognized that he needed more care than I could give him."

"He seems very healthy otherwise," I said.

"Is that a polite way of saying Daddy is quite a forceful character? Today, he was his old self with you. In fact, I think he took a genuine liking to you. I love him dearly, but when he's off, I don't have time to look after him the way he needs it. My brother, on the other hand, owns an adjacent farm and is a physician over in Brian County. Daddy stays in a nursing home not far from Barry's office."

"Running the farm certainly seems like a complex job," I said.

"I love it, but I admit it has grown more difficult and for that reason I'm thinking of putting it on the market. With the prices paid by developers for large tracts of land, we'll make out nicely."

"What will you do then?"

"I've longed to be an artist."

I followed her eyes to the far wall of the library where two watercolors hung. One was of the house, a moody, surreal piece. The other painting was of a corral of horses, the creatures appearing to move restlessly in response to an approaching storm. While I was hardly an expert in the field of art, I was impressed with the professional quality of the work. "Those are yours?" I asked.

"Two of several dozen I've completed in the last two years. The others have all sold. I have an open invitation from a New York City gallery to exhibit my work."

"Sounds like a nice transition."

"Perhaps. Even if I don't make it, I enjoy the effort." She studied me for a moment. "So how long have you been divorced?"

"Is it obvious?"

"You're doing all this traveling on your own. That was a clue."

"Papers were filed this spring. I think things got finalized while I was on the road."

She drained the glass of brandy in one swallow. "Are you lonely?"

"A little."

"Will you sleep with me tonight?"

Totally unprepared for the offer, I stammered, "I don't know."

"Is it the arm?"

"Of course not." But was it? I didn't think so. I just had never slept with any woman but Gloria. I was fat, out of shape, and frightened at the prospect of failing at something else in my life.

Lana stood, walked toward me, and unbuttoned her denim blouse. Beneath she wore a sleeveless man's undershirt. Beneath that, her breasts were firm and full, actually burgeoning. She dropped the shirt, revealing the harness that restrained her prosthesis. Unfastening two straps, she pulled her stump from the socket and tossed the contraption onto the sofa. Then she removed the stump sock. The stump ended halfway down her forearm, well rounded, with smooth white skin. She dropped onto my lap. We kissed and I sensed a stirring in my groin. When I came up for air, I said, "I'm quite sure it's not your stump."

"I can feel that. What then?"

"I hardly know you. I feel like I'm taking advantage of this situation."

"But I'm taking advantage of you, Professor. As I recall, I found you attractive in class twenty years ago and I like you now."

"You remember that far back?"

"Women remember when they are attracted to someone." She took me by the hand. We ascended the stairs to a wing of the house separated from the other rooms by a short corridor and a set of thick doors. The bedroom extended the length of the dormer, spanning nearly thirty feet. A king-sized bed occupied a prominent place at one end of the room. Lana slipped off her blue jeans, then her top, fully revealing her breasts. She stood in pink briefs. Her hips were round and full, her legs muscular. "Your turn."

I stood in the center of the room, frozen. What could this woman possibly want with me? She had a stable full of handsome young men less than half my age, capable of performing in any position. I'd be lucky to do one pushup. "The light is on," I said.

"That's the idea. I want to see you."

"You saw me earlier."

"All of you." She stepped toward me. I stepped back. "Alec, if you find me unattractive, say so. Otherwise, strip."

I kicked off the slippers, and then divested myself of the jeans and a borrowed shirt. Standing in my shorts, I said, "You first."

She slid her fingers around the waistband of her pink shorts and wiggled them to her ankles. Her pubic hair had been trimmed to a narrow band. Muscles rippled in her thighs and calves as she stepped out. "Do I detect a stirring in those shorts?" she said.

"Sorry," I apologized.

She moved toward me, reached out, and tugged at the cotton boxers until my penis popped above the elastic waistband. With the boxers now at my ankles, she stroked me several times. "Over here."

Leading me to the bed, she positioned me on my back, climbed aboard, and inserted me between her legs. As she eased her curvaceous body onto to me, I felt her tightness. Up and down, up and down she moved, as if riding a hobbyhorse. Her breasts rose and fell with each cycle, her enormous nipples bobbed before my eyes. As her pace quickened, our breathing deepened until we were gasping for air. Finally we came. Lana Prescott blasted a scream into my ear. When it was over, she dropped onto me, her generous breasts pinning my shoulders to the mattress.

I lay quietly beneath her weight, feeling the warmth of her body, enjoying the lingering excitement, a thrill I couldn't remember ever having before.

After a time, I grew uncomfortable. "Lana," I whispered. "Can you move?" I stroked her back. "Lana? I can't breathe."

I wiggled an arm loose and with considerable effort, heaved her onto her back. Lana was smiling, her eyes closed. I never knew a woman could have such a fierce orgasm. Had I read that some women could actually pass out from the intensity of a super come? Maybe. I couldn't recall. Stroking her face, her skin felt cool. "Lana," I called loudly, "don't fool around. Are you alright?"

I placed several fingers against her neck, checking for a pulse. Nothing. I compressed her chest, working up a rhythm that I had learned from a refresher CPR course taken the previous summer as a mandate at the university. Five, six, then seven minutes passed. Lana's body lay quietly inert. No pulse. About to yell for help, I remembered the old man and instead got dressed, covered Lana with a sheet, and slipped downstairs. With no idea how to contact Dirk, or whether that was even wise, I dialed 911, gave a short, dressed up version of the situation, and asked that a doctor and an ambulance be sent immediately.

Less than a mile down the main road, the emergency medical team, a woman and two men, responded within minutes. They raced up the stairs, checked Lana's vital signs, applied resuscitation for another ten minutes, then pronounced her dead. I couldn't believe it; death by sex.

As the rescue squad packed up, I sat on the edge of the bed, my face in my hands, wondering what I could possibly do next, when a bassoon voice startled me. Looking up, I saw a tall, ghostly figure emerge from the hallway. "I'm Dr. Bennington," the man said, more as a reminder than an introduction. Dr. Bennington appeared to be well into his seventies, with a full gray moustache and an air of authority. The emergency staff greeted him deferentially, and then left the room at his request. He closed the door and turned to me. "You the lover?" he asked.

"I barely know the woman," I said. "I was her former professor and came by to do some research. This just happened."

"Well, don't sound so guilty. I've told Lana for years she needs to take things easy. She had a bad ticker. It's a miracle that she has lived this long." He tapped his chest with an index finger, apparently to indicate where the heart was located. "She hadn't had sex in nearly two years. I know, cause I was her last. Before you, that is. Boy oh boy, she was some woman. It broke my heart to tell her we had to give it up. Well, she was always high spirited, wasn't about to listen to anyone. I was afraid at first she'd be tempted by those studs who worked for her. But Lana had good sense, liked older men, and never would fool with her employees. She swore she'd give up on the sex, but wouldn't slow down otherwise. Anyway, you ought not to feel guilty. She always told me when she had to go, this was the way. Funny thing, I almost came by the other night with this very thing in mind, cause my wife hasn't been her usual self lately. But I didn't feel I could be the one, being her doctor you know. Anyway, wherever our gal is now, you can be damn sure she's grateful to you. Now just give me a minute or two to say my good-byes."

"But what will happen to the farm, her father?"

"Lana's brother will be over by and by. He's just a couple of miles on the other side of the hill. The two farms adjoin one another." He studied me for a moment, perhaps discerning my discomfort. "In fact, if you don't have any more business here, why not just run along. I'll write that Lana died in her sleep. No need even for an autopsy, since she's got a long history of heart problems I can attest to."

"But I was supposed to perform some magic," I insisted.

Dr. Bennington stepped to my side, placing a hand on my shoulder. "Seeing the contented expression on Lana's face, I think that's exactly what you did, young man. You see, only Lana and I shared the fact that, in addition to her coronary problem, she had a very advanced brain tumor. Inoperable. This gal knew exactly what she was doing when she took you on. She probably didn't have any more than six months before she'd have a stroke that would cause the beginning of the end. That's no way for a woman with her spirit and love of life to go, lingering in some hospice.

"And if you were thinking about performing tricks for those orphans, don't fret. I got a steer roping contest and a bar-b-queue planned that'll knock them in the aisle. Now you hit the road before the family starts arriving and they claim you as some distant kin. That's how the Prescott's are. They catch you here and you'll be part of the family, have to hang around for the next week telling stories, making runs to the liquor store. They'll roast a hog, have barrel racing contests, and invite most of the county to the wake. Your vehicle out there in the yard will be buried behind three rows of farm machinery. You won't be able to move it for a month of Sundays."

I liked Dr. Bennington and had the briefest of fantasies that he might return to medical school to study psychiatry so I could see him for therapy, listen to his fatherly support, and know that my life would be in his hands. As we shook wordlessly, I wanted to embrace him, but resisted. Instead, I slipped quietly down to my room, packed up the few items I'd laid out, and headed to the laundry for the rest of my clothing.

CHAPTER 22
LET'S FACE IT: S..T HAPPENS

Sometime earlier in the evening, Lana had managed to iron my laundered clothes and arrange them on a hanger. I folded each item carefully into my luggage, donned my tennis shoes, and hustled through the house. As I descended the porch steps in the dark, I heard Lana's father bellowing from somewhere inside. I threw my luggage into the trunk of the Taurus and climbed behind the wheel. Maneuvering carefully down the long driveway, I eased past a car headed toward the farm; I presumed brother Barry and wife.

The nearest interstate exchange was several miles along the narrow two-lane road. As I turned onto the entrance ramp, I remained in my state of shock and disbelief at Lana's death. Having no desire to travel that evening, I took the next exit where I found a lone country motel. Pulling into the nearly empty parking lot, I got out of the car and headed to the lobby where an attendant sat behind a slab of thick glass. She glanced up, sniffed, then said, "You been walking in shit today?"

After checking in, I located a plastic bag, dropped the tennis shoes inside, sealed the bag with black electrical tape I found in the trunk, and returned to the parking lot where I dumped the bag containing the shoes into a community trash bin. In the trunk of the car I found my bottle of scotch. Retrieving the booze and a bucket of ice, I poured a generous drink and stretched out on the bed with the television running in the background.

I couldn't shake my feelings of guilt about Lana Prescott's death. If I had only known of her condition, I would have never agreed to have sex with her, regardless of Dr. Bennington's dismissal of my culpability. And what of my promise to produce a magic show for the orphans? A steer roping contest and a magic show were just not in the same league. I could only hope that Lana Prescott, wherever she was, would understand.

The cell phone sat on the bedside table next to my wallet and keys. I hit a speed dial number. After several rings, Rodney's voice-mail message came on, preceded by an unidentifiable rock tune. When the band finally wrapped up, I said, "Rodney. It's Dad. I was thinking about you. How's your summer going? I hope well. (Pause). I guess we should talk more often. No need to call, unless you want to." Unexplainably, tears floated along my lower eyelids. "I miss you, Rodney," I concluded, and then hung up.

Late the following morning, I awoke with a hangover to the noise of pounding on the motel room door. I immediately concluded that brother Barry had grilled Dr. Bennington who, grief-stricken, broke down and told the entire story of his affair with Lana, implicating me in her death. Certain that the state police were about to file murder charges against me, I was relieved to open the door and find a woman with sad eyes, a saggy body, and long, stringy hair, in the hallway. She held a stout stick forward from which dangled a plastic bag containing shoes. The stench nearly overwhelmed me. "These yours?" she asked.

I nodded.

"The garbage guys won't empty the bin. You can't leave these out there." She allowed the plastic bag to slip from the tip of the stick, the shoes bouncing as they hit the threshold. Bending forward, I retrieved the bag and closed the door.

A long, cold shower helped sooth my hangover. As I shivered beneath the spray, I continued to feel guilt at contributing to the death of a vibrant woman. Granted, I had no idea Lana Prescott had heart problems, let alone a brain tumor. She seemed healthy as a horse as she pulled the calf from the mother cow the previous day. Why had she not warned me? Was it a forgone conclusion she was to die from her next orgasm? More importantly, why had she sacrificed herself to me in particular?

I wanted to somehow grieve over Lana Prescott, but instead faced the cold spray until my skin grew numb. Then I dressed and, with my shit-kicking shoes in the trunk of the car, hit the road again.

An hour later, my stomach had settled enough to get half a bowl of oatmeal down. In the parking lot of the restaurant, I spied a garbage bin. As I approached with the plastic bag, the restaurant manager stepped up behind me and said, "Don't even think about leaving those shitty shoes here."

Even with the shoes stowed in the trunk wrapped in two layers of plastic, I smelled the ripening manure. Rolling down windows didn't help much, but I felt better about it. Driving at sixty-five, I gulped fresh air as it roared through the car's interior. After several hours, I stopped at a rest area. With the shoes in plastic and concealed within two additional layers of brown paper grocery bags, I headed for a dumpster when a state policeman called out. I looked up. He stood by the Taurus. "This your vehicle, sir?"

"Yes sir, it is."

"Where's it been?"

"The smell?"

Before I could explain, he held his nose and pointed at the bag. "That excrement? You can't dump excrement in a public bin. You'll get a two hundred dollar fine for doing that. Now you'd better move your vehicle out of here and take whatever that is with you. You're stinking up the place."

"They're only shoes," I protested.

Travelers at the rest stop shunned the Taurus, circling the vehicle in expansive arcs. The police officer jerked his thumb, the authoritative international directive to head down the road. In this case, *or else*. I climbed into the car, the bag on the seat next to me, and pulled onto the highway. The patrol car followed me to the state line.

Once in new territory, I considered tossing the shoes over an embankment along the road, but feared the state police had already been alerted and were watching via a sky satellite. The bag returned to the trunk.

At the next exit, I found a used car dealership. The salesperson came strutting out of the trailer that served as his office, a smile clamped across the lower half of his face. Stopping halfway across the lot, he pinched his nose. "You ain't unloading that piece of crap on this lot."

"I'll do anything," I said. "I'll buy a car and give you this one free."

"You'll pay me a hundred bucks to burn the damn thing."

We quickly struck an agreement. I cleaned out my belongings, leaving the junk in the back seat and the shoes in the trunk. The deal involved a Dodge Dart with a cracked rear window, three dented fenders, and missing hubcaps. The salesperson assured, in spite of the appearance of the auto, the engine would purr like a kitten.

Fifty miles down the road, the water pump gave out. When the tow truck arrived, the driver recognized the heap. "Sid's Select Auto Sales back in Scamperville. Old Sid's got two dozen of these sweethearts behind the barn. Bet he told you the engine purred like a kitten."

"Something like that," I said.

"Hope you didn't pay more than two hundred."

I shrugged. "Any salvage?" I asked.

"Tell you what," the driver replied. "I'll give you fifty bucks for parts and take you by my brother-in-law's. He'll fix you up with something that'll at least get out of the state."

Two hours later, I drove off Big Dave's lot in a 1996 Buick Skylark that had barely a scratch on it and an engine that actually sounded as if it might last until I got home.

CHAPTER 23
DEATH BECOMES HIM

Number nine on my list of former students to interview was Wallace Stromberg, an undertaker practicing in a small town in Virginia. As I neared the little community, I called ahead and got an answering machine with Stromberg's melodic voice oozing sympathy and advising that he was on a job at the local cemetery, but available by cell phone twenty-four hours a day. When I dialed Stromberg's cell phone number, my call apparently rolled over to his hard line. Stromberg might be available; the trick seemed to be making that initial contact.

A passerby I accosted knew of Stromberg as the local funeral director and provided me with directions to the cemetery. He informed me that Stromberg, if there, was undoubtedly digging a grave personally. I made a left, then two rights, and found the cemetery at the top of Culver Hill, a site populated with old oaks and blue spruce. A narrow macadam pathway wound its way like a mourning ribbon back and forth across the hillside. I pulled behind the only vehicle in sight, a black Cadillac limousine. Two dozen feet from the road, shovels-full of dirt were flying in rapid succession beyond the edge of a gravesite onto a well-stacked mound.

As I approached, I called out, "Mr. Stromberg?"

Another shovelful. I hovered at the brink of the pit, looking down at a man in his early thirties, rosy-cheeked, rotund, balding, with splotches of mud on his face. He worked in a dark business suit, white shirt, and somber gray striped necktie. "Indeed," he said, looking up. "Might you be Professor Simon from State U?"

"I am. How did you know?"

"Working close to the spirit world as I do, I have all kinds of knowledge, past, present, and future." He grinned. "A more honest answer would be that Armand Pennington advised me that you'd be around by and by."

"You know the Lioness?"

"Who?"

"Armand. You know her?"

"Indeed, Professor. Armand Pennington and I have been chums since college days. In fact, I took one of the last spots in your class while she was off having an abortion. She's never quite forgiven me. She needed that course in her sequence and ended up having to do a third year of French, which of course, she no longer regrets."

"You and she are the same age?"

"She's actually a year older, thirty-two. You'd never know it though, would you?"

"But she is, that is, was dating a twenty-three year old boy."

"Ain't love grand?" Another shovelful of dirt landed on the pile. Then Stromberg paused and looked up at me. "You don't remember me, do you, Professor?"

There was a note of expectation in his voice that raised my anxiety. Had he failed my class? Worse, had I written some despicable comment on a paper about which he's been ruminating all these years? I shook my head. "I must say, I don't. I hope your experience wasn't a bad one."

"On the contrary, I took one of your extra credit seminars. Your recitation of Mark Anthony's eulogy at the death of Julius Caesar so enthralled me, I decided to take over my father's mortuary business, a decision that has delighted us both. I grew convinced it was possible to stir the souls of the living while immortalizing the departed. And the power of those moments; the audience so fertile, so vulnerable.

"You see," he continued, scraping together another clod of soil and sending it spinning over his shoulder, "I have given considerable thought to the issue of death during these past ten years. Death is, without a doubt, the most significant stage of human development, more momentous than even birth. It is a stage of mystery and intrigue. Perhaps because of that," he raised a finger to the air, "with little to go on, humanity has sought to ascribe many myths to the experience.

"The ancient Egyptians believed in an active afterlife that required artifacts from this world. There are Eastern religions that postulate stages of reincarnation. Christians, as we know, espouse that the Lord sent Jesus Christ to guide us through the portal, to another place. There *is* a portal, you know. We even speak in those terms. The Great Beyond. Passing over." He paused, jabbed the pointed spade into the clay, and studied me. "So what do you believe, Professor?"

Hunching alongside the open grave, I said, "I haven't given it much thought."

Another shovelful of dirt flew through the air accompanied by sound effects this time, a grunt. "If that were true, Professor, you would be a very unusual person. Most of us think of death, yet stop short of imagining ourselves going through the process. As I mentioned, I have had great occasion to consider death, to develop my own particular spin. What if, for example, every branch of contemporary religious thought was wrong? Suppose death is merely a staging room for a recycling process? Not as in reincarnation. But what if we are all actors assigned roles to play? What if the universe was simply a gigantic stage on which we, as humans, carry out plays for the amusement of the gods, as the ancient Greeks supposed? What if Fred and Barney from the flint stone age beat each other to death with clubs, then found themselves in the staging room, patting one another's backs, congratulating each other on a job well done? Actors. All actors, waiting for another role somewhere in the universe. Do you get the ramification?"

I shuddered at the imagery. Hoping to lead away from the philosophical topic of life after death to a more immediate question, I said, "May I ask whose grave you are digging?"

"You may. It is the grave of the mayor."

"The mayor of this community?"

"The very same."

"What did he die of?"

"Oh, he's not dead yet."

"But his death is imminent."

"Very."

"Is he ill?"

"Not exactly."

"But you know he is likely to die soon."

"This is a small community, Professor. I know many secrets."

"In that case, perhaps you know something of Armand. For example, have you heard from her?"

"Yesterday," he replied. "A text right in the middle of a funeral."

My suspicions were correct. "When I spoke with Mrs. Ryder, she said her son and Armand nearly died in a lava flow accident in Italy."

"I'm sure she did."

"But you spoke with Armand. There is no doubt."

"I did, Professor. She and her young protégé are safe and sound at this very moment. Apparently, there was a misunderstanding, a case of mistaken mis-identity."

"Someone mistakenly thought Armand and young Ryder were among the dead?"

"Something like that."

"Do the Ryders know the truth?"

"Professor, what I don't do is meddle in Armand's affairs."

"But it's cruel to let Mrs. Ryder believe her only son is dead if he is not."

"May I simply say, the matter is in good hands."

Suppose my wild suspicions were accurate? Armand embezzled the money from the bank, faked their deaths, and then set up a meeting with the Ryders to divvy up the loot. Maybe that was none of my business, but why, then, was I jumping through these hoops? With the Lioness absorbed in an entirely new endeavor, cutting up the multi-million dollar pie, what possible interest could she have in me?

Wallace Stromberg carefully edged the corners of the grave, smoothing, leveling, sizing for an accurate fit. His gestures appeared to be almost caressing in nature. "May I ask why you are digging the mayor's grave personally?"

"I dig all my graves personally. We have a groundbreaking ceremony, and then I dig. Family members are so enthralled with my earnestness; I have their complete attention at the time I deliver the eulogy at the gravesite. This appearance of self-sacrifice purchases an extra measure of credibility and, of course, eases some pain at bill-paying time."

"To some, that might appear to be a bit cynical," I suggested.

"Of course. I manipulate their minds so they may see with clearer vision, listen with more attuned hearing. For what they wish to know, Professor, is whether their loved one's life has been worthwhile. And do you know why? Because, the experience of the death of another makes us consider our own mortality. We wonder if our own life has meaning. It is a question we all consider at one point or another, Professor. And, as I recite the deeds of the deceased, ascribing value to his or her time on this orb we call earth, the mourners listen and ask themselves, 'For what will *I* be remembered?'

"Which leads to the ultimate question, Professor. For what will any of us be remembered? Mozart, of course, is remembered for his music. Van Gogh for his paintings. Napoleon for his Waterloo. But for what is the average person remembered?

"Do we worry about it? Indeed we do. Being remembered is the closest one gets to immortality. Our biggest fear is that our life was lived for naught, that we would be soon forgotten. Each of us wants to have counted, to leave a legacy. True, some have actively sought and achieved their fifteen minutes of fame. Consider the epidemic of social media. Selfies. Postings of scrambled eggs and drooling bulldogs and kittens wearing buntings. More evidence that most live that life of quiet desperation and avoid addressing the question in a timely manner. For, in truth, none of us wants to face the reality of death.

"And then, Professor, there is the question of standards. By whose standards is one's life evaluated? Does being a good person count? Is it production? Are Mozart and Van Gogh and Shakespeare truly remembered as people? Or simply for the artifacts of their age. And what of those who merely get by? Does getting by in life count?" Stromberg leaned on the shovel, now grinning up at me. "What makes us count as human beings, Professor? Perhaps you, yourself, have wondered."

"I have," I confessed.

"And your conclusion?"

I wanted to fall back on Silverman's contention that none of it mattered. Doing one thing was as good as doing another, as long as we didn't violate any of the cardinal rules of conduct. I considered what had been held forth as the gold standard over the centuries. No killing, no stealing. That made sense. Was coveting another matter? And what of adultery? The entire country was going to hell on that one. Cursing had to be out the window as a rule. *Always* honoring mom and dad and the elders of the church? The cover on that got blown with the first sex abuse scandals. Other gods?

Was that like jumping teams? But what about free agency? And what of those who gave up, decided not to believe in anything? Did any of the rules count for them? Production alone couldn't be the answer, I decided. What of the serial killer who deliberately committed his crimes because he wanted to produce an effect to be remembered?

Stromberg tapped his fraternal ring impatiently against the shovel handle.

"I'm thinking," I said. "It can't be production."

"Not production, fine. Then what in your case, Professor? What will *you* be most remembered for?"

The Lioness had her hand in this; that was plain to see. Somewhere in a weak moment, I had confessed my fears, my angst. And she purposely brought me to this place. To Stromberg. Her agenda? Forcing me to face my truths. But why? What business was this of hers? I wanted to be angry, to scream out, *How can you, a mere youth, and a schemer to boot, how can you have the gall to confront me with my frailties?* How can you be so presumptuous as to force me to answer a question I have avoided my entire life?

"Are you afraid of the answer, Professor?" Stromberg asked. "I don't blame you. For any answer must, at best, be maudlin, mustn't it? Will you be remembered for a touch of kindness shown to a stranger? Or a special gift? Perhaps for a lifetime of professorship, conveying information, creating scenarios such as the one that inspired me so powerfully? Or simple dedication to duty, the daily grind, showing up? Perhaps love for a worthy creature in our global universe.

"Have you listened to the eulogies of others? *He was tireless. She, so loving.* In truth, Professor, we are remembered only after we are gone. For how else can it be? If we are alive, we are still a work in progress, to be experienced, not merely remembered. If we are alive, there is time to change. To learn. To love. To repent. To forgive. To heal. And in this great universality in which, like it or not, we live, all human, all destined for the same end, all seeking the same solace, what more can we want than to be a work in progress? We are life, Professor. That's the answer. We are *life*."

The shovel suddenly flew over the edge of the grave and landed with a thud. "Well, my job is nearly done," Stromberg said. He groped along the edge of the grave, locating a canvas bag that I hadn't noticed. Pulling the bag into the hole with him, he reached inside and withdrew a pistol, a revolver. "Fear not, my good man, for the life I seek is not yours, but mine."

I hovered closer to the edge of the opening, dumbfounded. "But why?"

"By virtue of my status in the business, I could answer, 'Because I can'. However, that would be disingenuous. In truth, I cannot stem my curiosity. These many years, I have worked arduously to put others into the ground, or into the fires, then to the urn. In the early days, I merely wondered. Wonder led to speculation. Finally, my passion grew until I have reached a point of no return. I must know Death. I can't stand *not knowing*. I cannot continue in this business, this splendid business dedicated to guarding the vessels of the spirits who have departed for the other world, without myself seeking the journey."

"I thought this grave was for the mayor," I said, hoping to distract him until I concocted a plan to save his life.

"I *am* the mayor."

"But why must *you* die?"

"Because I've got to know. Where do these souls or spirits or whatever you may wish to call them go? What is this new realm? Regardless of one's beliefs, it must truly be a marvelous transition." He flipped open the revolver's chamber, checked the rounds, then continued. "Reflect on the intricacies of earthly life, the complexities of the most modest creatures. The sparrow, the toad, the simple groundhog in the field, the human child. If what we call nature has created and maintained such dazzling specimens while bound by the principles of earthly physical law, how much more splendiferous creation might be without such constraints. I tell you, Professor, I fairly tremble with delight as I contemplate passing through the portal from the earth-bound to the spiritual. Within moments I shall have my answer."

Stromberg held the muzzle of the revolver to his head.

"Suppose you miss," I said, my tone pleading.

"Miss? How?"

"Suppose the bullet doesn't kill you. Suppose you become a vegetable, destined to lie inert in some county nursing home for years, maybe with just enough brain power to realize each and every moment that you hadn't made it."

"A scary proposition, Professor. However, you must remember, I'm in the biz. I know what it takes to mash the human cerebellum into three ounces of gray slime. You are looking at a fifty-caliber handgun loaded with enough firepower to completely decapitate a stallion. Once I pull this trigger, I will disintegrate from the neck up. My single regret is that you have to be a witness. But someone must report the findings accurately. I can't leave wild speculation as my legacy, can I?"

"Suppose I walk away?" I said.

"You won't. Walking away isn't in your nature, Professor. If it were, you'd have walked away from your unhappy marriage years ago, instead of waiting for your wife to find a lover. You'd have walked off from Homer, the fat-assed dog, who pisses in the rear seat of your old Nissan. And you'd have walked away from an employer who rarely appreciates your efforts, who piles on, who demands useless reports, expects more for less, fully anticipates that you'll lease your soul for the opportunity to work at what you love most in life. That's who you are, Professor. Armand enlightened me. And so you won't walk out on me, a former student seeking the answers to the most fundamental questions of human existence."

"Then I'll stop you," I said, fully realizing the futility of my suggestion, because there was no way to disarm Stromberg before he pulled the trigger. I merely hoped the threat, a show of concern, might dissuade him. But he called my bluff.

"Try."

"Think of those who will be deprived of a Stromberg send-off if you do this. There are people in the community who have counted on you to highlight their memories. After all, you have a reputation, don't you? How disappointed will your community of admirers be if you precede them before your time? Some might even consider that a selfish act."

"Why don't you tell me it's against the law to commit suicide, Professor? Or that I'll leave a wife and two children behind? Or that my death will be a tragic, useless waste? Aren't those the arguments? Or perhaps that, at age thirty-one, I have so much to live for? No, Professor, none of those arguments hold sway. For it is the journey that matters. And I am off on mine. Not only to discover what secrets death holds, but also to resolve a considerable debt I've incurred through my gambling enterprises. You see, I can't afford to go on."

"At least tell me of Armand. Is she sitting on millions of dollars of embezzled bank funds?"

"Adieu, my Professor. Adieu."

CHAPTER 24
SILVERMAN'S CONFESSION

Stromberg was correct regarding the weapon he'd chosen; instantly, he lay headless. I looked away, the shock wave of the weapon's concussion ringing through my ears. There must be instances when vomiting was totally spontaneous. I emptied the contents of my stomach by the edge of the grave, and then stumbled away.

The sheriff and two deputies arrived six minutes after my call. They were minimalists when it came to conversation. For that matter, I had little to say myself. I hung around for forty minutes while photos were taken by one of the deputies and Stromberg's assistant retrieved the headless corpse using a rope and an awkward balance beam. The sheriff then asked me to stop by his office at the courthouse to give a formal statement.

On the drive to the center of town, I thought about what to say. The reason for my presence had become standardized fare by now. Mobile professor conducting a pilot study: *Personal interviews with former students to determine the future of the instructional rubrics for teachers of history.* The description almost sounded purposeful. Am I authorized or sponsored on my project? Of course not. This was a cutting edge investigation. How many professors take time from their summer vacations to humiliate themselves? Only mediocre professors with the threat of going to jail hanging over their heads.

Of the hour I spent with the sheriff, only ten minutes were devoted to my statement. The balance of time was given up to interruptions, telephone calls and clerks wandering to and fro with questions on a variety of violations, from dog licenses to undocumented rubbish piles. The sheriff treated me with a deference rarely afforded a university professor in the field. I quickly learned that Stromberg had actually spoken of me on occasion, how my inspiring lectures had led him to give new meaning to *the eulogy*. And I had correctly second-guessed the sheriff's disappointment at not having Stromberg available to memorialize his own deliverance from mortality.

When we had completed our business, the sheriff flashed a strained smile and I feared he was about to ask me to remain long enough to deliver Stromberg's eulogy. But he didn't. Perhaps he read the sadness in my expression. More likely, the notion had never crossed his mind.

As I drove off, I thought of those lectures. That particular semester, I had taken exceptional pains to focus on personal lessons drawn from history. Conceivably, without my inspiration, Stromberg would have stayed with pharmacy, filling prescriptions at the local supermarket. I imagined him giving a snotty-nosed kid a lollypop as he rung up the one hundred and fifty dollar prescription for the child's antibiotic. He would have undoubtedly been superb at answering questions, eloquent, patient, and above all, sincere. I pictured his rosy-cheeked face framed in the plexi-glass window above which hung a sign, *Consultations*.

Back on the interstate, I spied an arrow pointing to a parking area labeled *Scenic Overlook*. I pulled off. The view was spectacular, the rolling hills of green Virginia. A scattering of frail barns dotted the hillsides as far as I could see. Then, as spontaneously as I had vomited, I cried. Sobbed was a better descriptor. I lost track of time. When the gut-wrenching pain finally subsided, I wiped my eyes with a tissue and sat calmly, clueless as to the root of my outburst. It could not have been for Stromberg, for I hardly knew the man. Were the tears for me, for time lost, for the road not taken, for the sprinkling of surreptitious pleasures grazed with a blushing heart, for the more than half-empty glass that only I could fill? Or perhaps for the lonely childhood about which my therapist insisted on reminding me.

That's when I decided it was time to once again phone Silverman.

Doctor Silverman was as buoyant in temperament as ever. "My boy, what a delight to hear from you. I was saying only yesterday to Mrs. Doctor, 'Where is my traveling Professor?' And today, here you are. So, how's tricks?"

"Doctor, I'm coming apart at the seams."

"I love that expression," he replied. "So quaint. So visually descriptive. In professional parlance, we might say, 'you are losing your marbles'. Yes?"

"Doctor, I had sex with a women, a former student. She died right on top of me. Then, I saw a man blow his head off. I threw-up, then cried. I mean, I cried my heart out. What's wrong with me?"

"Nothing that a good night's sleep won't cure," he said.

"It's more than that. I feel like something in my past is catching up with me."

"My boy, with all due respect to your profession, the past is highly overrated. For years, we shrinks have blamed everything on the past. Yet, the past is powerless. It's a bunch of memories that we make up from the present moment.

"Let me test you. Have you ever discussed a movie with a friend, insisting that the plot went a certain way, or that a particular event happened to a character, only to see the film again and discover you had it all mixed up? Now, suppose the characters in the movie acted based on your recall? The movie might be very different.

"So it is with memories from our past. We live our current lives as if all that in the past happened exactly the way we recall. And even if it did, so what? We must cut our ties to the past, my boy. Only this moment counts."

"Well, I'm afraid something in the present moment has gone haywire and is affecting my life in a very negative way," I insisted.

"Why didn't you say so? That's a different story. Let's make an appointment. When will you return?"

"I'm not certain. I still have one envelope to open. Until I do, I have no idea where I'll end up or when this will be over."

"What are you waiting for?" he said. "Open, open. We may be on the verge of discovering your destiny."

Easy for you to say, I thought. You've been in your cushy office by day and your cushy bed by night, snuggling with Mrs. Doctor while I've been rousting about in Mom and Pop motels, eating grease, and crapping in porcelain receptacles with one-size-fits-all seats worn smooth beyond registered trademark recognition. "I'm afraid," I admitted.

"Afraid? What could you possibly fear?"

Reflecting on the previous eight weeks of travel, I said, "Death, insanity and seduction."

"Welcome to the real world, Professor."

"Is there a chance you could be any less supportive?"

"If you feel I am suffocating you, I'll back off. Perhaps it is a case of counter-transference. I'll speak to my therapist about it in the morning."

"*You* are in therapy?"

"Of course, my boy. Where do you think I get my ideas? From aliens in the closet?"

That's exactly where I thought his ideas came from. Not that aliens couldn't have good ideas. It's just that I'd hope Silverman would translate their relevance to my life. "Does this mean that your therapist knows about me?"

"All about you, my boy. For the past two months, you have been the focus of his attention, because, of course, you have been the focus of my attention. My therapist's opening welcome has become, 'So how goes it with the Professor'. He knows about the Lioness, the attempted bank robbery, the divorce, and Homer, the fat-assed dog. He knows about your travels, beginning with Hasbach the wonder-boy, through the transgender judge, and now I'll fill him in on your latest escapades. He is a virtual DVD of information on Professor Alec Simon."

Hanging up, I decided never to speak to Dr. Silverman again. At least, not without a better reason than being lonely, frightened and confused. Those problems I would now handle on my own.

Feeling exhausted from the day and the grind of the trip, I checked into a motel. I still hadn't the courage to open envelope Number Ten. Somehow I feared Silverman was right; the last envelope would deliver my destiny, likely a *coup de grace*. Hitting the remainder of the scotch while watching an old John Wayne western, I ordered pizza, and sat toying with the nine by twelve envelope. I puzzled. What could it contain? And why was I so terrified to know?

Pizza came; I ate, then, in a stupor of booze and carbs, lifted the flap. The shock wave of adrenaline sent me sitting bolt upright. Student Number Ten was, of course, none other than young Jeffrey Ryder.

But why? He'd already spoken to me of my class, how I'd saved his college career, endearing me to his parents. At the risk of thinking poorly of the rumored dead, the young man was a bootlicker, drooling over the slightest nod of attention, playing the dolt among a cast of characters who towered above him in intelligence and resolution. He'd apparently been out of his element from the moment of birth with an ambitious mother, an omnipotent father, and later in life, a high-spirited, feckless courtesan as a companion. What was there to discuss?

"Big deal," I shouted to the walls, drunker than I had supposed.

"Shut the hell up," came a response.

I passed out, face down into the empty pizza box.

CHAPTER 25

THERAPY BY ANY OTHER NAME

W hen I arrived home, I found the house vacant. Apparently a personal emergency in his homeland had cut short my tenant's schedule. He left a flowery note taped to the kitchen faucet and an envelope with full payment for the entire ten weeks. I considered returning the check by overnight mail, but as I contemplated a trip to Europe, decided to hang on to it. Money was tight and if I intended to travel, to confront the Lioness and her young suitor personally, I needed the cash. I would provide the visiting professor from Sri Lanka his refund after my first fall semester paycheck.

Reneging on my secret promise to never speak to Silverman again, I placed the call. My therapist was ecstatic to hear from me and canceled two appointments in order to squeeze me in.

"I missed you, my boy," he said as I settle onto the sofa. "I feared your peevishness might separate us forever."

I had obviously forgiven him for whatever imaginary transgressions I thought he'd committed and detailed my every experience during my travels, rehashing even incidents I had reported during our telephone conversations. After running beyond the usual hour, I said, "You're charging me double, I presume."

"Nonsense. A session is a session." He refocused, cleared his throat, and gestured. "Now, you are certain the Lioness is alive and well? And the young man?"

"I can only infer."

"And the father may be in cahoots?"

I shrugged. "My question is, do I travel overseas to investigate in person? Or do I return to my humdrum life?"

"Such a scheme that woman has concocted. You can't *not* go. I insist."

"Perhaps I'm risking adding conspiracy-after-the-fact to my rap sheet."

"My boy, at this moment, it is all wild speculation. You'll arrive; you'll do your duty by interviewing the young man, presuming he is alive. Then you'll get the entire story from the Lioness. Depending on what happens at that point, you'll make a decision about your life. That's the best you can hope for, I'm afraid."

That Silverman derived such vicarious excitement from my dilemma continued to irritate me. I wanted to blast him, but in truth, I felt he was my only source of refuge. Was I so friendless, I wondered, so hard up that I counted my deranged therapist as my closest ally? There were colleagues at work with whom I socialized on occasion. But that was collegial socializing. And the newly formed purging group where we seven had taken the opportunity to confess our past, as well as current, transgressions? Perhaps I could find some support among them, but I wasn't counting heavily on that.

Somehow I had managed to isolate myself in a world surrounded by others. I had my work, a sparse family life, and my secret ambition to create magic. That the latter had led me to these troubles I found particularly egregious and ironic. Magic, my alter ego, my ticket out, my salvation. My idiotic adolescent performance hung over me like a Damocles sword.

Finally, the Silverman clock ran out and I slinked from his office with little resolved beyond my conclusion that, as I was getting worse, my therapist was showing a level of joyfulness unbefitting his role. Was my relationship with Silverman a variation on the theme from *The Picture of Dorian Grey*? Was I becoming more twisted and ugly, as he grew more winsome and clever?

That evening, I made the decision. Meet with the Lioness in her den of thieves, complete an interview with Young Ryder, if possible, and then push for a commitment that my humiliation would end, then and there. Most importantly, get that tape. I no longer wished my freedom and reputation to be hanging in the balance. Regardless of what I knew or didn't know about her scheme, I would demand to be unencumbered, to live my life with the bank episode behind me.

Then reality struck.

How was I in a position to dictate the conditions of my release? The best I could wish for was a benign resolution based on the graciousness of the Ryder clan and the evolution of the interests of the Lioness. If, in fact, she possessed millions in bank funds, she was sitting on a pearl in her own oyster. I could only hope that whatever titillation she had found in putting me through my paces had run its course.

When I re-examined the Ryder envelope, I discovered a second mailer overlooked in my earlier state of intoxication. Contained in the smaller white envelope was a page of detailed instructions that suggested the Lioness has anticipated the unfolding of events far in advance. She knew this moment would come, for she had planned matters down to the finest element. I was to be at a particular location in London, England, within the week. The directive was unequivocal as reflected in her concluding remark: 'Don't show up, Professor, and the tape goes directly to the authorities.' The intention of the Lioness was clear. I'd be dragged into her scheme one way or another.

⊷ ⊶

Locating a cheap last minute airline ticket through the internet, I checked my office, spoke briefly with my department chairperson, and repacked my luggage. I allowed several extra days for the trip, figuring I might visit an historic site or two and legitimately deduct a portion of the expenses as work related. That was, presuming I wasn't returned to the States by a pair of U.S. Marshalls.

With a half day to kill, I decided to contact Finbar about the self-discovery group. He told me not only were they intact, they were meeting that very afternoon. Extending a cordial invitation, he assured me the members would be thrilled to hear of my summer exploits. I decided to attend.

To my surprise, the entire group of six, plus a new member, showed up. I was greeted warmly by all and introduced to Mary Ann Moody, university vice president for marketing. She was perhaps in her late forties, recently widowed, and the only genuine volunteer to the group; meaning no one suggested she attend for the good of the faculty.

"I'm so excited to meet you," Moody said. "The boys have told me enough about your adventure to whet my appetite. What a splendid idea to interview former students. Did you come upon that idea on your own?"

Apparently the boys had been tight-lipped about the bank job.

"Let's say it was an assignment I carried out in my own best interests," I replied. Mary Ann Moody, as a rookie in the group, seemed content with my explanation.

After a recounting of the group's trials and tribulations over the summer, there was a suggestion from Finbar that Moody had something on her mind she was yet to reveal. "Feel free," Finbar encouraged. "You'll find these people surprisingly open-minded and accepting."

"I don't doubt that," Moody replied. "Perhaps in time. I'm still getting comfortable. For the present, I'd like to watch and listen. That is, if no one minds."

"Your intentions for being here are good," Finbar said. "That's apparent. I'm sure we'll hear from you when you're ready." He glanced about the group. "Well, if there are no objections, I'd like to turn our attention to Alec."

Suddenly, I was in the spotlight and less confident about telling my story than I had felt when agreeing to attend the session.

Leaning toward me, Finbar said, "Looking over your shoulder, so to speak, has not caused you to turn to salt, Alec. You have survived your adventures." Finbar glanced first at Pollard, chemistry, then Pickering, accounting, Axelrod, computers, briefly at Moody, and finally at Eagerman and Wesley of biology, before adding, "You cerebral, left brain types all recall the biblical reference, I presume?"

"Lot's wife," Eagerman said impatiently. "Don't be so smug. Let the man get on with his story."

"Yes, Alec, tell us," Finbar said. "What was it like to venture into your own past? Rather ironic for an historian, I would imagine."

They were all staring at me. Perhaps it was their show of interest, or my pent up frustration, possibly even the addition of Moody, a woman who, in the short run, appeared to be a warm and sympathetic soul. Whatever the reason, my emotional damn broke and I spewed forth a narration on the summer's adventures more sonorous than *The Rhyme of the Ancient Mariner*. By the time I had finished nearly an hour later, half the group sat in tears, the other half in shock, over my exploits.

"That poor woman," Finbar wept. "Giving herself to you knowing it would mean sudden death."

Wesley said, "But how can you live with yourself, Alec, knowing you were the source of her demise?"

"Now," Finbar said, "we're here not to judge. Alec had no idea the woman would succumb to his amorous attentions."

"I think it's romantic," Moody said. "She gave herself to her former professor. Perhaps this was her life-long dream."

"It *was her* idea," I insisted, appreciating Moody's support, even though I couldn't imagine anyone's life-long dream as having sex with me. "I would never have given in had I known of her medical condition."

"Tsk, tsk, my boy," Finbar reassured. "No way to know such matters." He sniveled, and then broke into roiling laughter. "Please tell us again about the shoes. Oh, my, what a rich story."

The others picked up on his guffaw and commenced roaring with laughter. Eagerman finally slid from his chair onto the floor, pounding one fist on the carpet. Pollard wheezed and sucked air as he held his side. Moody smiled appreciatively. Only Axelrod remained sober-faced, absently checking his fingernails, and then stifling a phony yawn as he rolled his eyes at me. While I never felt one way or the other about Axelrod, I did appreciate his temperate response to my plight. Speeding down the highway at seventy miles an hour with the windows open so as to breathe fresh air hadn't seemed funny to me at the time.

Finally the laughter subsided, and Axelrod took on the group's focus. "You can laugh all you wish, gentlemen, but I feel sorry for Alec. He's had a difficult time of it, for the most part, not of his doing. That's the bloody shame of it, when we set something in motion over which we have no control. Alec's one impulsive act has nearly ruined him."

"I wouldn't go as far as to say that," Pickering said. "He's alive, he's here, and he's making me pee my pants."

Axelrod rushed in to stem a fresh outbreak of hilarity. "It's easy for us to chuckle at another's foibles. Never judge another until you've walked in his shoes."

This remark brought more waves of laughter, surging to a level that caused even Axelrod to break into a smile. I remained calm hoping that they would soon be drained and I could slip away and go home to get drunk.

After more thigh slapping and chair pounding, Pickering said, "Tell us one more time how the cop followed you to the state line." He wiped a tear with the back of his hand.

"Stop this nonsense," Axelrod shouted. The group sat stunned. Coming abruptly to attention, several groped for handkerchiefs with which to dab tears from their eyes. Finbar cleared his throat.

"We're only allowing ourselves to release a little tension, George," Finbar said. "There is no need to overreact."

"The man has had enough. Can't you see the pain he is in?" Axelrod covered his face with his hands.

"But what about you?" Finbar asked. "You seem to be the one in pain."

Axelrod shook his head. "She's back," he confessed with an uncharacteristic sob. "She's back and she wants me."

"Who's back?" Pollard asked, the edge of his usually crisp tone muted with concern.

"Angela. President Packer's wife. She called me last week to say she misses me and can't stand living without me. She's leaving Packer and wants to move in with me. She'll be arriving sometime this evening."

"Well, how do you feel about it?" Finbar asked, his tone with more feeling than I can ever remember hearing from my therapist.

"I'm frightened," Axelrod said. "I've been a widower for four years now. Living alone, fending for myself. I don't know if I'm ready for a relationship." He looked around, his expression appearing to be that of a teenager confused by hormonal stirrings.

"The worst part is she told me to purchase a hairbrush, a particular kind. She likes over-the-knee spankings with a hairbrush before having sex. I've never hit a woman in my life."

Wesley expelled a slow whistle, followed by: "Fifty Shades of Grey."

Finbar reached forward and touched Axelrod gently on his forearm. "You're not hitting her, for god's sake. It's part of sex-play. Some women like that. Some men for that matter, too." He looked around the group, then quickly added, "Not I, of course".

Moody added, "My sister, Monica, is a big fan of the birch."

Axelrod said, "But when we had sex before, she never asked me to do anything like that."

"It's a sign of trust," Moody replied. "She's opening herself to you. She's making herself vulnerable. I felt that way with Monica when she first showed me her collection of riding crops and canes."

"But that's not all. She says she has a thing she wants to try on me. It's a thing she's had a while and she's never gotten to use it."

"A thing?" Finbar said. "What kind of a thing?"

"I'm too embarrassed," Axelrod said. "I couldn't say, not ever."

"Well, if you won't tell us, how can we help you?" Finbar said. Finbar was clearly in the lead on this, with Moody as a strong second. The rest of us sat fascinated as if we were watching a car wreck, afraid to step in to help because of doing harm, yet unable to look away.

Axelrod took a breath. "It's a thing a woman can wear to have sex with a man," he blurted out.

The room grew still. All breathing stopped. Even Finbar glanced away for a moment. Maintaining his composure, however, he turned back to Axelrod, his tone kindly. "I see. That sort of thing. Well, how do you feel about it?"

Finbar was sounding more and more like a genuine therapist. I wondered if he might have an hour to spare before I left town in the morning.

Axelrod squirmed in his seat, a gesture that resulted in the rest of us shifting our positions as we averted our eyes. "How do you think I feel? Can you imagine? Naked, down on all fours, my rump in the air, her behind me with this...thing...."

"We have the image," Finbar interrupted. "I think it's more the concept we should address rather than the actuality. Conceptually, how do you feel about the idea? That is, if Angela gets pleasure from this sort of thing, can you handle it from your end."

At this, Pickering guffawed and was back pounding his thigh, then the chair seat between his legs before slipping onto the floor and slapping the carpet with his open palm. His gasping for air momentarily riveted our attention, providing relief from Axelrod's ungainly description of himself on all fours.

Then the contagion set in. The members were soon howling, rolling around in our chairs, sliding this way and that with several eventually folding onto the floor in spasms. I tried to control myself, but finally gave in. Even Moody had drawn up her legs and was shaking with laughter, her face pressed into her thighs.

Axelrod's abrupt dash for the door sobered us. "No," Finbar called, "don't leave. Please, George. No harm meant. It was merely my poor choice of words. Come back and sit. We'll see you through this." More chuckling at Finbar's last reference, but his stern surveillance of the group quieted us down.

Lumbering back to his place, Axelrod slumped into his chair. "I don't expect you to understand, but all this scares the hell out of me. I never intended for any of this to happen."

"Yes you did," I said, shocked at my own words.

The members turned to me with mixed expressions of anger and terror, as if I had just pulled a knife. "What are you saying?" Finbar probed.

"I think Axelrod did what he did with purpose." I stared directly at Axelrod who stared back, his eyes lit with panic. "I know you don't want to admit it. I didn't either. When someone first accused me of walking into that bank and deliberately giving the teller a hold-up note, I thought they were crazy. It was a gimmick. But I know now I did it with intention. I was tired of my humdrum life, tired of not being taken seriously by many of my colleagues, by my own wife. I was prowling for excitement."

"You certainly got *that*," Wesley injected.

"Go on," Finbar said, seemingly intrigued by my thesis.

"I think Axelrod did what he did because he is tired of his life. I think he wants love or sex or companionship and doesn't know how to go about getting it, so he pulled his stupid prank, just as I pulled mine. We are both trying to take control of our lives, to make something happen that hasn't been happening."

Rather than discounting my rashly proffered diagnosis, Axelrod nodded and stroked his chin with a gesture of consideration. "I hadn't thought of it that way." He surveyed the others. "I really wanted to have sex with Angela the first time I laid eyes on her. It was at the fall reception for President Packer. I went through the receiving line and was taken in by her long dark hair, her bright eyes, that smile." He paused in apparent reflection. "When she approached me about those private computer lessons, I sensed something in her manner. Somewhere deep inside, I sensed she wanted to get to know me, to become intimate."

Wesley again. "You certainly helped her accomplish that with your hands-on approach."

Only Axelrod smiled at the quip. "Yes, I did, didn't I. I think Alec is right, I did want all of this to happen. It was just a very foolish way to start. I shudder to think what my life would be like if she had protested."

"You'd be reading your e-mail in the prison library," Pollard said.

"But that's not how it unfolded," Finbar countered. "Now that you have gotten what you presumably wanted, you must decide what you'll do about it. Are you accepting this woman, Angela, into your life when she shows up tonight? Hairbrush and all the rest?"

"My god," Axelrod said, squirming now in apparent pleasure, "it is all rather intriguing, isn't it?"

Wesley seemed to have lost touch with the group. "I see a pony ride in your future with you as the pony." He chuckled at his own line.

Finbar cast a frosty look at Wesley. "I don't want to insist you leave, Samuel, but I will if you don't stop your adolescent remarks. This man's entire future is at stake."

Wesley appeared chastened as Finbar turned back to Axelrod. "If tonight is the night, are you prepared?"

"He means, have you stocked up on hemorrhoid creams," Wesley said, pushing Finbar, breaking into laughter.

Finbar ignored the comment, rather than setting up a confrontation, a decision I considered prudent.

"Do I have a choice?"

"You can explain to her that you are not interested," Finbar said. "After all, the woman seems to be a rational being. She'll turn around and go back to her husband."

"That's out," Axelrod said. "She's already filed for divorce and has given up any claim to the house or their belongings. She's bringing half their savings, a sort of dowry, I suppose."

"So you can't very well send her away," Pollard suggested. "Have you considered a trial run?"

The group turned to Pollard as if he had just offered the sure cure for a dozen potentially fatal diseases. "Of course," Finbar said, breaking into a smile. "Agree to give it a try with the condition that, if either of you is unpleased after a set period of time, it's off. That would be a simple solution, right?"

"I haven't bought the hairbrush yet," Axelrod said.

"I suggest the two of you go out tomorrow and buy it together," Wesley said. "She'll be thrilled. You can even tell her you're going to try them out on her right there in public."

"Let's not get carried away," Finbar said.

"What an excellent idea," Axelrod said, brightening. "We could make the entire event into an adventure."

The room fell into silence as we all pictured George Axelrod standing at the notions counter in Swank's Department Store swatting Angela Packer on her curvaceous bottom with a hairbrush.

After a moment, Wesley said, "What about the other?"

"The other?"

"You know. Getting stuck from behind."

"Perhaps that's negotiable," Finbar suggested. "George could ask Angela if she really must go all the way."

"I think he should go through with it," Moody said. "He might like it."

Finbar spun toward Moody. "You can't be serious, Mary Ann. It would be worse than the prostate poke we've all had to endure."

"But that's usually performed by a male in a medical setting. Suppose this woman is sensitive, warms Axelrod up to the occasion? At first, he may resist, but imagine she speaks in soft, encouraging tones. Axelrod relaxes, then feels the next stage as she presses against him." Moody paused and glanced around at the transfixed expressions.

"Go on," Wesley said. "Don't stop. What then?"

"I think we get the idea, Mary Ann," Finbar said. "The scene is somehow more erotic as you describe it. You're suggesting that when Angela Packer is hovering behind Axelrod, he'll have a very different experience."

Moody smiled slyly. "He'll never know until he gives it a try."

"May we ask?" Wesley said boldly.

"You may," Moody replied.

"Well?"

"I didn't say I'd respond. You'll have to look me over and make that decision for yourselves."

"I think we're overreaching this a bit," Finbar said. "I've been reading up on group leadership this summer and it is clearly important not to generate sexual energy among members." He glanced at Moody. "Nothing personal, of course, Mary Ann. Your eloquent description is appreciated if it helps Axelrod get past his reticence. But you know what I mean."

"Have you ever thought of having a frank discussion about sex?" Moody asked.

"In here? I don't think the topic has ever come up quite in this way before."

"Perhaps it should. Sharing our experiences, our concerns and fears, can enlighten us all. We're all mature adults. And I'm certain, together, we have a wealth of knowledge."

"Speak for yourself, Mary Ann," Wesley said. "I have two reactions to sex, chills and sweats. I get laid twice a year, once in the winter and once in the summer."

Mary Ann Moody smiled. I liked her proposal, but given I was flying to London in the morning, I had no vote. Yet I wanted to support the suggestion. "Great idea," I said. "This summer has opened my eyes. There's much to learn out there."

"That may be our problem," Pollard said. "We all have a lot to learn, but from whom? We're a bunch of old farts, with the exception of Moody, of course, and most of us have only screwed one or two people in our lives. What could we have to offer each other?"

Pickering spoke up. "Who says?"

"Really?" Wesley replied, eyebrows arched.

"I just don't like to be cast as an old fart. Molly and I have experimented with a thing or two."

"Your thing and someone else's?" Wesley said.

Finbar jumped in. "Gentlemen, please. Save the jousting for the next college faculty meeting. If we have consensus and are serious about pursuing such a discussion, we'll approach it like a book club. Each of us will have an assigned reading over the week and we can come back and lead a discussion on the topic. If we each throw in any personal experiences we're comfortable sharing, that should make for quite an interesting and informative series of groups sessions."

"Where shall we get a book list?" Eagerman asked.

Eyes fell on Mary Ann Moody. "You're the most contemporary of us, Mary Ann," Finbar said.

"Boys, I can recommend some great books written from a woman's perspective. How's that for a place to start?"

"And there is the internet," Wesley said. "And the local bookstore."

"I'd say with those resources, we'll have a very adequate reading list," Finbar said. "Raise your hand if you're in."

All hands go up but mine.

"Prude," Wesley muttered.

"I'll be on my way to Europe in the morning and there is no telling when I'll be back," I said defensively.

"Then we'll carry on in your absence."

"If you're leaving again, Alec, tell us your plans," Pickering said. "We've hung in with you this far."

"Yes," Finbar said, once again adopting the leadership role, "tell us about the next stage in your adventure."

"I'm off to London in the morning. I won't find out more until I'm over there."

"Do be careful," Pollard said. "We don't want you drawn into some scam that leaves you holding the bag."

The others nodded their agreement.

Eagerman suggested, "Have you considered going to the police and explaining the entire mess? After all, you didn't rob the bank, didn't even have that as your intention. I'll bet if you hire an attorney and lay this all out, you'll be off the hook in no time."

"If I'd done that originally, perhaps," I said. "Now that money has been stolen from the bank, my explanation would seem self-serving. And should the Lioness implicate me, I'd be a cooked goose."

Silence, as I suspected they pictured me on a roasting rack, belly up, smoldering.

"Good luck," Wesley said. "And stay out of the cow pastures over there."

At that, the room virtually exploded with laughter. I waited for the opportune moment, then slipped to the door and headed home to tie one on.

CHAPTER 26
FLYING INTO HER ARMS

The flight to London was long, but uneventful. After arriving at Gatwick airport, I took the train to Victoria Station, then the underground to the Marble Arch stop near Hyde Park. My destination was a small but lavish residential hotel just a short walk from the tube station. At check-in, after learning my expenses were covered, I was given a plain white envelope inside of which was a single piece of stationary. One word: *Wait.* No signature.

The room was small, but comfortable, with an open view of Hyde Park. At the end of my second day of site seeing, I received a message in the form of a telegram at the front desk. The instructions were to fly to Stromboli, Italy, that afternoon and head directly to St. Benedictine's Hospital. A confirmed e-ticket awaited me at Heathrow Airport.

I repacked, checked out, and grabbed a taxi to the airport. After a long wait among throngs of tourists, I reached the security checkpoint. Removing my coat, I slipped off shoes, emptied my pockets and, after several tries, cleared the metal detector. My bags had been unpacked and loosely reassembled twice. Finally on the plane, I sat back and tried to doze among the happy tourists drinking champagne and singing in at least four languages.

We landed, more searches, more security and passport checks, and finally I was on the street where dozens of drivers hawked at travelers spilling out like gravy through a colander. Having been to Stromboli just once, I located an information station and discovered that the bus into the city was, inexplicably to the agent on duty, running on schedule. Hauling my luggage to the nearest stop, I waited. When the bus arrived, people fought to get on as others struggled to get off. I waited for the fray to quiet down, then got the last spot by the door. The bus rolled onto the highway and a half hour later, we were downtown.

Two blocks south of the first city stop, my destination, a small family-run hotel, sat tucked between a bakery and a wine distributorship. Once again, the Lioness had apparently paved the way. I was greeted warmly at the desk by the owner's son, who carried my bag and refused a tip. After freshening up, I inquired about St. Benedictine's Hospital and initially received a dour look purported to be sympathetic. When I explained my appointment to meet a friend, the cluster of family employees brightened. I received a chorus of directions, nodded my appreciation all around, and set out to find a taxi.

A block from the hotel, I found a driver leaning against his cab reading a newspaper. Using my limited Italian vocabulary, I asked for a ride to St. Benedictine's, and got an enthusiastic nod. The hospital, as it turned out, was a mere three blocks from the hotel. Thirty minutes of twisting through traffic brought us to the front door.

Patient registration had Armand Pennington listed on the second floor. Given a visitor's card to wear about my neck and directed to the aging elevator, I chose the stairway.

I located the Lioness in a ward of eight beds, propped against the metal headboard reading *Vogue* and working on an ice cream bar. She looked up as I approached.

"Professor, right on time. But you look dreadful. Have you not slept?"

"I'm fine," I said. "You, on the contrary, look beautiful." I couldn't resist.

"You are too full of flattery, Professor. But I like it, so we'll let it stand." She flipped the magazine closed. "Now we can get out of here."

"Are you well enough to travel?" I asked with genuine concern.

"Totally," she replied. "They've kept me here an extra day because there was no one to sign me out. Now you can do that."

"Are you able to walk?"

She smiled. "If you will take my arm."

We stopped at the nurses' station, then took the aged elevator to the first floor. After interminable signing of papers at administration, we were escorted to the curb with the Lioness's luggage. The taxi ride back to the hotel seemed much shorter and soon we were together in the small room that overlooked a lush courtyard.

"Wine, Professor, please. Find us wine of some sort and something to eat. We will celebrate." She tossed bills at me, some floating to the floor. I groveled after them.

Scurrying about the neighborhood, thirty minutes later I had a feast of humble foods spread on tabletops about the room. Cheeses. Salamis. Breads. And of course an array of wines, including champagne, which I placed in a bucket of ice bartered from the front desk. "*Surpresa,*" I said. "For the Lioness."

She stared at me. "Why do you call me that? The lioness."

Time to explain. But not before the second glass of champagne. "Here," I said, handing her a glass, "let's drink. Then we can talk and swap stories."

We drank as we sat by the window gazing beyond the courtyard. Dusk had settled in and the evening stars were evident in the feathery blue sky. As the wine doused my system and the aura of the moment washed over me, I thought, here sits one mediocre professor with a goddess wearing mauve silk pajamas and smelling of rose pedals and gardenias. How more fortunate could I be?

Armand turned to me. "Why do you call me the lioness?"

"Because when you recognized me on that occasion at the Ryder's, I knew I was trapped, that I was in your power. At that moment, you became the hunter, thus the Lioness. I, in turn, became the hunted, the gazelle."

"You are strange, Professor. You are a romantic. Quite honestly, I don't like romance. It's very impractical. I like men who are practical and decisive."

"I can change," I said. "I can be anything you wish."

"And I like to be adored."

"But I can adore you. I *do* adore you."

"Enough to do anything for me?"

"Anything."

"You would kiss my feet?"

"With passion," I said.

"You would steal for me?"

"You saw my recklessness at our first meeting," I said. "Before even knowing you."

She held forth her glass. "More champagne. And tell me about your summer. Did you have a pleasant time?"

I poured. What could I say? My brain was spinning. Should I be artful or truthful? I would tell her what she wanted to hear, if I only knew. Perhaps a blend. The summer? Interesting. An eye-opener. Enlightening, yet disquieting. I was flattered by some comments about my teaching, discouraged by others. Romance? No, not really. Had I fallen in love with any of my former students? Hardly. A dalliance, at least? Well…. It was truly not of my doing. She practically forced herself upon me. What chance did I have? It was less than a one-night stand. And then, she died. Right there on top of me. No laughter, please. That was perhaps the most disquieting experience of my life.

Of course, there was Stromberg. How horrible. Did I mind that you told him my entire life story? My pain and frustration? My weaknesses? My dislike of Homer, the fat-assed dog? How could that possibly trouble me when I know you had only my shallow interests at heart?

Did I look forward to seeing you again, to our reunion? With every fiber. I have thought only of you since we parted. Was I ready to collect my reward? Yes. *Oh, yes.*

As I prepared to regale the Lioness with my adventures, enthrall her with my promise of eternal love, she drifted across the room, eased into bed and slipped into a soundless sleep. Blurry-eyed from too much drink, I nibbled at the food, then packed the abundant remains and trucked them to the front desk where the family was delighted to have a late night meal. Trudging back up the stairs, head spinning, I climbed into the narrow space the Lioness had not occupied with her sprawl and lost consciousness.

CHAPTER 27

MURDEROUS FANTASIES

The following morning, my head throbbed as I rolled over and looked at my watch on the nightstand. Ten a.m. The Lioness was up; the sound of sloshing water could be heard from the shower. She had laid out her apparel for the day and her luggage sat open, clothes draped here and there. The room had the appearance of someone packing to leave.

I staggered down the hallway to the community toilet. When I returned, the Lioness was dressed and had most of her belongings packed. "We're leaving," she said perfunctorily.

"Leaving?" I echoed, my head throbbing. "Why are we leaving?"

"I wish to be in a country where they speak my language. We're flying to London this morning. Please hurry. I don't care to miss our flight."

I stood freshly showered in my shabby robe. Rummaging through the dresser, I pulled out clothes to wear, others to pack. By the time I had my things together, the Lioness was at the front desk checking out and arranging for a porter. A strapping young man, one of the owner's sons, the one who had shown me to my room the previous day, appeared with a rickety hand truck and piled our bags high. We met him at the curb where he loaded a taxi the Lioness had commandeered. When she had tipped all around, we settled into the narrow backseat of the rough riding rig. Each bounce along the rough terrain jarred my skull. I forced myself to defeat the urge to toss up the salamis and cheeses from the previous night's repast. The Lioness settled back with a fashion magazine, appearing cool and resolute.

At the airport, she waved small packets of euros here and there and our bags were quickly checked. We then awaited the plane's departure. Once aboard first class, the Lioness ordered champagne where as I asked for a club soda and two aspirin. The flight was smooth, uneventful. We hardly exchanged ten words while in the air. The Lioness continued to read as she sipped her drink, then dozed until we were on the ground.

At baggage claim, she once again swirled bills through the air, this time pounds sterling, and we were soon through customs, our luggage whisked to the curb and loaded into a cab. She gave the address of our destination and we settled back. Now for the first time since rising that morning, she turned to me with a smile.

"So, Professor, what shall we do first? Perhaps a fine lunch, then we'll take a cab to where we'll do some shopping. You must lose that dreadful sports jacket or whatever you call it. You look like a little rumpled man. We'll buy you some fine apparel, then see some sites."

We did just that. The hotel was again in the neighborhood of Hyde Park, but a much more luxurious place. She had reserved a suite, two bedrooms. "This doesn't mean we won't make love necessarily," she said, matter-of-factly, as she hung garments in her closet. "But I must have my rest and I find I can best do that on my own."

I placed my few belongings in the adjacent closet and watched as the Lioness worked to space her wardrobe properly to avoid wrinkles. Several dresses and a suit were laid out for the hotel concierge to arrange for pressing.

We ate a late lunch of smoked salmon and chilled vegetables in the gold-embossed restaurant with windows that looked out onto the park, again champagne for the Lioness. I stayed with club soda. Then we rode in a taxi to Harrods where we went on a whirlwind shopping tour. She picked out three suits for me, half dozen shirts, shoes, socks, even underwear. The necktie choices were the most trying, with the Lioness torn among several of a dozen silk ties, most costing as much as fifty pounds each. Finally, she threw up her hands and said, "We'll take them all."

The cost of the purchases were placed on her credit card and she directed the clerk to have the alternations made and the items delivered to our hotel by seven that evening. The threat of 'or else' was implied. Two twenty pound notes pressed into his hand brought assurances that the matter would be executed according to her instructions.

Clearly, the Lioness knew her away around London, most likely the result of her travels with Ryder Senior. I wished to ask her about the Ryders, in particular young Jeffrey, but we simply hadn't taken time. Soon, however, I would feel compelled to get to the topic.

Time for refreshments. She led us to a petit mansion within which was a private club. Although the obsequious staff showed no apparent recognition, her welcome was most respectable. After escorting us to a booth, the host brought champagne and we settled in. The Lioness reached into her cream colored bag and withdrew a package of cigarettes. I sat shocked at the sight of her lighting one and blowing forth a stream of smoke with all the gusto of a teenager on a street corner.

"I didn't know you smoked," I said, the surprise obvious in my tone.

She puffed again. "There are many things you don't know, Professor. Won't it be a delight to learn all about me? I can be quite charming, when I'm well taken care of."

"I'm sure," I agreed, stupidly. Deciding this might be as good a time as any to ask about young Ryder, I did. "Is Jeffrey doing well?"

"You mean after our scrape with the volcano? Absolutely. He received a few burns and bruises. Poor boy whined like a castrated lamb. He was very happy to see Mommy and Daddy."

"Is it then over?"

"Over? Is what over? That silly little tryst? The poor boy loved to brush my hair and paint my toenails. I let him touch my breast one time, fully clothed of course."

"But I thought you had an abortion."

"I did. But not from anything to do with him. It was his father, you dolt."

The reference to dolt bit me, but I stayed the course. She was talking and I wished to learn more about the Lioness and the Ryders. "So you and Papa Ryder did have an affair."

"We had an arrangement. We have each now fulfilled our part of the agreement, and *that* has come to a close."

"You aren't in love with Jeffrey, planning to marry?"

"The implication that the boy and I were serious was intended as a cover. It has served its purpose, for the moment, at least."

"Nor are you in love with Ryder Senior?"

"Professor, have you learned nothing in your lifetime? How ever many years old are you?" She leaned across the table, blowing a thin stream of smoke into my face. "We fucked. Period." Her remark, although spoken softly, brought quick glances from the surrounding male clientele.

I coughed, blushed, then coughed again. My response was petulant, but spontaneous. "Sorry," I said, apologetically. "I was only curious."

She sat back, posturing regally, cigarette to her lips. "Don't be curious. I don't like it when you are curious. What I did with Ryder senior, as you refer to him, is none of your business."

"Including the millions you embezzled?" The words were out before I could stop myself. What surprised me was my sudden change in attitude. I didn't care. Aware that my confrontation would likely elicit a calamitous response, I thought; screw it. I may be a dolt, but I know when I'm being abused. I'd sit still for almost everything, but not idle abuse. Threats? Absolutely. The Lioness had ruled nearly three months of my life with her threat of revealing the security tape. I understood that. I *accepted* it. Even Gloria understood my tolerance for threats. She had made many over the years, and I nearly always acquiesced. But on the several occasions she tried abuse, she was forcefully rebuked. And the Lioness would be as well, even if it meant jail time.

Apparently reading my shift in disposition, she crushed her cigarette in an opulent cut crystal ashtray and offered that cranberry jam smile I'd fallen in love with. Leaning across the table once again, she mouthed her words slowly, accentuating the soft curves of her lips. Her voice flowed like a ribbon of silk. "To be exact, it was nearly twelve million, Professor. And it was not a split. I insisted on sixty percent. After all, I was taking all the risks. And *I* had the skill to pull it off. Ryder Senior only wanted enough to cover the losses he incurred through his gambling and philandering. That way he got to keep his house and his car and, above all, his job." She reached for my hand and patted it several times. "Now, I hope that has satisfied your curiosity on the subject." She cocked her head. "No? Then ask. Please ask now. For what I will detest about you is your incessant curiosity, your prying, your twisting our conversation around to this topic, or any topic, for that matter, and wanting to know. I am not an encyclopedia that you can simply take off the shelf when you wish and flip open to some page and begin to question. If you wish to interview me, then do it now, please. My hope had been that you would get to know me over time, but I can see that will be impossible. You cannot seem to live in the present moment, Professor. You must know where I have been and I presume where I am going while ignoring the fact that you have me to yourself at this very moment. You are squandering this moment, you foolish man." Her voice had elevated in volume to the point that, not only were patrons squirming, but the host, who had behaved so graciously upon our entrance, now stood in the doorway of the lounge, apparently calculating an intervention.

I tossed a smile in his direction and signaled for another round of drinks. He hesitated, and then turned, I hoped to follow up on my request and not search out a bobby on the street.

Returning my attention to the Lioness, I said, "My summer adventure, what did it have to do with any of this?"

Her voice, once again, grew controlled, silken and smooth. "If you must have details," she began, "the moment you pulled your silly magic trick, the thought occurred to me that you might be the perfect foil for my scheme. I decided to use the videotape to keep you on a string long enough for me to work my own magic. My plan would include you, but only if I had been caught or if Ryder *Senior* had gotten cold feet and pulled a double-cross.

"In either event, you were to be the brains behind the scheme and I the mere dupe, terrified by your threats to reveal my liaison with Ryan, thereby destroying his career and his family life. I would claim that you learned of my computer expertise through our social interaction at the Ryders and forced me to agree to transfer funds to a numbered account in Switzerland. We conspired at that little chalet in the woods, where I have a champagne glass with your fingerprints on it and a security tape that the owner provided picturing the two of us sitting on a rock by the brook, naked, chowing down. Up to that point, the facts might seem circumstantial. My word against yours, as it were, until I produced the videotape from the bank. I would tell the authorities that your silly trick was your cue to me to make the transfer of the money." She paused long enough to draw a deep breath of tobacco smoke. "After all, what other conclusion could they come to? Your words, '*I want to make a withdrawal'.* You completed your trick, delivered your message, and then left the bank. Abruptly, I might add. Young Jeffrey, whom you had somehow drawn into your scheme, pursued you in his naïve attempt to talk you out of the theft, but you ignored his pleas. Not only that, you took advantage of his family's hospitality."

"So sending me cross-country to interview former students? That was your way to keep me on a string."

"It was perfect. At dinner when Ryan asked about your former students, I decided that would be an excellent way to keep you busy while I pulled off the transfer of funds. I wanted to know where you were and what you were doing at all times. I couldn't have you off on some sabbatical to Australia or wherever. Not knowing your whereabouts, I'd have no one to blame. If matters had gone poorly, I could easily report to the authorities that you were the mastermind. You kept tabs on me throughout the entire escapade. How could I confirm that? By revealing your exact location day by day over that three month period." A thin ribbon of smoke drifted between us. "Clever, huh."

Our drinks arrived, the barman cool in his appraisal.

I sat stunned. The Lioness's revelation gave new meaning to the word cuckold. When the barman was out of earshot, I recovered enough to ask, "But how did you choose those particular students? Did you take time to research them before you drew lots?"

She leaned forward, close enough that the fragrance of her spicy tobacco breath seared my nostrils. "A purely random selection, my dear Alec. I went back to the beginning of your career at the university and picked the numbers that came up. With two exceptions."

"Stromberg," I said. "And Jeffrey."

"Stromberg was my benchmark, a way of determining you were completing your assignment. When you showed up, he sent me a predetermined text message."

"While he was digging his own grave?"

"It's possible."

"Do you know he killed himself?"

"He had advised me of his plan. I really didn't know, though, that he would choose to do so in your presence. I hope that wasn't too disturbing."

"He blew his head completely off."

"He was always rather dramatic, as I recall."

"And he had debts?"

"Beyond imagination."

"Drugs? Gambling? That's what he implied, at least."

"Yes. He had developed quite of range of pastimes, including rather expensive trips to Las Vegas and here, to London."

"Did you travel with him?"

"That's none of your concern."

"Was he one of your lovers?" I asked, my voice again petulant.

The Lioness tossed several pound notes onto the table and stalked toward the exit. I followed, my face flushed, less from embarrassment at her grand exit than from the realization I continued to be a living cliché. As Silverman pointed out, I had a tiger by the tail, except in this instance, the tiger was my Lioness and I refused to let go.

When I hit the street, there she waited, the cranberry smile having returned. She hooked her arm in mine. "Now, Professor, what would you say to a late afternoon cruise on the Thames? There are so many beautiful sites that can be seen only from the water. Then we shall return to our rooms. I had planned an evening on the town, but I find myself rather tired. So we shall have a lovely champagne supper by candlelight delivered to our suite. We shall look out upon the park as the sun sets in the Western sky and toast our good fortune. And then, Professor, if you are very, very good, you shall make love to me."

But for the latter promise, she was true to her word. We took a marvelous cruise on the Thames, and then found a taxi to whisk us to our apartment where she ordered a sumptuous feast to be delivered precisely at eight p.m. We retired to our separate rooms to rest and await the appointed cocktail hour.

Although I had been disappointed initially at the Lioness's choice of a suite with separate bedrooms, I was now grateful for her foresight. Perhaps she knew how tiresome she could be; although I doubted that. I suspected the decision was based on her wish to be alone and perhaps to promote an air of aloofness and mystery. No matter. I was simply happy to have the opportunity to take a long shower and rest my weary mind.

After throwing on a pair of shorts and a robe, I poured a drink and sat by the window looking down upon the park, watching pedestrians scurry through the early dusk, wondering how much longer I could play my role as a docile supplicant. Time spent with the Lioness had worn on me, yet I wished to avoid raising her ire and risking more threats of exposure. The thought occurred to me that perhaps we had no deal at all, that my foolishness had indentured me to this beautiful, selfish woman for life, that I could never get away, that the Lioness had no intention of returning that tape to me and setting me free. I would remain her dupe forever, the perpetual threat of being accused of masterminding the great bank robbery.

While I was hardly a violent person, and the thought of taking another's life appalled me beyond comprehension, I stared into the deepening shadows sympathizing with those about whom I'd read who simply felt they had no way out. If I were truly trapped, could I even remotely entertain the thought of magically making the Lioness disappear from my life? In the gloom that now settled over the park below, I found myself considering that very option.

After all, other than my brief association with her through the Ryders, and our short-lived European travels, sharing hotel rooms, we had no traceable connections. The hotel staff could certainly attest to the possibility that the woman who had reserved the suite, seemingly self-absorbed, might be the sort to take long, languid baths, drink champagne with gusto and perhaps fall asleep in a stupor and slide beneath the water. That was always a possible scenario, especially lacking evidence to the contrary.

Of course, should I remain on the scene until the autopsy was complete, I ran the risk of a more thorough investigation. Unfortunately, somewhere along the line, if queried, Ryan Ryder might add his perspective. Perhaps he already knew of my indiscretion, of the tape, even have a copy in his possession. Those were elements of the situation about which I could make no prediction. They would certainly have to be considered and dealt with.

As I thought through the bathtub scene, however, I concluded it was too personal, too fraught with danger. A scream, a struggle, water stains on the wall, any indication that all was not as it seemed, might put me in jeopardy. No, this required a more subtle approach, something more natural, and definitely more public.

I poured another drink.

The streets of London could be dangerous, as were the streets of any large city. Taxis careening around corners, buses plunging from stop to stop. I had noticed the Lioness often failed to check the direction of traffic, was at times oblivious to the fact that oncoming autos approached from the opposite direction than that to which she was accustomed. In fact, I had restrained her several times. If instead I restrained myself, even stood a short distance from her to avoid the temptation to intervene, and she lunged ahead as she was wont to do, who could predict the outcome?

Unless I walked away, there would be an investigation into our relationship, the beautiful young princess and the frumpy middle-aged professor. Scotland Yard would learn of my recent divorce proceedings and my cross-country travels. Along with the FBI, they would grill members of the self-discovery group and discover the existence of the security tape. Offers of immunity would be held out to the lot of them for their testimony. Of course, anything short of her instant death placed me in even greater peril. I pictured her lying in the street, affirming that I was the brain behind the embezzlement, that I wished her death so as to collect the entire nearly twelve million, less Ryder's cut. Perhaps she would even claim I had recruited her as a former student at State U.; that I had brainwashed her and manipulated her to play out this role.

The worse fear, however, was of serving as her caretaker. Imagine how difficult and demanding a patient she would be. Were I found guilty of first-degree-failure-to-restrain, a judge might dole out just such a punishment. I would prefer my demise by lethal injection to a life of servitude to the Lioness. Yes, her death would have to come swiftly and free of my involvement. A very natural accident.

The knock on the door startled me.

"Yes?" I called out, swallowing hard.

The Lioness pushed the door ajar, appearing in a negligee with two glasses, a bottle of champagne, and her cranberry smile. "I missed you, Professor. But you are deep in thought. Let me wash away your trivial concerns."

The thought that this woman might be clairvoyant suddenly terrified me.

She placed the glasses on the table, poured, and handed me one. I now had two glasses from which to drink. She drifted behind me, trailing her fingertips along the nape of my neck, then reached beneath the robe and encircled each of my nipples. I felt a strange arousal that bucked against the disdain I'd developed for this woman who had so ingeniously entrapped me.

"Has dinner arrived?" I asked, hoping to use our meal as an excuse to avoid the tempting position she appeared ready to place me in.

"Are you *always* hungry, Professor?" she asked. Her fingers now trailed along my stomach which, I was pleased to say, had shrunk during the efforts of my summer travels. While I hardly looked athletic, my appearance pleased me more than it had in several years.

"I seemed to have worked up an appetite," I said, my tone threaded with an edgy enmity. She couldn't help but react.

"My poor Professor," she said. "I have treated you badly, haven't I. And you are pouting. Well, I shall make it up to you. When we have dined on lobster and snails and sumptuous caviar, I shall treat you to a romp in my bed. What would you say to that?"

Before I could deliver a response, I was saved by a knock at the door.

The Lioness did the honors. When she returned, she said, "Your wish is my command. Dinner is served."

I slipped into comfortable clothes and joined her in the living room. Glowing candlelight spilled onto the feast, the scene mellowing my mood. After seating the Lioness, we tackled the first course, snails roasted in butter and garlic. I thought briefly of Gloria, how disgusted she would be with the appetizer.

We ate, the Lioness drank, and the first hour slipped into the second as we finished with coffee and a chocolate lemon chiffon dessert. Because the Lioness appeared in a genial mood and slightly intoxicated, I decided it might be the ideal time to broach the subject of my freedom.

"Will you object greatly if I return home?" I asked in a tone as matter of fact as I could muster.

"Are you bored with me, Professor?"

"More with myself," I said. "It's time I get back to work. I have courses to prepare for and students to see."

"You don't fool me, Professor. I know what you are up to. You resent me. You think me indolent and self-indulgent. Well, you are right. I wish to be adored and you thought you would like that, didn't you? But you don't. You make a poor sycophant, Professor. And do you know why? Because of your ego. You have this fraudulent little ego." She illustrated her assertion by holding two fingers close to-gether. "You are unable to give in, to give fully of yourself. I, on the other hand, am quite capable of giving in with the right person. And I'm very capable of taking as well. And that is another thing you do poorly, Professor. You do not take well. You measure what you take, as if fearful you will have to give back ounce for ounce. I, however, have no such qualms. I will take and take and take. Joyously. With gusto and abandon. And I have no concern about giving back. Not ever."

She paused to drain her glass. I opened another bottle and poured. She tasted the fresh champagne. "Ah, much better."

"May I go home?" I asked.

"How does it feel to have to ask permission of a beautiful wom-an? Does it excite you, Professor?"

Once I might have said, 'yes, I'm excited by the challenge'. But, in truth, I was simply tired. Not even disappointed. Merely worn out. I said none of that, of course. Instead, I said, "You have me in a delicate position. I don't want to ruin my life over that silly indis-cretion. If you let me go, we can have a truce."

"You won't tell about the embezzlement and I won't send the tape to the police," she said, sloshing champagne as she spoke. "Perhaps you don't think I've thought of that, but I have. I think we'll have to call a truce. Otherwise one of us will have to kill the other of us and I don't think either of us is the killing kind. Are we, Professor?"

I stared at her silently, now certain she had read my mind. In my silence, I wished her to draw whatever conclusion she chose. Finally she pulled herself from the chair and stumbled into her bedroom. As the door swung closed behind her, I heard her say, "A truce, Professor. Be gone by the time I'm sober in the morning."

Changing into my own clothes, I slipped out to an all-night internet kiosk and found an open seat on a morning flight to the States. Then I returned to the room and packed my few belongings, leaving the newly purchased items hanging in the closet. I slept restlessly. When daylight arrived, I carried my bags downstairs and found a taxi to Victoria station where I caught the train to Gatwick airport. Three hours later, I was aboard a plane heading west, tired, but happy to be going home.

CHAPTER 28
THE DOUBLE-CROSS

Apparently, the police had been tipped off, because two detectives met me at the airport as I came through customs, taking up positions as my escorts. My luggage was confiscated and I was driven downtown in an unmarked police car. Perhaps the Lioness was to blame, but I was inclined to suspect that, with the fund transfer completed, Ryder Senior calculated that by implicating me he might deflect focus from himself.

Admittedly, I was shocked by the encounter, but in a short time, the demeanor of the detectives put me at ease. They were courteous and clearly uncertain as to my status in this triangle; suspect, material witness, or schmo caught in the crossfire. Settling into an interview room, they offered refreshments, then began their debriefing.

"You don't need a lawyer," a lanky blond-haired man said. Rollins was his name. "Because you're not a suspect in anything. Not yet, at least. If you want a lawyer, that's okay. But then that ups the ante. You get my drift?" The drift was apparently a threat: Call a lawyer and we'll give you a reason to need one.

"I'm not sure how I can be of help?" I said. I modulated my voice to the extent I could to convey a sense of innocence.

Rollins launched into a few casual questions, such as what had I done in London, had I gotten to the Tower, and so forth, and then said, "Okay, professor, enough small talk. We're on to you. What we don't know are details. In other words, we know you've been up to something. Just not what. Now we want you to tell us in your own words. That's what we'd like, for you to come clean and make this easy on all of us. Otherwise, we'll be here a long time. None of us wants to be here a long time. In fact, none of us wants to be here at all. Get my drift?"

I was clear *I* didn't want to be there. Somehow, I had the impression they had no choice. They did this for a living.

"I flew to London to meet a friend," I said.

"You didn't meet anyone in London, Professor. You flew to London, then on to Italy and that's where you met a woman. A very attractive woman, by all reports. You took responsibility for her when she was discharged from the hospital. Then you flew together *back* to London. She spent a lot of money on you in the time you were together. She's very slick. We don't have a read on her yet, but we will very soon."

"Initially, I thought we were to meet in London. What I didn't know was that my presence was required for her to be discharged from the hospital in Stromboli."

"And what is your relationship to this woman?"

"Friends. More like acquaintances," I said. "Because I came to see her in the hospital, she insisted on buying me things."

"Clothes, Professor. Not just things. Clothes. We all know professors need clothes. I've never seen such a frumpy lot. Why is it professors can't pick out clothes? And why do their clothes always look so baggy? Do you pick out baggy clothes on purpose? You look worse than cops."

The door opened and a woman stepped into the room. She had lots of curly blond hair and large breasts. Her waist was slender and her hips full. She moved with certain deliberateness. Her voice was soft. "That's enough, Rollins," she said. She looked down at me, blue eyes shimmering. "Professor, please tell us about this woman you met."

"Acquaintances," I said. "That's all. We're just acquaintances."

"Can you give us her name?"

I considered the question. Yes, I knew her name. But would I tell? Of more concern, however, was why *they* didn't know her name? Unless they were testing me. After all, the bank lost nearly twelve million dollars and one of their tellers skipped town. That seemed like a slam-dunk to me.

Perhaps the Lionesses' European travels had confused them. The scrape with the volcano, injuries to young Ryder, modest as they apparently were, and a visit from Mom and Dad, may have thrown off their investigation. And, of course, the Lioness had left town with the bank president's son *before* the discovery of the missing money. Jeffrey's injuries provided an excuse for the couple to remain out of the country longer than scheduled, so the authorities could have easily overlooked the obvious; that the three of them, the Lioness, and father and son Ryder, were a team.

The real question for me was, should I be the one to connect the dots?

"Do you?" Rollins said.

What would I lose by telling them her name? Won't they find out eventually? If the Lioness discovered I squealed, what could she do? Rat on me? Hand over the tape? Yes, that's exactly what she'd do. Now that I had gotten to know her sunnier side, I concluded she'd take down everyone on the playing field, just for spite.

However, even if I held out now, how long could I last? Eventually, I'd have to cooperate if I wanted to save myself. The rule could be this: Don't offer up anything I was not asked. But answer all questions truthfully. After all, I wasn't guilty of anything but stupidity. Then again, the road to prison seemed paved with stupid acts just like mine.

"Armand Pennington." I blurted out.

"That's the woman's name?"

I nodded. "Yes. She was dating a former student of mine. When I heard the pair had been injured in an eruption of a volcano, I called his parents to learn of their whereabouts. By the time I got to Stromboli, Mr. and Mrs. Ryder had already taken their son home. Only Ms. Pennington was there. She was so pleased to see me, she suggested we go to London for a few days to aid in her recovery. We did. There, she insisted on purchasing clothing for me which, incidentally, I decided not to accept. Then I came home."

Rollins pressed on. "You expect us to believe that story?"

"It's true," I said. "You can verify everything by checking with the Ryders and the hotel registries and the airlines." I looked squarely at Detective Rollins. "I have nothing to hide."

Her name was Ruby. No one seemed to want to give her a last name. I liked her matter-of-fact style. But her presence was short-lived. A phone call took her from the room. Her replacement was a young man who appeared to be a junior grade detective just out of the academy. His name was Taft. Taft apparently had been watching through the two-way mirror. He jumped right in. "What did you do on your summer vacation, Professor?"

"Visit former students," I said proudly. Now it all made sense. What a wonderful, considerate project for a professor to conduct on his summer vacation. How many professors could claim to have done *that*?

"We've done a complete investigation of your summer travels, Professor. We know everything. That is, everywhere you went, everyone you saw. What we don't know is, why? Let's take the famous author, Zack Henley. You spent nearly an entire afternoon there. Why?"

"He was reading scripts to me."

"You expect us to believe that? We know for a fact he won't even tell his publisher the plot of a story until it is ready for the presses. Why would he tell you?"

"I'd say because these weren't his best sellers."

"Watch your tongue, Professor. Henley only writes bestsellers. He's our hero. He knows how to write a detective story with real cops in it." Taft circled me, I presumed to enhance my sense of intimidation. "Okay, how about the girl student you visited next? You screwing her?"

"Sarah McCoy? She's just a child."

"When we interviewed her, she wasn't just a child. She tried to get Rollins into the sack if he promised to lay off you. She has a shrine with your picture plastered on it in her room surrounded by a half dozen dildo-shaped candles. She said she lights incense and pleasures herself while she dreams about you."

"I think she's love-starved," I said. "I had nothing to do with that."

Rollins retook the lead. "Let's move on. The surgeon in Colorado, he's a different story. Hates your guts. Thinks all you professors are free-loaders. And I must say, I'm inclined to agree with him."

Somewhere on my travels, memories of Cecil Worksworth's class performance had returned to me. He and his roommate apparently used to record the answers to quizzes on the bottoms of athletic socks. On one occasion, Cecil wore his roommate's socks by error and got a hundred percent on the quiz I'd given to the earlier section of a European studies class. When he handed in his paper and I saw his answers, the scam became immediately apparent. Although I gave him the option of a make-up exam, I did require him to leave the classroom barefooted. I was younger then and considerably more foolish. Perhaps he never forgot his embarrassment. He certainly never forgave me.

"I'm sorry about that," I said. "I don't know how much I contributed to the doctor's attitude, but he certainly has one."

"That's it? That's your best explanation? A brilliant surgeon has an attitude and you blow it off? Suppose he performed surgery on *you?* Suppose you were rushed to the hospital and he was the only surgeon available to save your life. Did you ever think of *that?*"

"I'd rather pass on the thought, thank you." I had, in fact, thought of exactly that. Lying in an emergency room, staring into the blazing overhead lights, Dr. Cecil Worksworth's image emerging, hovering, grinning, salivating. The flashing blade. I always hoped that very few of my former students would become doctors or lawyers.

"Don't be flip, Professor. We can always fly the good doctor in for a cavity search."

"I'm sorry, detectives, I just don't know what you want from me. True, not all of my former students have fond memories of my classes. Some have no memories. But I feel I put out a reasonable effort to gain some feedback about my teaching. That's all I can claim." By this time, I'd nearly convinced myself that my travels were truly intended to get feedback about my teaching, unrelated to keeping my sorry ass out of prison.

"And then you had the nerve to go and disturb Andrea Winforth, the only African American judge in Jackrabbit County. Such a wonderful, high-spirited woman who fought for and saved thousands of homesteads from the evil encroachment of the federal government. We heard all about your intrusion into her life from Deputy Oliver. You were lucky he didn't pistol whip you and send you out of town with a two by four up your rear."

"Yes, I confess to the intrusion." Dare I tell them, it was the good deputy taking it in the rear? Probably not. "The judge and I had a spirited discussion during which I told her how much I admired her rather androgynous life style."

The two men exchanged a glance. "You told her that?" Rollins said.

"Yes, I did."

"And Oliver didn't haul off and slug you?"

"He was out of earshot."

"Damn good thing. Otherwise, you would have been a goner. Of all the things Oliver hates most, it's big words."

Taft said, "Let's continue our journey, Professor. You've got a lot to answer for. What about Stiles, the drug runner? What's your association with him? You didn't expect to get an honest answer out of that freak, did you?"

"I didn't," I confessed. "But I didn't want to discriminate against him because he was in prison. Besides, leaving him out would introduce a sampling error."

"What were you sampling, Professor?" Taft asked. "Drugs? He let you try some of his personal stock, maybe some he wanted you to peddle for him on the outside?"

"No, sir. He only bragged about how much money he had put aside."

"A thrifty young man, is that what you're saying? Sold drugs and put it all away for a rainy day, eh? You expect us to believe that?"

"That's what he told me."

"That's his illusion, Professor. Welcome to the real world. *He* wants to believe he put away all that money. When he was arrested, he didn't have two pieces of crap to rub together. Oh, he told you a story about how much money he has stashed around the world, didn't he? He told us the same story, even gave us bank account numbers. We checked it all out. We examined the paper trail down to the last zero. The dumb son of a bitch made it all up to try to sucker us in. He figured if we thought there was a lot of money out there to recover, the prosecutor would make a deal with him just to get the cash back. But there was no way the dough was there. Unfortunately, Stiles began to believe his own lies. Even after we disproved his every claim, he continued to brag about having all that dough."

I wondered if Stiles was truly delusional or simply shrewd, letting the police think he was unstable so that, if he ever got out of prison, there would be less likelihood the authorities would follow him around to get a scent of that money. There seemed no point to running that scenario by Rollins and Taft, so I simply shrugged and steeled myself for the continuing onslaught.

"Okay, Professor, let's jump ahead. We'll skip the next two former students you visited. Deter Crouch is off-limits. We know of his contributions to world peace and his connection to a well-known government think tank. Most of his work is highly classified. And the loser, Ambrose Archer, is on house arrest with those nice nuns, so we can give him a pass. We know that local law enforcement are delaying his prosecution, trying to get him to turn tricks for them. So let's go to the broad, the one you screwed to death. You got an explanation for that?"

"Ms. Prescott had a bad heart," I protested. "I didn't know that or I wouldn't have given in to her."

"You gave in to *her*?" Taft said.

"She wanted to have sex. So I agreed."

"You must have some magic package, Professor, for her to want to have sex with *you*. What'd you do, flash it at her and she went ape-shit? She just couldn't control herself, eh?" Taft chuckled.

"Her doctor said she hadn't had sex in several years."

"Damn near a virgin, I'd say. We know you didn't actually kill her. But if you hadn't had sex, she'd be alive today, right?"

"Perhaps," I conceded. I decided to forgo any reference to her inoperable brain tumor. "We took a liking to each other, that's the only reason I did it."

"We saw photos of her on the ranch, Professor. We understand how you could take a liking to her." Taft looked at Rollins. "She reminds me a little of Ruby. Got those kind of tits."

Rollins frowned. "You never saw Ruby's tits," he said.

"How do you know?"

"I just know."

"I suppose *you* did. You see them? I mean really see them?"

"I never saw them, you know, like naked. You don't have to see them that way to see they are big."

"You'd have to be blind not to know they're big," Taft said. "You ever bump into her? You know, accidentally on purpose?"

"What do you think I am, a creep like you? Besides, she'd break your arm if you tried a trick like that. We had a kid fresh from the academy assigned here once. He made a serious pass at her, you know, figured he was some kind of young stud. They did surgery on his hand for six hours just to get all the fingers back in the right order. That's the last move anyone's made on her since. That was five years ago. So don't fool with Detective Touch or you could wind up with your you-know-what in your ear, and I don't mean that in no figurative way."

Taft looked down at me. "What are you listening to? You never heard any of this, you understand?"

"If there is nothing else, I'd like to go home. I think I have a fever."

"Just don't leave the country, Professor."

"That's not likely," I said.

As I stood, Rollins leaned in, lowering his voice to a whisper. "You know that book, *The Rise and Fall of the Roman Empire*?" he said.

"Yes, I know the book."

"That's history, right? You wouldn't have an extra copy laying around, would you? My father-in-law has been yakking about getting a copy. I just thought, you know, being in history, you might have a bunch of those laying around. Like we got brochures on AIDS and *Don't Use Drugs*. You might have books people can pick up."

"I'll check my personal library."

CHAPTER 29
HOME AGAIN, HOME AGAIN...

The little house appeared as a haven to me as I pulled into the driveway. After unloading, unpacking, thoroughly showering, and climbing into my tired old sweats, I poured a stiff drink and sat on the small sun porch, the floor of which was cluttered with dried leaves from plants that had succumbed to neglect. As I sipped the booze, considering for that moment how I'd been drinking a great deal more since my bank escapade, I slipped back in the chair with my eyes closed and let the fatigue drain from my body.

The sound of a car in the drive tempted me to open my eyes, but I resisted and, instead, speculated. Who could it be? Young Ryder wanting an effusive discussion on Italian art? Rollins, the detective, looking for my spare copy of *The Rise and Fall...*? Ryder Senior challenging me to a dual at dawn over the heart of his mistress? Martha Ryder searching out Gloria's recipe for slick gray gravy? The Lioness ready to rip another layer of epidermis from my trimmer, shapelier body? Stromberg resurrected from the dead, about to give me a full report on his experience at passing over?

I forced my eyes open.

Detective Ruby Touch climbed from her patrol car and stood in the drive, one hand poised on the butt of her forty-five automatic, looking into the sunroom directly at me. Her face broke into a smile. I stepped to the door and swung it open. "Detective, please come in."

I watched her advance, generous hips rolling from side to side against the thick gun belt, breasts tightly swaddled. I hadn't seen her clearly in the interrogation room. Now, in the golden sunlight, her countenance shone beautifully, like a delicious Greek goddess, her blond hair curly, flouncing about her face. What I didn't like about her arrival was the package she carried, the size and shape of a videotape.

She climbed the three steps to the sun porch and stepped inside. I smelled a fragrance, something natural, maybe soap or shampoo. She extended her hand. We shook, then I closed the door. "I'm having an early cocktail." I looked at the clock on the wall; three-thirty. I felt the need to explain, "It's been a long day. And I'm on London time. Would you care for one?"

She shook her head. "Do you have a DVD player or a VCR by any chance?"

An involuntary shudder ran from my head to somewhere half-way down my legs. An urge to regurgitate cinched my stomach, but I fought the impulse and led the way to the living room. "Both." I pointed, stepping back as if the machines were a set of vipers about to strike. "The VCR is right next to the DVD player. I'm sure the former is one of the few remaining in town."

She withdrew the tape from its sleeve. "Let's use the tape. It's somewhat clearer than the DVD copy."

"I'm hoping it's the seventh game of the nineteen fifty-two World Series. Any chance?"

She shook her head, curls shimmering in the ambient light. "No, I'm afraid it isn't."

"A trip to the Grand Canyon? Your kids at Disney World? The shooting of Lee Harvey Oswald? The crash of the Hindenburg?"

"It's a security tape from the First National Bank."

I sat, gargled with a swig of whiskey, then felt nauseated. "A security tape? Hmmm. I wonder what that has to do with me?"

"That's what I'd like to know." That's what *I'd* like to know. Not we; but *I.* She had gone into business for herself. Please, no more interviews with former students. I'll do anything. Almost anything. You want this house? It's yours. The Buick? You've got it. I'll paint your nails, cut your grass, be a surrogate visitor to your relatives, the ones you don't wish to see during the holidays. Use me for target practice on the firing range with an apple in my mouth. Just no more travel, no more interviews, please.

As she was about to press the 'play' button, she turned to me. "Professor? You look distressed. Are you okay?"

Her voice wasn't tough at all. It was melodious, gentle. Soft. Alluring.

"Alec?"

Alec? She called me Alec? Not Al. What happened to Professor? Alec?

I sat upright. "Yes."

"Are you okay? Shall I come back?"

"No. Don't come back. I mean, don't leave." Just don't show me that tape. I couldn't stand the thought of going to prison. Not now. Not yet. I have so much to do with my life. *What?* I'd figure that out. But stuff. Things I haven't done. Breathe fresh air. See blue sky. Walk. Talk. Laugh. Anything. Everything. But not prison. I know there are a lot of people in prison, but I don't consider that an endorsement.

"May I show you this tape?"

May you? Stop torturing me. *'May I strap you into the electric chair for the remainder of your life?'* "Of course," I said.

"You're not okay. Can I get you something? Have you eaten? Let me fix a meal. I'm really a very good cook. And I like to cook, too."

"Thank you," I said. Her words calmed me. "You're much too kind. Let's just get this over with."

"Sure. Then maybe I'll have that drink with you. That is, if you don't mind."

The celebration drink. That's when her cohorts in law enforcement show up at the door. She'll drink my scotch while they cuff me, read me my rights, ogle her tits, and stuff me into the trunk of their squad car for the bumpy ride downtown.

She hit the play button. Flicker, flicker, lines, black and white picture, the cage. The Lioness. Who is that man with his back to the camera? Whoops, the camera angle flips. Such technology. Now the camera shows the back of the Lioness and the face of the man. My face. *MY FACE.* My hands. The note. My finger pointing at individual words. Crumpling the paper, stuffing it into my mouth. Swallowing. The paper reappearing. Flames. Empty hands. Nothing.

"Do you know her well?"

"Armand? Not well," I said, my voice now a computer generated monotone, less intonation than you might hear from a NOAA weather broadcaster.

"I thought that perhaps, since you were performing a magic trick for her, you knew her before your travels to Europe."

"I was simply trying to be entertaining."

"We've had our eye on her. Now we know she's one of the perpetrators involved in the bank's loss. When we discovered this recording at the bank, we were just hoping you could provide us with any additional information you might have."

At the bank?

"The content of security tapes are now recorded on computer disks so they can be regenerated for situations just like this. Of course, tapes can't normally leave the premises."

Can't leave the premises? How is that possible?

"To prevent someone from doctoring a tape, they are electronically encoded just like the markers placed on clothing in a department store. Any attempt to remove a recording from the bank sets off an alarm."

So there is no way the Lioness could have had a copy of this tape?

"No one could have this tape outside the bank. In fact, no one can view this tape without a special authorization code."

But she was involved with the president of the bank; wouldn't she have access to that code?

"The code is changed frequently by the insurance carrier and delivered by a special electronic message. It would be difficult for any bank employee, even the president of the bank, to get the code without special authorization. That wouldn't be given without cause. And, of course, the details of that authorization are fully recorded."

So there was no way the Lioness could know what that tape really showed.

"One thing I was curious about? The camera can't pick out the words on that slip of paper." She smiled. "What did you write on that note that generated such a puzzled expression on her face?"

Computer generated voice: "I wrote, 'I want to make a withdrawal...'."

"Did she know what you meant?"

"She thought I was deaf? She wanted to call someone to sign for me."

"And did you have an account at the bank?"

"I did." Thank god for that, I thought.

"But you really didn't know her at that time? You went up to a teller with whom you were not acquainted and gave her a slip asking for money. Good thing she believed you were deaf. Otherwise, she might have thought you were trying to hold her up."

"Yes. What a laugh that would have been."

We gazed at each other. Her smile was better than the Lioness's, not the cranberry glaze, but a smile that was warm, genuine, with lips that curled into a pronounced ridge. Her white teeth were square, strong, appearing to be good biters. I wondered if she had ever bitten a suspect.

She glanced at her watch. "Now I'm off-duty."

"That drink." I said. I went to the kitchen, poured scotch over ice, freshened mine, and returned. "This is all I have just now. I mean, the only kind of drink. I have a gallon of it. Gloria drank wine. I don't care for wine. I usually drink gin. But I'm out."

She took the glass, touching my fingers as she did. "I don't care for wine either."

I sat. The television picture flickered. "Do you mind if I turn that off?" I asked.

"I will." She reached for the remote control and pushed the power button. Retrieving the videotape, she asked, "Do you keep souvenirs?"

"If I kept a record of all my mistakes," I said, "I would need my own planet."

She laughed. "You too?" She stood with the tape. "Trash?" I nodded toward the kitchen. She found the plastic pail beneath the sink. When she returned, she said,

"I think we're done with that."

Sigh. Relief. "Yes, I'm glad we're done with that."

"So, do you live alone?"

"Yes."

"Your wife, I think Gloria is her name, she's gone?"

How did she know? "Gone for good. We were officially divorced some time this summer. As you know, I was on the road, so I don't have an exact date. Of course, if it's important, I could always call the courthouse."

She shook her head. "My divorce was final a year ago. How are you handling yours?"

I hadn't thought much about it. "I guess I'm handling it alright. And you?"

"Fine. He was seeing another woman. I'm glad it's over."

"She was seeing another man. But I think it was over long before that."

We sat in a comfortable silence, sipping our booze, eyeing one another. Then she said, "Do you mind if I remove my gun belt." It was a statement. She stood, pulled out her pistol and removed the clip, then cleared the chamber. She laid the weapon carefully on the carpet beneath a table. Then the belt dropped away with its array of technology, mace, cuffs, a radio that had been switched off. "I don't like this stuff underfoot when I'm relaxing." She stepped to the sun porch and glanced out to the driveway. "My partner is picking up the cruiser. I don't live far from here, so I can walk home."

When she re-entered the room, I said, "Will you be arresting her?"

"Armand Pennington? When INTERPOL locates her, we'll want to ask her some questions. She's traveling with the bank president's son just now. We thought the dad was the brains behind the theft at first. It took a little digging to figure out it was the boy who set this up. He seemed like such a nice, almost simple kid when we questioned him initially. Then he left town again to join her. The parents, of course, are devastated. They blame the woman, but the boy was clearly a major player. The puzzling news is that the money isn't where they claimed it to be. Apparently, the boy was more shocked than anyone. We still don't have the money in custody. Even the FBI is at a loss."

I thought of those new clothes the Lioness had purchased for me and was glad to have left them behind. Otherwise I might be in possession of ill-gotten gain. "What will happen to the woman and the boy?" I said, speaking of them with detachment, as if they were a couple I'd merely seen go through their antics on *COPS*.

"If they accept a plea bargain, and the money is actually returned, it will be up to a judge to make that decision. Neither has a record and the crime was non-violent. Ultimately, it will depend on a pre-sentencing report."

"Will it go easier on them if they give themselves up?"

"Usually that's the case."

"Since I know the boy from the university, I could make an appeal to him. Perhaps out of respect for his former professor, he would listen to me."

"You'd be willing to do that?"

"For the parent's sake," I said.

"That might require you traveling overseas. Confronting the couple. And the authorities would have to be poised to move in for an arrest whether or not they accepted your offer."

I thought, it's the least I can do after what the Lioness put me through. And she didn't have the security camera tape after all.

The telephone rang. I answered it. It was Mrs. Ryder Senior. "Oh, Professor," she began, "I'm so glad you are back in town. Young Jeffrey has fully recovered and returned to Europe to continue his travels with that woman. Now the police wish to speak with him again about the missing money. I was hoping that perhaps you had been in touch with him, since I understand you were kind enough to travel all the way to Italy to visit him in the hospital only to discover that we'd already brought him back to the States. And I have that package for you."

Yes, the package.

"Mrs. Ryder," I said, watching Detective Ruby Touch watch me, "how nice to hear from you. I can't imagine what the police might want of young Jeffrey, but perhaps I can be of some help. If I meet with you and Mr. Ryder and the police, we can devise a plan to bring Jeffrey safely home. What do you say?" Well modulated, very professorial.

"I'll ask Ryan, but I can't imagine that he would not agree. We so do want our son back." A deep breath on her end. "That woman." Humph, humph.

Yes, *that* woman.

"At this very moment I'm speaking with a member of law enforcement," I said. "I'll be glad to set up the arrangements, if you and Mr. Ryder agree. Suppose you contact the police directly," I continued, watching Ruby Touch shake her head, "or better yet, call me back with Mr. Ryder's answer. Then, I'll speak with the police and offer my services. Okay?" A confirming nod from across the room.

"Professor Simon, you are a wonderful man. God has a place in His house for a man like you. I'll get back to you shortly."

I hung up. "The plan is afoot," I said.

"Sherlock Holmes."

"You're a reader?" I said, approvingly. "What now?"

"She'll hopefully call back this evening. The dad will want a lawyer present. Your motives must be clear. You are doing this because, as the parent of an only child, you deeply understand their devastation at having their son accused of something he could have never done. This is heartbreaking. You want to put yourself out for their cause."

"Do I have to remember all that?"

"In your own words."

"Do police detectives usually make house calls, alone, so close to being off-duty?"

"During the interview, I sensed something about you I liked," she said. "I admit, making this sort of house call is very unusual for me."

"This is very unusual for me," I countered. "I don't usually get myself involved with bank thieves."

"You don't have that reputation."

"You checked up on me."

"Part of the job."

"I must admit, you seem like a person I'd like to get to know better," I said.

"At the moment," she said, "that is out of the question. We don't wish to contaminate our professional relationship until this matter has been settled."

"I wouldn't mind."

She smiled. "Call me when you hear from the Ryders. In the meantime, I'll check with my boss and set it up." She stood, walked toward me, and paused within a hot breath's length. "As soon as this is settled, perhaps we'll have dinner."

"I'd like that," I said.

Ruby Touch buttoned her blouse to once again conceal her cleavage, collected her paraphernalia, and left. I waited for the Ryder call.

CHAPTER 30
SAVING JEFFREY RYDER

W e had gathered in the lawyer's conference room, the Ryders, Attorney Paisley along with another senior officer from the bank, the prosecuting attorney, the assistant police commissioner, a captain, a special agent with the FBI, Detective Ruby Touch, and me. Detective Touch was dressed in a business suit, her weapon snuggly concealed beneath the contour of her jacket.

"You have no hard evidence against the young man," Attorney Paisley said. "He is only wanted for questioning. That's our understanding."

"A search of his room at the Ryder's mansion revealed brochures, information on opening a Swiss bank account along with a partial account number, and maps of their travel route through Europe," the captain said. "That's enough for a start."

"But that evidence is circumstantial. There could be a logical explanation."

"Let's say our warrant is a way of labeling this as more than a guest appearance." The prosecutor turned to me. "And Professor, you'd be willing to travel to Europe and meet with Jeffrey?"

"Yes, sir," I said. "I feel it's the least I can do, under the circumstances. I have a son of my own. If he were in trouble, I would appreciate any help I could get."

"And we do appreciate it, Professor," Martha Ryder said. "We want our son home safely. Whatever it costs. Isn't that right, Ryan?"

Humph, humph. "Well, of course, my dear. And, regardless of the circumstances, the bank would like its money returned. If Jeffrey has any complicity in this deed, I'm sure it is by association only." *Who could have guessed the trollop would turn out to be such a big time thief? She could have married into it, but, instead, she got greedy.*

"What guarantees do we have that you will respect young Mr. Ryder's rights if he should turn down the Professor?" asked Attorney Paisley.

"This is an international case," the prosecutor said. "He'll be extradited according to international law. That's all I can offer just now." He added, speaking to the Ryders, "This is quite an opportunity to negotiate for this young man. Should you fail to give us the information we need to locate the boy, there will be no second chances."

So officialdom knew that the Ryders knew. I wondered how? E-mails? Phone calls? Letters? Weren't those scofflaws brazen? Young Ryder reaching out, concerned that Mom and Dad might worry?

Exchanging a glance with Martha, Senior Ryder's countenance changed, the arrogant façade replaced by a look of defeat. "In truth," he began, "they are both back in this country. Jeffrey stopped by two nights ago. He didn't stay long. He just didn't want us to worry."

Gasps all around. "They are here?" the assistant police commissioner said. "You could be charged with…." The prosecutor cut him short with a wave of his hand.

"It is imperative that we move ahead with this plan. Otherwise, all bets are off."

"My apologies," Ryan Ryder said. "I have a telephone number I can give to the Professor. He'll have to leave a message and set up the arrangement."

"Cell phone?"

"Yes."

"Professor? Are you willing?"

"Of course," I said. "When?"

"Let's move on this now."

Ryder Senior produced a cell phone and handed it to me. "The number is programmed," he said. "Number two on the keyboard."

I hit two and pushed the dial-up button. Three rings before the message played Jeffrey's sweet voice. I left an abbreviated version of what I had rehearsed; *Mom... Dad... concerned... future life... lots to give... everyone makes mistakes...forget and forgive... seven years isn't that long....* The recording ended with a "beep". I handed the phone to Ryan Ryder.

"I liked everything except that last part, the seven years," the assistant police commissioner said. "Where'd you get that idea?"

"Dragnet?" I said.

No one smiled except Ruby Touch and she brushed her smile away with an index finger along her upper lip.

"That's that," the attorney for the Ryders said. "As soon as you hear something, Professor, please let these people know." He handed me a list of law enforcement phone numbers to call. "It's all in your hands now."

"You won't need these," the captain said, reaching for the list. "We'll be in on this all the way, Professor. Your home, office, and cell phone all will be tapped. We'll know the instant he calls. Detective Touch will accompany you. She'll carry a phone that will roll over calls from both your home and office. The sooner we move, the better." I nodded, but couldn't get *Dragnet* from my mind, deliberately avoiding eye contact with Detective Touch.

"Then, we're agreed," Attorney Paisley said.

Hands were shaken all around.

"Oh, by the way, Professor, this is for you." Martha Ryder handed me a package wrapped in plain brown paper very much the size of a videotape.

"Thank you." I took it, avoided all eye contact, and followed Detective Touch to the street.

When we were in my car, she said, "Do you know what it is?"

"This?" I said, innocently, clutching the package.

"It looks very much like a video tape."

"Yes."

"Let's go to your place. We'll beat the phone technicians and play it."

What was there to dread? I asked myself. "Sure. Great idea."

Not really a great idea, but what could I do? Not surprisingly, the tape was identical to the tape Ruby Touch had played, except the clarity had been enhanced considerably. Both my words on the slip of paper and the expression on the Lioness's face were most evident.

"I guessed correctly. She had never laid eyes on you before," Ruby Touch concluded.

"No," I said. We were sitting side by side on the sofa facing my twenty-five inch television screen. Ruby Touch had removed her coat. Her bosom strained the buttons on the men's broadcloth shirt she wore.

"You went into the bank and handed a note to the teller requesting money when you could have simply filled out a withdrawal slip? Why?"

"I wanted to perform a magic trick for a perfect stranger?"

"That's your answer?"

"I don't have a better one."

"She had this tape all along. Was she blackmailing you?"

"I wouldn't exactly call it blackmail."

"Your summer travels? This tape has something to do with those travels, doesn't it?"

"At first I genuinely thought she had my best interests at heart, forcing me to interview former students so I might get a fresh perspective on my teaching. In Europe, however, she told the truth.

Her motivation was to set me up to look like the brains behind the stolen money. If things went wrong, she would produce this tape as evidence of my complicity."

"But you didn't even know each other."

"Not at first. And never very well. But she had this uncanny sense."

"So you spent the entire summer looking up former students because you thought she would turn you into the authorities?"

"Something like that."

"Alec, you would never have been prosecuted for a stunt like this. She would have had to talk a pretty good game to convince anyone that there was a tie in between this scene and the missing funds."

"She's a pretty good talker."

"Is it possible that you took on her assignment because it was a chance to do something more interesting and exciting than anything you had planned for the summer?"

"Is it?"

"Well, what do you think?"

I wasn't thinking. I was watching Ruby Touch. Could this really work? A tired history professor and a cop? "I never thought about it." I had actually let Silverman do the thinking. Of course, that had been another in a series of mistakes.

"Alec Simon, you can relax. You are not going to prison for this silly prank. Actually, it's kind of clever. Now, if you had taken it further, if she had offered money beyond your deposits and you had accepted it, then you might have gotten into trouble."

"So I did all that traveling for nothing?"

"Maybe you did it because you needed to do it."

"Maybe."

"And now?"

"I don't know."

"Good. It's time you put those worries behind you and begin living more in the moment."

"That's what Silverman says."

"And he's right."

"Do you know about Silverman?"

"Your psychiatrist? Yes, I know all about him."

"So you know things about me and I know nothing about you."

She smiled. "Let's ditch the tape." A car in the driveway. "The techs are here." She retrieved the video from the machine and carried it to the kitchen to deposit in the trash.

An hour later, the house was fully wired. One technician remained behind to monitor calls.

"Now what?" I asked.

"We wait," Ruby Touch said.

The call from Young Ryder came that evening. Detective Touch had dozed off on the sofa after her relief called in sick. One technician had been replaced by another. While reading a piece in *The New Yorker*, the telephone rang and I jumped at the break in the silence.

Jeffrey's opening words were, "Professor, what a mess."

"Yes," I replied. "Your parents are concerned."

"They gave you this number?"

"They would like you to turn yourself in."

"But I'm right here in the city. It's not like I'm on the run."

"I think the police would like to speak with you again."

"Do they know?"

"I think they know everything. They would be willing to make a deal."

"I don't need a deal. I need everyone to leave me alone."

"I don't think that's going to happen, Jeffrey."

"Look, Professor, you don't know what I've been through. I mean, with Penny. She promised she would leave her husband if I pulled this off."

"She's married?"

"I did what she asked and now she's reneged. She wants the three of us to go off together. And I really don't care that much for him. He farts a lot."

"I can hardly blame you. All the more reason for speaking with the police." She was married all along?

"But I don't have the money."

"Armand, that is, Penny, has the money?"

"I don't know where the money is. She gave me the numbers and I transferred it electronically, but it never got deposited in the Swiss bank account. It's lost."

"Perhaps someone else stole it," I suggested. What a novel thought.

"Yes, that's what I am thinking." He paused. "Is this call being traced?"

"Are you on a cell phone?"

"You're stalling, Professor, aren't you?"

The technician looked at me, gesturing with two fingers. Two minutes? Two seconds? I couldn't tell.

"Does anything I said make sense? About your life?"

The technician whispered, "He's out front. *He's right out front.*"

We all stepped onto the sun porch. There sat Jeffrey in his black Mustang, cell phone pressed to his ear. Ruby eased out the rear door, circled the house, and was on him in less than a minute. Young Jeffrey continued to talk to me as she led him to the front door.

"Professor, I've lost all hope. What is my life about, anyway? That's what I can't figure out. Do you have any ideas?"

We stood opposite one another, perhaps two feet apart, phones pressed to our ears. He had the good sense to hang up first.

"Life is about a lot of things, Jeffrey. Stealing money doesn't have to be one of them."

"It's too late."

"No. You still have a chance to make things right. You want to do what's right, I know. That's why you called me back. You wouldn't have called if you hadn't wanted to make things right."

I ran out of platitudes and clichés. Fortunately, the FBI interrogation team of four gray clad agents arrived. The lead investigator wanted to take Jeffrey downtown, but I persuaded him to keep it low key and stay at the house, at least until we discovered how cooperative Jeffrey might be. I made coffee and suggested to Ruby she send one of the underlings out for snacks and soft drinks. The head interrogator was a young man, dark hair, soft spoken, not much older than Jeffrey. He sat across from Jeffrey, smiling.

"You say you don't know where the money is? Any idea how it got lost?"

"I don't think it was ever sent from the Federal Reserve Bank. I mean, I did the computer transfer, so it showed on paper, but the money never went anywhere that I could find."

"So you think it is still at the Federal Reserve?"

"Or in the basement."

"In the basement of your father's bank?"

"There is a basement vault that could hold that much money. You see, I might have gotten confused about the computer codes. If I did, then the money would have been delivered to my father's bank instead of wired to Switzerland. I was nervous and things got very unclear for me in those last few minutes."

"We'll check." He nodded a *check-it-out* directive to one of the local detectives. "Now, about your partner. Ms. Pennington. Do you know her whereabouts?"

"She and her husband left the country. I don't know where they are headed."

As I watched, the different demeanor Jeffrey Ryder presented struck me. Gone was the frolicsome boy, wildly excited about two postage stamps from Zaire. Here sat an articulate, albeit anxious, young man no longer halting of speech or gesture. I wondered for a moment if he, not the Lioness, had been responsible for arranging my summer itinerary. And had she shared my peccadillo at the bank teller window with him? Of course, she had. They had had a good laugh over the silly, absent-minded professor, wandering aimlessly cross-country, creating mischief.

"She left you to take the rap?"

"She'd spent a lot of money, then freaked out when she learned the Swiss bank account we'd set up was empty."

"Does she think you took the money?"

"I couldn't have without her involvement. We developed a simple security system. Each of us had half the account numbers. Only when we put them together could we make the deposit."

"What about afterward?"

"We never knew the other's numbers. We had arranged in advance to read them to the bank officer over separate telephone lines."

Now I marveled at the sophistication of this young man. As slick a crook as there ever was.

The prosecuting attorney arrived with the family's attorney and went into conference with law enforcement. Someone gave young Ryder a cup of coffee. I exchanged glances with Ruby Touch who had chosen to remain in the background. Finally the conference broke up and Attorney Paisley stepped onto the scene. "Jeff, for the moment, the government is holding you as a material witness and on one charge of obstructing justice. We'll get you out on bond this evening. Since you have turned yourself in and are cooperating, that won't be a problem. Once we determine what actually happened to the money, we'll have a better idea of where this thing is going."

Young Ryder stepped up to me and extended his hand. "Thanks, Professor. If anyone else had called, I'd have blown them off. Hearing from you made all the difference."

My appeal to the criminal element dumbfounded me. Ambrose Archer, Jonathan Stiles, and now, Jeffrey Ryder.

"I'm glad you've done the right thing, Jeff," I said, modeling my tone after Attorney Paisley's. "You won't regret it."

In the moments that followed, I thought of the old western in which someone invariably says, just before the curtain drops; *'Well, sheriff, I think I'll be off now.'*

Ruby Touch remained behind. I poured drinks and ordered pizza. As I hung up from the pizza call, I looked up and there she stood in the bedroom doorway clad in her broadcloth shirt, the tails of which draped across her full hips. A single button bridged the material across her straining bosom.

"I'm officially off the case," she said.

"But why me?"

"What do you mean?"

"Why are you attracted to me? You are a gorgeous woman with a great deal of sex appeal. You have the most curvaceous figure I've ever seen. I'm in my fifties, actually fifty-three, paunchy, out of shape. You hang around young, virile detectives. I've only had sex with two women in my entire life. The first divorced me, the second died post-coitus."

Ruby Touch unbuttoned the last restraint.

"On second thought, maybe my track record isn't that important," I said. "I'll leave cash for the pizza driver."

CHAPTER 31

LOOSE ENDS

The following morning, I stepped out to retrieve the newspaper and my neighbor, Brody Fine, hailed me from his yard where, properly attired in strap-on kneepads, he attacked an early fall resurgence of dandelions. "Busy place, over there," he said. In his dandelion pursuing crouch, Brody resembled a gopher-stalker, gleefully ready to stab a curious varmint with his forked de-weeder.

As I reached down, holding my shabby robe tightly around my legs, I replied, "Yes. I've had a few guests."

"Law enforcement. Catching up with you, Al? Probably caught you voting Democrat in the summer primary." Brody chuckled.

"Actually, they were asking about you. You knew my tenant disappeared before his lease was up, didn't you? The cannibal?"

Brody leapt to his feet. "My god, Al, I had nothing to do with that. Honest. Sure, I looked through the window a couple times to see what he was eating. But that was it. Cause there were these strange smells all the time coming from the house. I think he was using herbs or something to cook with. He used to come back from shopping with these baskets of stuff, looked like small heads. I remembered what you said. You know, about him being a cannibal. I figured he's eating herbs with small heads." He folded back the edge of his fishing vest to reveal a five-pointed tin star. "It's part of being on neighborhood watch, looking through windows."

I smiled. "Have a nice morning, Brody."

"You're kidding me, right? They're not asking about me. They couldn't know that I used your spare key...." He stopped.

"Brody," I said, "you didn't."

Brody hung his head. "You can't be too careful, Al. Suppose he was cutting people up right there in your kitchen?"

"I hope he would at least have invited you to dinner," I replied, stepping into the sun porch and closing the door on Brody's final protest.

The authorities did find the money, eleven and a half million dollars in original Federal Reserve bags stored in the basement of the Ryder bank. Apparently Young Ryder had gotten confused about the transfer codes and sent the money to his father's bank instead of overseas to the Swiss account. Since deliveries of cash weren't unusual at the bank, and Ryder Senior was out of the country, a conscientious clerk signed the documents and had the money relegated to the basement vault. The engorged bags had simply sat quietly collecting dust.

Young Jeffrey was given six months probation by an understanding judge who, coincidentally, had received contributions to his re-election campaign from Ryder Senior's personal account. After a brief deliberation with the family, the judge determined the boy was actually too naive to have stolen the money, as evidenced by his use of the wrong transfer code. Overjoyed, the parent's applauded the judge's official ruling: *Not-too-guilty by reason of naivety.*

At the urging of Attorney Paisley, Jeffrey contacted the Lioness, explained his error, and, after her yelling ceased, convinced her to return from her Canadian hideaway to face the music. She agreed, albeit reluctantly, and was given a year suspended sentence and five years probation. The more severe penalty was awarded on the grounds that she had fled the country and was old enough to know better. Senior Ryder also managed to convince the judge to make a condition of her probation that she not see his son during that period. She readily acquiesced, making no mention to the authorities that Ryder Senior was to have been a recipient of a portion of the money had the transfer of funds been successful. Perhaps the Lioness let him off the hook because she had no intention of sharing the loot anyway.

Armand's so-called husband turned out to be an old boyfriend she had recruited as a ruse to keep young Ryder focused on his role as business partner, rather than suitor. The boyfriend knew nothing of the scheme.

By the time the fiasco was straightened out, I had dropped my reference to this sociopath as *The Lioness* and thought of her by her given name, Armand, a change of which I was quite proud. The lioness had been de-clawed.

CHAPTER 32

HOMER'S FINAL FART

R uby Touch and I launched a torrid affair. Her visits to the house were frequent and extended, our activities carried out with considerable gusto. I purchased new shades for all the windows and retrieved my spare key from beneath the flowerpot on the back stoop. I also paid a considerable sum of money to have a nursery team plant a fully-grown hedgerow between my house and Brody Fine's. Brody, of course, was no longer speaking to me, a fact that strongly suggested my life was moving in the right direction.

Ruby, by now, had established a ritual, standing on display in the bedroom doorway as I watched her pop that last button. At her instigation, we also experimented with variations, such as her wearing the thick leather gun belt beneath her shirt, a peaked uniform cap, mirrored sunglasses, and exotic spiked heels. On several occasions, I wore only my academic robe, mortarboard hat, and black dress shoes, while chastising her for a tardy homework assignment. I was reluctant to introduce the hairbrush.

One Saturday, after a morning of languid lovemaking, the side doorbell rang. Ruby looked out. "It's a man with a dog, Alec. Perhaps you'd better go to the door."

I descended the short flight of stairs in my sweats and swung open the door. There stood Ackerman Fink, the general contractor in whose magnificent mansion Gloria now resided. At the end of the leash squatted Homer, the fat-assed dog, glaring up at me with those limpid eyes.

"Professor, I'm sorry to bother you, but I can't take it anymore. He misses you. He whines and scratches at the door. He won't let me walk him. It's been a nightmare. He's not been well and Gloria says you're the only one who can handle him. You got to take him back."

I looked down. "Is that right, Homer?"

Homer farted.

"Please?" Ackerman said.

The look of distress on Ackerman's face moved me. "Has he pissed in the rear seat of your car yet?"

"He's crapped three times on my leather upholstery. The stains and the stench got so bad, I had to replace the car."

"Does Gloria still feed him liver?"

"Liver? I don't know. Do dogs eat liver?"

"I don't mean to speak unkindly of the dearly divorced, but I think Gloria has a passive-aggressive streak."

"Will you take him? Please? You know, if you want any work done around the place, I can send some men over. I'll do it first thing Monday morning. Like, for example, I notice your roof is looking a little shabby. It's a day's job at most. I'd only charge for the materials. Or painting. I got two guys who can paint the entire place in two days, tops."

I thought I saw a tear in the corner of an Ackerman eye.

Reaching for the leash, I said, "Homer misses Rodney. Although they didn't talk much, they did grow up together. Homer always had a soft spot for his younger brother."

"Whatever," Ackerman said. "Thank you, Professor. I'll give you a few days to think about what you need done." He fumbled in his wallet and pulled forth a business card, the corners of which were frayed. "That's my cell phone number there." He pointed with an index finger. The nail had been chewed nearly to the quick. "I always answer that. Now, remember, I want to hear from you. I'll do anything. Okay? And thanks."

The big man scampered down the driveway as if the devil were after him. Homer and I stood together and watched. Then, looking down at the pooch, I said, "You want to walk?"

Ordinarily, Homer would swing his rear end about and clickety-clack down the drive. Instead, he nuzzled my leg, a first when he wasn't attempting to hump me, then pushed his way into the house. As he struggled to ascend the shallow flight of stairs, I noticed a lump along one side of his chest. I lifted his short legs to help him handle the ascent, one he had always managed with as much aplomb as a dog of his dimensions could muster. Once on level ground, he click-clacked to the faux fireplace and curled into a ball.

Ruby stepped to my side. "He doesn't look well, Alec. Shall we take him to a vet?"

"Let's wait," I said.

She joined me as I positioned myself next to Homer and stroked his brow and neck. For one brief moment, he raised his head and looked into my eyes. Then he rested his head on one paw, took a last deep breath, and released it with a gentle shudder. I watched his breathing subside. Moments later, Homer lay dead.

We sat in silence for nearly a minute before the wave of sadness swept over me. My first sob was a shudder that nearly matched Homer's. Then my body shook as I wept unabashedly. Ruby enfolded me in her arms and held me tight.

We ignored the passage of time. When my emotions finally settled down, I accepted her kiss as she wiped my tears with a gentle swipe of her thumb. "Goodbye, Homer," I said as I looked into Ruby's eyes. Then I broke into sobs once again as she rocked me back and forth.

When I finally composed myself, we showered, dressed, and I called a local veterinarian's office. The answering service agreed to contact the doctor, who in turn expressed her willingness to meet us at her office to accept Homer's remains. Ruby did the honors, nestling the inert body into a blanket and placing it gently inside the trunk. She drove the short distance, carried the carcass inside, and handled the paperwork. We agreed to cremation. She selected a silver urn and handed the vet her credit card to cover the expenses.

Driving back to the house, we sat in the driveway for several moments, I holding her hand and stroking her palm. "Thank you," I said. "I don't know what came over me."

"You simply chose to show me what a kind, gentle, and loving man you are," she said.

"I never knew I had those feelings for Homer."

"Perhaps there are a lot of feelings you don't know you have, feelings looking for a way out. Homer's passing opened that door."

I briefly thought of Stromberg and whether he might be on the other side welcoming the pooch. What an alliance that would be.

We kissed there in her car sitting in the front yard. When I came up for air and glanced toward the house, there stood Rodney. Spontaneously, I jumped out and ran toward him. We embraced.

"Hey, Dad, who's the chick?" he said, looking beyond my shoulder. Since 'chick' was not a term Rodney has previously used, I ascribed the expanded vocabulary to a summer at the beach.

Ruby walked up the driveway, a gorgeous spectacle with her glistening hair and broad smile. "This is Ruby," I said, reaching for her hand. "Ruby, this is my son, Rodney. A young man of whom I'm very proud." Much to my pleasure, they embraced as old friends.

"Dad, I want my own place," Rodney said as we walked back to the house.

"Good," I said.

"You mean it?"

"Of course. It's about time."

"Great. Now I've just got to find an apartment and get a job to pay for it."

"I don't want to interfere," Ruby said, "but I have an apartment that could be available."

Rodney asked, "How much a month?"

"Don't worry about that. The lease has been paid for the next few months. Try it on, see how you like it."

"Gee, that's terrific. But what about you?"

Ruby looked at me.

"Ruby is living here now, Rodney. That is, if you're okay with it."

"Fantastic, Dad."

I told him the news about Homer.

"I know," he said. "When I got back from the beach two days ago, I went to Mom's figuring I'd take care of that obligation first. You know, thinking if I spent a couple of days there, maybe she'd understand that I didn't want to live with them. Anyway, I saw Homer and we all knew he was very ill. Mom had taken him to the vet who said nothing could be done. I think that's why she sent him back here. She wanted you to have a chance to say goodbye."

Perhaps moving Rodney into Ruby's apartment at such a tender age, just eighteen, showed me to be a foolish, indulgent parent. But I had faith that Rodney would use the experience wisely. It took no more effort than packing two pieces of luggage, a computer, and a backpack. He chose to leave his skateboard with me. Other than stocking the refrigerator, there was little to add to his living conditions. Ruby handed over a key, reviewed with Rodney the infrastructure of the place along with some rules, and we celebrated at a restaurant that served delicious Mexican food. At the end of the evening, we dropped him at his new digs and there were hugs all around. There was a look in Rodney's eyes as he bid us goodbye that I'd seen before, one of ambivalence. I started to say, 'Hey, you know the door is always open for you at home', but decided against it, perhaps because I knew he knew and that we both felt good about it.

Ruby offered to drive to the house, and I accepted. As we rode in silence, I thought about Rodney and his experience of growing up. It was not an easy road, I knew, even if family values are at the one hundred and ten percent level with both parents present and the extended family network weaving a safety net resilient enough to catch a locomotive. And growth rarely happened with the continuity of a ribbon of soft ice cream oozing from the nozzle of a smoothie machine. It was more like climbing a scary scaffolding toward an uncertain destination, a plateau beyond the clouds. Most youngsters, I'd noticed, required a time to pause and catch their breath, a chance to survey the landscape from each new perspective and decide whether to continue upward or to set up camp for a while. For Rodney, I guessed, this was a chance to enjoy a sense of freedom, to become accustomed to new heights, and perhaps most of all, to relish, at least for a period of time, his sense of accomplishment.

CHAPTER 33
FACE TO FACE WITH DR. SILVERMAN

I decided I owed myself one final face-to-face therapy session with Dr. Silverman. He was not his usual buoyant self as I took a seat in a leather chair, foregoing the couch.

"My boy, my therapist is ill and must give up his practice," he said morosely.

"My condolences," I replied. *Does this mean you are now without any semblance of constraint?* I thought, perhaps unkindly.

"It's time I'm back on my own, anyway," he said, sounding more concerned about the transition in his own life than his mentor's health. "So enough about me. Let's talk about you. How does it feel to be off the hook?"

"Mixed, I suppose," I said with candor. "There was a certain excitement to my summer experience."

"That is easy to say now," he said. "Remember how you whined all summer, calling, complaining?"

Once again, he was right. "That's true. Now that I'm on the better side of the thin ice, it doesn't look so scary."

"What is this cliché, 'better side of the thin ice'? I've never heard it. Is this Scandinavian? Is your family Scandinavian?"

My family were not Scandinavian, not to my knowledge. I had no idea where the phrase had come from and didn't wish to spend therapy money debating the source of my cliché. I'd never use it again. However, I admitted, "For some unknown reason, I've been using strange and unfamiliar words and phrases lately."

"It is possible someone from the spirit world is channeling through you." He looked at me with a sober face, no grin. Then, "Okay, enough about clichés. Fill me in. What has been happening since you've been back?"

I told him about Rodney moving out, Ruby moving in and my new sense of confidence.

"Be careful of this flight into health," he said. "Sigmund Freud was right when he said patients have a tendency to show signs of health when they approach the apex of their neurosis. You are not yet well, my boy. You are reaching the crest of the mountain and resting short of your goal, claiming victory, rather than continuing your journey to the other side. You see, the cliché, 'it is the journey, not the destination, that counts', is true in many of life's endeavors, but not in the process of psychotherapy. You've got to reach the goal to claim the prize."

"And what is on the other side?" I asked.

"What is *usually* on the other side is the parent," he replied.

"The parent?"

"Yes. *The* parent. Usually one. Sometimes, two. But most often, one. You must deal with one of your parents."

"They are both dead."

"Irrelevant. They could have both been dead when you were born and you would have to deal with one of them at least. Let me guess. In your case, I would say *the mother.*"

"My father, I believe," I said.

"I was close." He smiled. "What does it matter? A little joke. Of course it is your father. I don't wish to be too perfect as a magician, otherwise I might discourage you from the delight of self discovery."

"What is it I have to do exactly?"

"This is where I leave you at the edge of the path. You must go it alone."

"In other words, whatever I've got to do about my father, *I've* got to do. There is no map, no guideline you can offer?"

"Isn't that just what I said?"

"Can you at least point me in some direction?"

"Anger toward parents is often a predominant emotion in children. Also guilt. Or a need to be loved. I would say those are the big three. Like the Detroit automakers."

"And how do I express any of these emotions?"

"You may wish to write a letter to get those emotions outside of yourself. Or, if there is a gravesite, go there and express them aloud. Combining the two is another option. Write the letter, and read it at the gravesite."

Suddenly, my therapist was sounding very serious, very sensible, and more profound than I would have liked. I decided at that moment I preferred him insane. "Is it like a magic spell?" I asked.

"Yes," he said, "you have the idea. Very much like a magic spell. That's all the past is, really. A spell. Once we figure that out and do the right incantation, we're done with it. We get on with our lives."

"I say the correct incantation and I'm set free?"

He appraised me silently for a moment, pressing long, angular fingers against one another, his head bobbing, pensive, as if considering an invocation of his own. Finally, "Yes, if you follow your heart and offer up your true feelings, you will be set free."

"Is this why I have pursued my secret career as a closet magician?"

"My boy, I wouldn't put much stock in such a direct correlation. Lay persons often look for one-to-one relationships, hoping to wrap their psychic pain into a nice, neat bundle. When you are over the top of the mountain, the landscape may look different than you had anticipated. This is what we can never predict with certainty and why the ethical therapist must refrain from offering up the cure on a silver platter. The enemy may metamorphose before your very eyes. Kind of like a virus. Or an edition of the *Matrix*." He smiled impishly. "And then where the hell are you?"

CHAPTER 34

FROM DREAMS TO REALITY

Fall classes started that following week. I had never been so happy to be back in my classroom. After greeting five hundred freshmen with an exuberant 'Yahoo', I pulled a rabbit from a hat, made a dove disappear into a food processor and reappear without having lost a feather, performed six different card tricks, and took requests for the following week.

At the first faculty meeting, I took a leadership role for the first time in years and, much to the puzzlement of my colleagues, even volunteered for two standing committees. When nominations came due for the University Senate, I wrote in my own name, ran, and not to anyone's surprise, won a seat by overwhelming acclamation. Of course, my name was the only one on the ballot to represent our college.

Three weeks into the semester, things were running smoothly. Arriving home from a particularly long day, I poured myself a drink, and sat with the newspaper in my lap and the evening news on the television. Ruby had taken several days off from her law enforcement job and put in long hours cleaning, cooking, and stashing food in the freezer. As I relaxed, I had a wonderful sense of domestic tranquility. Before I knew it, I fell into a deep, dreamy slumber, maybe the kind that broadsided *Sleeping Beauty*.

In my dream, as best I could recall, Fulmer Hasbach received the Pulitzer Prize for Literature based on a collection of unpublished story plots. His acceptance speech was four hours and thirty-three minutes in length, fortunately condensed by the magic of the subconscious. Upon completion, Sara McCovey led him from the stage to a church sanctuary where Dr. Cecil Worksworth married them. Ryan Ryder emerged from the church with the president of State U. to announce that he was putting up one hundred thousand dollars to establish the Professor Alec Simon Distinguished Lecturer's Chair in History to honor my efforts with his son, Jeffrey. Everyone threw rice.

The president of the university stepped to the microphone. *"This is quite an honor for you, Professor Simon,"* he said, suddenly now at a news conference in his office.

"Ladies and gentlemen, without further adieu, I give you Dr. Harry Silverstein."

Applause.

"Thank you, Mr. President. And by the way, it's Silverman. Harvey Silverman."

I lay dumbfounded in my coma. They had selected my shrink for a eulogy.

"What is the purpose of life?" Silverman began, raising hedge-like eyebrows on a super-sized face with bug-eyes that leered at the small gathering. *"More to the point, what is the purpose of Professor Simon's life? The story of Professor Simon's life is about waking up one day and asking, has he made a difference? The fact that Professor Simon wished to be an illusionist, what does that say about him? We may never know. Professor Simon has to make the decision for himself as to whether his life has been worthwhile."*

Silverman then turned to me. *"Most importantly, Alec, it is time to wake up and live."*

"Alec, wake up. Wake up. Wake up, Alec. The telephone is for you."

Reaching for the remote receiver, I struggled to sit upright on the sofa.

"Yes?" I said, dazed by my dream.

"Professor Simon, this is Cynthia, the Dean's secretary. Sorry to bother you at home, but I was working late and thought you might want to know that Mr. Ryder is giving the history department a plaque honoring your work with students. It's going to hang right outside the men's room. Would you prefer oak or walnut?"

"Oak or walnut?"

"And he's giving one hundred dollars to our library fund."

"A hundred dollars?"

"Yes. And the plaque has an inscription. Can I read it to you? It says: 'Professor Alec Simon will be remembered most for....'"

"For what?" I asked.

"That's it. Mr. Ryder thought it would be best for you to fill it in."

"I see."

"And, a young man by the name of Ambrose Archer was around to see you. He said he owed you twenty dollars from when you visited him in New York City. When I told him you were home, he wanted your address. He looked a little seedy, so I didn't give it to him. I hope that was okay."

"Yes, that was a good decision," I said.

"He said he'd keep coming back until he found you."

I glanced up at Ruby leaning against the bedroom doorframe. This time her blouse was tightly buttoned. Two pieces of luggage sat at her feet. I said into the telephone, "Thanks for the call, Cynthia. I'll have to get back to you on the plaque." I hung up and turned to Ruby. "Going somewhere?"

"I didn't know how to tell you, Alec. I've taken a job in Seattle."

The cooking, the cleaning, a going away present. As easily as she had come into my life, Ruby Touch left with barely a ripple.

CHAPTER 35

DEATH BEFORE RESURRECTION

O nce again, Silverman was right. I had lingered short of the crest of the mountain, hesitant to go further. Now it was time for the visit, the one I knew I had to make, and one perhaps for which I was now ready. It was time to return to my roots in the most basic sense.

I wondered about it, the draw of the past. Was it simple curiosity? Or a need to nourish some dormant element within? What did I need from my father after all these years? Our family life, such as it was, had ended many years earlier. He died of a heart attack while sitting behind the wheel of his eighteen-wheeler at a rest stop on Interstate 95. We had not seen each other, even spoken on the telephone, the previous two years. I learned of his death from one of his fellow drivers, a simple postcard, on one side a photo of two bathing beauties extending their sand-coated posteriors. The note read: *Alec, your old man is dead. Sorry. Hal Moss.* The card arrived six months after my father's funeral. When I called an uncle, whom I expected handled the arrangements, I was told not to worry, all was in order. Three months later, I received the settlement from my father's estate, a cashier's check for three hundred and seventy dollars.

Hal Moss had come to our rented house twice when I was five or six and stayed for dinner on the second occasion. He was young and blond and had flirted with my mother, much to my father's embarrassment. For some reason, that image stuck in my mind for many years. As I grew older, I wondered about the scene, the interplay between Hal and my father. It was as if my father had been taunted that night and felt helpless to defend his honor.

One day the thought occurred to me that perhaps something had been going on between them, something more charismatic than merely their alliance as driving pals. I wondered if Hal Moss was the reason my father was home so infrequently? And was their camaraderie the source of my mother's frustration and the reason she threw herself so completely into her study of the dance?

While Mother was beautiful, and loving in a certain cool and distant manner, it was clear, even to a child, that she wanted something more in her life than parenthood. Her talent as a dancer was adequate, but she would never be star of the show. Without love, without stardom, I watched her heart grow bitter. She eventually surrounded herself with aging dancers, sharing tales of what might have been were it not for the tilt of the spotlight, a competing Broadway show, the snowstorm that had kept away an important critic, or the miraculous recovery of the superstar for whom she had once been an understudy. And occasionally, if I were to arrive home from college unexpectedly, I would find her sitting with her glass of sherry, turning the tear-stained pages of her scrapbook. Sometimes, I would sit with her and listen to her tales of life in the wings of the great dance theaters of America.

Traveling home the Christmas of my senior year, I found Mom in her wedding gown, stretched out on the sofa, the scrapbook propped by her side, open to a photo of her one starring role, a show that had closed three weeks after its debut. An autopsy concluded she had ingested a fatal dose of sleeping pills along with a considerable volume of vodka, apparently a day before my arrival.

Her funeral was actually quite beautiful. Her dancing friends, all long retired, attended the service, held on a Saturday afternoon in late December. A woman, who had danced with my mother in a review at the Fox Theatre, delivered the eulogy. "Sugar Simon," she said, "will always be remembered for her devotion to her art. She was a star in all our hearts." I had no better tribute, so I declined sharing my few words of comfort with the small group. Instead, I said, "Let's dance." I couldn't have made that proposal to a more receptive group. We danced away the afternoon, then said our good-byes.

I had stood alone beside the open casket, studying the radiant smile my mother offered, even in death. She was a trooper upon whom the footlights of fame had shown but dimly, fading early. Somehow tears would have demeaned her life, so I simply whispered, "Break a leg up there, Sugar." And I kissed her cool forehead.

Her union insurance paid for the funeral and her headstone. That helped. At the time, I was struggling to pay off my modest credit card debt each month. My father was on the west coast. He wired his condolences, to on one in particular.

CHAPTER 36

WAS THERE ANYONE AT HOME?

My parents. They were some pair. Skip and Sugar. Planets orbiting in different planes from the very beginning. That's how I thought of them on my father's birthday as I drove the hundred or so miles to the cemetery. Ironically, they were closer in death than in life, buried in adjacent plots, separate headstones. My mother's headstone was nearly four feet high, marble, with an engraved angel trumpeting her arrival, very much like I presumed she would have wanted to make her appearance in heaven. My father's remains rested in a plain metal urn beneath a stone, unadorned but for the simple Latin inscription; "*Sit tibi terra levis.*" *May the earth lie light upon thee.* Perhaps I had offered the quote that first year of college in an effort to impress them with my academic prowess. Skip had remembered. The headstone had most likely been purchased by Hal Moss, colleague, companion, perhaps much more to the father I had never truly known.

As I stood before my father's headstone, I wondered why I had come. I felt a sudden gnawing. What was the hunger about? *My childhood?* Unlikely. I had become a realist in that regard. *Words of praise?* I had actually gotten a few here and there, but always mixed with the gritty disillusionment of his reality. *Assurances of love?* Skip had offered little love to my mother. Could I have expected more?

A voice called my name. Looking up, I saw Stromberg perched on the edge of my Mother's gravestone, his head intact.

"Alec, your mother says, 'Hi'."

"Must you sit on her headstone?" I asked, more surprised at his audacity than by his sudden appearance.

"She invited me. She knew you were coming and sent me as a courier, so to speak."

"And for what reason?" I asked.

"To tell you she loves you. To acknowledge she wasn't much of a parent. To ask you for forgiveness?"

"Of course, I forgive her. She had a life, a career. Those were important to her."

"But she also had a little boy. You were important to her. She didn't realize how important until it was too late."

"That's a cliché," I said, experiencing a surge of indignation and self-righteousness. "If you don't pay attention to your life, it will always be too late."

"Don't get histrionic, Alec. Accept her simple apology. She says that someday you will understand."

"That's it?"

"Then there is your father."

"He sent you, too?"

"He sent a message. He said, 'Kid, you can't look to anyone but yourself.' Ring a bell?"

"Yes. It rings a bell. When he was home, that was one of his favorite expressions."

"Good advice. I wish I'd heard it when I was still in corpus."

I couldn't resist. "Is it very different over there?" I asked.

"There are very few rules. One absolute rule, however, is that you have to find out what it's like for yourself. But I can say this; you won't be disappointed."

I blinked. Stromberg had vanished. I looked about. There was absolutely no one within sight. A breeze stirred the tall grasses in a copse near the top of the knoll and the surrounding trees shivered. Several crisp maple leaves broke free of their tethers and sailed to and fro on their way earthward, landing and scooting across the surface of the tightly manicured lawn. Harbingers of the coming season.

Gazing one last time at my mother's headstone, I considered my vision of Stromberg and my sanity and decided I had the answer to neither. However, somehow I had crossed the top of the fabled mountain of which Doctor Silverman had spoken. His insights, once again, prevailed. The view was indeed different than I had imagined.

As I turned to leave, I spied another image, this one very real. An elderly man stood at the end of the row of tombstones, a peaked cap sitting jauntily on his head, a cigarette dangling from his lips. He wore a tweed sport coat slightly larger than his frame. Removing the cigarette, he lifted a hand to wave and offered a weak smile. Hal Moss had come to pay a visit on my father's birthday. What remarkable timing.

I walked toward him. He extended a gnarled hand, arthritic from years of clutching the wheel of the big rig. We pumped twice, then our hands dropped to our respective sides and he grinned broadly. He had an ingratiating smile.

"How's he doing?"

"Well enough, I guess. He's not complaining." I thought of Stromberg's comment.

"He was a tough old guy, even when he was a kid. Never could love worth a damn." Hal Moss blushed, then added, "You know what I mean. As long as we were together, I never felt that close to your dad."

"I can say the same thing."

Hal Moss chortled, then emitted a rattling cough. "You ever wonder about it?"

"I only recently drew the conclusion."

"I apologize, Alec. I really do. I was only thinking of myself in those days. That's all any of us did. It's no excuse, but it was the reason your dad wasn't home a lot of the time. It didn't matter to your mom that much, I don't think. But I never thought about you, how I kept your dad to myself." Hal Moss took several steps and I fell in by his side. We walked slowly, aimlessly, yet with purpose; walking was something to do as we exchanged the few words that perhaps had to be said. "You don't need to hear how it all began, I don't guess."

I shook my head. "Not unless it means something to my father's memory."

"It ain't much of a story. Kind of sordid." He flicked his ash. "One night, on the road, not long after we was driving together, we decided to get a motel room rather than sleep in the rig. Well, it was this little town in Arizona or Nevada, I don't remember exactly. The place was a crossroad, pretty busy, and a lot of working girls hung out there. We rented this one girl together. I think she was a blond. Anyway, after a while we found we were more interested in each other than her." He looked off. "We were together nearly twenty years. Back then, being gay was different. You just didn't come out, especially not if you was driving a rig. Looking back, I'm not proud of the secret we kept. I wish more than anything we could of been honest, could of been who we really were." He looked at me, his weathered face tired and drawn. "I just never thought about you."

We had reached my car. "Can I drop you somewhere?" I asked. I wanted to prolong our time, fascinated by the words of my father's lover. Part of me wished to find out more about my father, the man who bore me, then abandoned me for his own way of life.

Another part accepted that I'd be learning about a stranger. Hal Moss could only share a myth, one I could never fully grasp.

Perhaps Hal Moss knew the futility of saying more. "Thanks," he said. He flicked his cigarette into the crushed gravel drive. "I'll walk. The bus station is just down the foot of the hill. I'll be leaving to go out west for the winter. Got a sister in Arizona who takes me in when I need to get out of this weather." He extended his hand. "I'm not just saying this, Alec, but if it's worth anything, I know your father loved you."

Hal Moss turned and ambled along the side of the roadway. As I watched, I thought perhaps I'd look him up one day, at a time when I was ready to hear more. But then I knew I never would. It was time to go home.

CHAPTER 37

FATHERS AND THEIR SONS

Rodney sat on the front door stoop flipping a football, one he had gotten as a birthday gift years earlier. As I stepped from the car, he threw the ball in a gentle arc. I nearly had it in my grasp, and then the ball somersaulted through my arms and plopped to the ground, rolling several feet before coming to rest.

"Visiting?" I asked, bending forward.

"Do you mind if I come home? To live."

"Of course not. I'd actually like that a great deal." My tone did not conceal my pleasure at his decision.

He trotted out for a pass. I threw my best, but the football fell short, hitting the grass and gyrating end for end into the road. Rodney did as he had always been taught, glancing both ways before retrieving the ball. He turned toward me, fingers on the laces, and threw a gently arched spiral that slid into my arms, a toss that was nearly impossible not to catch.

"I've been thinking about my future, Dad," he said, ambling back onto the lawn. I lobbed a pass with height rather than distance. He caught the ball with the adroitness that eighteen-year-old boys exhibit, a casual gesture. The exchange was clearly secondary to our true purpose. The question was unavoidable. He asked, "How did you decide that you wanted to teach?"

How indeed? Would I tell him how haphazard and serendipitous the decision had been? How, in those early college days, a time when I chose a study break, I happened to meet a stranger who by chance mentioned the availability of a grant offered through a military organization for the study of the Second World War? How I applied, was twelfth on a list of applicants, and through attrition, wiggled my way to the surface to receive a scholarship? Was this lecture time, the opening every parent dreamt of, the opportunity to say how hard one has to work, the part-time jobs, the long study hours, the requisite sucking up to navigate the political landscape of a graduate program? Maybe this was my opportunity to forge a new parental role, to make another contribution to the evolving stage of Rodney's adult development.

Or, on the contrary, perhaps this was the occasion to simply pass along the family mantra: 'Kid, you can't look to anyone but yourself'?

Rodney stood ten feet from me, that nonchalant adolescent posture, tossing the ball into the air and fielding its return. I noticed that he had gotten his hair trimmed sometime during the summer. "I guess everyone's got to make his own decision about what he wants to do when he grows up, doesn't he?" he said. "Mom wants me to be an architect. But I don't know. How about your mom and dad? What did they want you to be?"

Invisible, I thought. Magic. 'Make yourself disappear,' my father would say.

Rodney studied me. "I guess they died when you were pretty young, didn't they?" He took a step closer, hugging the ball beneath one arm. "Mom says you devoted yourself to your students. You had chances to get promoted and to travel, but you only wanted to teach. She says you were asked to move to Europe to work in some ambassador's office because you knew so much about the countries over there and the world wars and the politics. You could have had a plush job, she said, where you would have hobnobbed with important people. I guess that's where I would have grown up, somewhere in Europe."

Was my son asking me what went wrong? How could I tell him? *Nothing.* Nothing went wrong. I'd done exactly what I had wanted to do. In that regard, I was my father's son.

As if intuitively reading his role in my life at that moment, Rodney stepped up and draped one lanky arm around my shoulder. He had gained height over the summer. "I'm glad we didn't move to Europe, Dad. I like living in this neighborhood. And I'm glad you like teaching. I know you were always there for your students. And for me." He encircled me with his other arm and gave me a hug, the kind you know is offered out of love, asking nothing in return. Then he stepped back. "So, you hungry? I think Ruby left some food in the freezer. I can take out a casserole and heat it up in a jiffy. How about a salad to go with it? I want to tell you about my summer job at the *Crab Shack* on the beach." We walked toward the house, arm in arm. "You know, Dad, I really liked Ruby. It was great of her to stop over to say goodbye." He looked at me. "Somehow, though, I don't think she's the one for you."

As I followed my son into the house, I realized that over one short summer, a new generation had emerged. My son was about to take his place in the adult world. And my reward, as a parent, was the privilege of watching that happen.

While my son went about the task of preparing dinner, I sat with my drink and wondered about Rodney's questions. In his search for his own path, he was asking how I had found mine. Perhaps this was his first effort to discover his origins, how who he was becoming evolved from those who had come before him. Had I sought out my father's gravesite with the same question in mind? Were headstones historic markers, not totally unlike those found along roadside parks, from which to begin the search? Were family memoires, ancestral search engines, the rummaging through dog-eared photographs of grandparents and great grandparents reflective of our effort to embrace the power of lineage, to attach to something greater than the brief twinkling of our own destiny? Perhaps we wished to glimpse our origins to confirm that we are not simply solitary embolisms, broken free, floating aimlessly on the river of time.

As the casserole sat in the microwave, the purr of technology massaging a block of ice into a palatable meal, I watched Rodney work at the cutting board, slicing vegetables for a salad. I had always believed that good teachers learned from their students, sometimes as much as students learned in return. Perhaps there were moments when this was true of parents and children. Stromberg was right; being remembered was not a part of life, but a part of death. I preferred to be a work in progress. Completion of the plaque, to be hung by the men's room door, would have to wait.

Rodney's salad was delicious and I praised him for a job well done. As he related tales from the beach, I saw more evidence that my adolescent son had undergone his metamorphosis into young manhood. His voice was deeper, his expressions more mature, his observations more complex. While I had liked his boyish ways, I liked the adult Rodney even more.

We ate, Rodney detailing life at the *Crab Shack*, about placating whiny customers, welcoming heavy tippers, feeding the poor family who begged for food at the rear door each Saturday night, and mastering the relentless seven day work schedule. As the anecdotes ran down and our dinner drew to a close, the tone of his narration shifted. Rodney shared his own observations, what he had learned over the summer, about work, and friendships, and love. "George and I have become great friends. Talley seems different, though. I thought we'd all get along, but he got moody, started to hang out with a different crowd. I don't think we'll be seeing much of each other now that we're back."

My son was shaping his own values. Sure, maybe he'd still ask my advice on occasion, but I was pleased to hear his own standards emerge. Perhaps, partly through my muddling efforts on the parenting team, Rodney had learned to think for himself, to trust his own judgment. To the extent I had contributed, I wanted that to be part of my legacy.

Then came the inevitable question. Rodney asked, "Someday will you tell me about your dad? My grandfather."

It was then I realized that, although the historian, I had kept my past hidden from my son. And of course, from myself. I thought again about my discussions with Silverman, about magic. Had my closet passion truly been a metaphor? That interpretation seemed too glib. Why could I not simply have a passion for illusions, for the beauty and the mystery that comes with the suspension of belief? But if it were that simple, then why the secrecy, why had I chosen not to share my passion with the world? Was I employing the literal form of smoke and mirrors to mystify my audience and myself?

My son studied me across the table, smiling a knowing smile. He reached out, covering my hand with his. His hand was larger than I remembered, a man's hand. I wondered when that had happened, when my son had grown such large hands, hands large enough to cover mine?

"Someday I'd just like to know," he said. "You know, about my grandfather."

CHAPTER 38
THE TRUTH SHALL SET YOU FREE

I passed Finbar on a walkway as I crossed campus and he asked why I hadn't been to the group meetings. I felt a little awkward, like the sinner who had missed too many Sundays at church, the preacher admonishing me for my absences. Well, I'd had a lot on my mind, I told him, but agreed to attend the next session. It was not that I had forgotten about the group. On the contrary, I had been tempted to attend and share some of my newly found insights. Somehow, though, I'd held back, fearful that by opening up, I would not only be vulnerable to the others, but would have to deal with the part of my life that stood before me, beyond some imaginary wall, a place I'd barely dared to glimpse. Like Scrooge, I most feared the *Ghost of Christmas Future*.

The group was smaller than when I had last attended. Moody and Axelrod had dropped out. Finbar explained that Axelrod was so ecstatic with his new love life, he had little time for anything else. He confided, during his final session, that he couldn't bring himself to reveal to the group the spirited routines Angela had introduced to their relationship. He felt *that* a betrayal of their love. Besides, he didn't wish to give others any ideas about this woman he now adored for fear, in a state of aroused passion, one of them might make an attempt to steal her away.

I applauded Axelrod. He had found his Xanadu.

No one knew why Moody had dropped out. Finbar inquired, but she merely shrugged and suggested she had gotten too busy with the semester's rush. While no one believed that to be the actual reason, this was her right, he assured the group.

"Perhaps she was frightened of revealing herself," Pollard suggested.

"Or she's resolved her issues on her own, whatever they were," Eagerman said.

"I, for one, am very disappointed," Wesley said. "Her suggestion that we discuss sex had me very intrigued."

"I'm afraid that topic was appealing to your prurient interests," Pickering said.

"Come now, gents, we're back to the old boys club," Finbar said. "Let's get along the best we can. I think we should lead off with an accounting from Alec. He's made his trip to Europe." Finbar turned to me. "So how'd it go?"

I provided a digested version of the trip, the faded relationship with Armand Pennington, returning home to the arms of law enforcement, and the final resolution of the missing funds and Jeffrey Ryder. I mentioned Ruby Touch as an agreeable footnote. Out of respect to my long-term career interests at State, I omitted my conversation with Stromberg as he perched on my mother's headstone.

Then I dropped the bombshell. "I met my father's lover."

"Was she anything like you imagined?" Pollard asked.

"He," I replied. "Yes, he was exactly who I thought he would be. I'd met him twice before, when I was a child."

"Your father was *gay*?" Wesley asked incredulously.

"Even back then," I said. "People could be gay."

"What Wesley means, I think," Finbar said, "is that you had never alluded to this in past conversations."

"I had never been certain. Now I know," I said.

"And how do you feel about it?"

"Sad. Not that he was gay. Sad because he had to hide it from me and the world."

"He had little choice back then."

"That's the worst part."

"Are you angry as well?"

"Relieved, I think. His relationship with this other man explains a great deal, why he was gone so frequently, his difficulty giving my mother the love she desperately desired."

"What was it like to meet your father's lover again face to face, as adults?"

"Reassuring. For both of us, I think."

"Now what?"

"That's what I'm wondering. Armand (I was now using her given name) saw that I was, as she put it, on *the verge* when she and I first met. Her interpretation of that was, I believe, to be 'on the verge of cracking up'. I thought so, too. Then, at least. Now I realize I am on the verge of my future, something new and perhaps very different. Before I'd been only frightened of the unknown. Now I am excited as well, wanting to embrace what might come next."

"And can you share with us the nature of your unknown?" Pickering asked.

"If I knew, it wouldn't be my unknown, would it?" I replied.

They scrutinized me as if I had made the deliberate decision to hold out on some secret store of fact or fancy. Perhaps, in my long absence, they were facing their own unknowns and thought facing mine with me would make it easier all around. They might have been right, but I was just not ready.

"We'll be sorry to lose you from the group," Pollard said.

Pollard's observation surprised me. While I had decided this would be my last session, I was puzzled as to how that came across so clearly. The others nodded, eliminating any need for me to confirm Pollard's assertion.

"In a way, Alec, I feel you are the one who has changed the most," Wesley said. "You exude more confidence than when you first came here. And I hear you are performing feats of magic in your classrooms. Quite an attention-getter."

Although I knew little about the dynamics of self-discovery groups, this seemed to be the time in which I was going to get feedback from each member. I listened attentively, interested and sometimes surprised by what the others shared. It turned out that the balance of the group's time did focus on me as the departing member. I was also asked to give each of the others feedback in return. When we finished, there were hugs all around, a surprising course of action among middle-aged white men with extended bellies, body boundary issues, and major egos.

I understood Axelrod no longer attending the group, but Moody's decision to not return puzzled me. Her office was on the far end of the campus. As a vice president for marketing, she had her own administrative assistant and a student staff of two. I announced myself to the receptionist, a work-study student in the business college who had taken one of my classes the previous spring semester. To my surprise, the young man recognized me. We shook hands as he extolled the virtues of my teaching, in particular how well I had underscored the importance of understanding the history of *anything*, including a business opportunity. I thanked him and waited as he announced my unscheduled arrival.

The vice president for marketing, who also had an appointment in the business college and taught a marketing course each year, was in conference, but would be free momentarily. I fiddled with a *Business Week* for less than thirty seconds before the door to her office opened and Mary Ann Moody stepped into the anti-room followed by Professor Axelrod. Axelrod rushed to me and grabbed my hand.

"Alec, so good to see you. Sorry I've missed the group meetings, but I do want to hear how it's going with you. Let's have lunch?" he said.

"Lunch it is," I replied.

"Wonderful," he said. He scurried along the corridor, a gangly, joyful creature.

Mary Ann Moody watched me for a moment then jerked her head toward the inner office. "Let's talk."

When we were settled into plush chairs across the coffee table from one another, I said. "Sorry I didn't first make an appointment. I've just come from the group."

"And you wonder why I dropped out," she said.

"I do."

"The group members have been making the rounds one by one," she said. "I'm flattered, I think."

"What's the prevailing speculation?" I asked.

"That I have sexual issues as in being gay, that I'm not over the death of my husband, that I feel a conflict of interest because I'm with administration, that I was bothered at being the only female, and that I found your presence a distraction."

"Did anyone come close?"

"Yes."

"The winner is…."

"That I found you a distraction."

"Who's speculation, may I ask?"

"Mine."

"Would you have let on?" I asked.

"To you? When you return to your office, you'll find a message from me. And another on your home answering machine. I was hoping we could have dinner sometime."

"Tonight?"

"Tonight I'm invited to the Axelrod's for dinner. Of course, I can slip away early and stop by your place. Say around nine?"

I was proud of myself on one account: I did not ask Mary Ann Moody, *Why me?* Instead, I said, "Nine is good. You know where I live?"

"I'll find it."

CHAPTER 39

SUMMING UP

Mary Ann Moody and I have been dating casually for about three months. She is a warm, open person with a wonderful sense of humor. While I would not have picked her, I'm pleased she has picked me. We are not soul mates, something that is clear to us both. Yet we are a good twosome to explore what is beyond the wall for each of us. Sometimes we venture into the outer world. Other times, we venture inward. We date others on occasion and share thoughts on our personal discoveries. Perhaps because we are investing in a growing friendship, there is little to hide. Our intimate relationship is also casual, caring and fun, and simply another dimension of our friendship. This may be the best of all possible worlds for each of us at the moment.

Rodney has received acceptance letters from a half-dozen colleges, at least two offering full scholarships, a fact that pleases me greatly for obvious reasons. Most likely, he won't attend State, but will go off on his own. I'll miss his daily presence, yet am excited for his new life.

Two weeks before Christmas, I received a package postmarked *Arizona*, accompanied by a note from Hal Moss's sister. Hal had died of lung cancer a month earlier. He wished me to have a dozen letters my father had written to him over the years, several of which contained references to me and our family life. My heart fluttered as I slipped a rubber band from the frail packet. My thumb brushed the postmark on the top letter, a letter mailed when I was just four years old. It occurred to me that I held in my hands original historic documents, not the works of a president or a prime minister, but the words of a simple man with simple needs.

I wondered how, if at all, the contents of these letters might enlighten my past. One point I had finally accepted was that it was not up to Skip, nor anyone else; it was up to me. And with that thought, a strange, peaceful insight washed over me. No longer was I expecting people to be who I wished them to be.

Was I ready to read the letters? Not just then. But, I planned not to wait too long, for their texture felt fragile, like old parchment, as if with time they would flake into dust. Of greater consequence, however, was their relevance to me, something that might fade even more quickly. Regardless of what pain the reading of their contents set in motion for me, I wished to feel the significance of their impact while I was vulnerable to them, rather than wait till a time when I might only peruse them with detached curiosity.

The self-discovery group continues to flourish under Finbar's leadership. He has taken several classes in the counseling department so as to improve his leadership style. Membership has grown to a maximum of ten with a mixture of younger faculty and staff, both men and women. Word of Finbar's kindly guidance has spread across the campus and there is talk of establishing additional groups under his mentorship.

I received an email from Ruby Touch telling me she had settled in, that she misses me, and that if I was out her way, I should look her up. She had been made chief of homicide for the county sheriff's department. I responded with a note of congratulations and a footnote of thanks.

Surprising to no one who knows her, Armand Pennington married the crown prince of a small oil principality, and after making arrangements with her probation officer to leave the country, was living abroad. London, of course. Jeffrey converted to Catholicism, enrolled in the seminary, and was studying to become a teaching brother at St. Joseph's Academy. He stops by my office from time to time to discuss the history of Christianity and to drop hints concerning my own salvation. Ryan Ryder continues his involvement with the bank, although as chairman of the board rather than president. He does, however, still travel a great deal on some sort of business while Martha and Cook create new recipes with which to experiment upon his return. Rumor has it that he has made numerous trips to London, at his own expense, of course.

Gloria and Ackerman Fink have married and are living in a wonderful new mansion designed and fashioned in her honor by Ackerman himself. A mutual acquaintance tells me she is happily devoting her time to accumulating replicated Greek and Roman statuary with which to surround their three acre pond, the one adjacent to the acreage upon which her guest house is to be constructed, sometime within the year.

Silverman's therapist died. I read of the event in the newspaper, was tempted to attend the wake, but decided instead to send a card. Several weeks later, I received a warm one-page letter extolling my virtues as a patient. *For Professor Alec Simon,* Silverman wrote, *there is always a place on the couch.* High tribute from one's therapist, I think. Hopefully, I won't need the reservation, at least for a while.

As far as the former students I'd visited were concerned;

Dr. Cecil Worksworth was voted doctor of the year by his colleagues. Unfortunately, the IRS is following up on an anonymous report that Dr. Worksworth claimed a sumptuous second home as an arm of his research foundation. The government agency is maintaining the doctor owes several hundred thousands of dollars in back taxes, interest, and penalties. I am guiltless in the matter.

Hasbach Fulmer, writing as Zack Henley, has another Tammy Gunrattle bestseller out. While I haven't read the novel, a colleague, who is a long-time devotee of the mystery series, tells me the plot centers around a university professor who is murdered by a former student for stealing the student's creative ideas. I've considered installing a security system.

Ambrose Archer, having been found absent-without-leave from his residence at the mission, received a three-year sentence and periodically emails my office from a prison in upper New York State. He assures me that, upon his release, he still plans to return the twenty he had borrowed. He asked whether I might be willing to sponsor his parole, and perhaps arrange for employment with the university, just until he's fully on his feet again. He also offered his services as a gardener in exchange for room and board.

Jonathan Stiles' death was cited under "Other News" in the local newspaper. He was found hanging in his cell at Leavenworth. While his death was allegedly self-induced, the investigation continues amid speculation that a former partner in crime had bribed a fellow inmate into killing Stiles and making it appear as a suicide. Rumor had it that the former crime partner, upon his discharge, discovered a sum total of four dollars and twenty-two cents in a foreign bank account that was presumed to contain millions in ill-gotten monies from drug sales.

Andrea Winforth was drafted by the state Democrats to run for a seat in the United States Senate. Were she to win, she would be the first African-American transgender person to hold a senate seat from that state. The polls were already showing her in the lead. Her nomination has caught the eye of the national media. In a number of the interviews broadcast on cable television, I observed Deputy Oliver hovering in the background, in uniform, his bald pate gleaming in the overhead lights. A glowing smile replaced his terse frown, suggesting how much he was enjoying the limelight.

Lana Prescott's brother made contact late one evening to say he had found a composition book among Lana's belongings detailing her academic journey at State, in both prose and poetry with accompanying sketches, and asked if I would mind if he sent the book along to perhaps be included in the library's local history archives. He also revealed that Lana's daughter would be attending State the following year and requested that I check in on her on occasion. Of course, I had no idea Lana Prescott had a daughter, but assured him I would be a doting Dutch Uncle as the opportunity presented itself.

Sara McCovy's dissertation committee chair did send a note to my department head asking that I serve on Sara's committee as an outside reader. My chair consulted with me and I agreed on the condition that my role be carried out by internet and telephone. I preferred not to have direct contact with Sara, given her apparent propensity to become overly-involved with men of authority.

Deter, formerly Peter, Crouch, received a commendation from an anonymous source in the CIA for thinking *outside-the-box*. Shortly afterward, Deter disappeared. Rumor on campus among his small group of admirers was that he had been drafted by the U.S. Government to serve as a shadow ambassador to a South American country. By pure coincidence, the country in question, operating with a functional, if rather unstable, democratic regime, was about to legislate taxes on several large U.S. owned corporations that had originally sought cheap labor and relief from the U.S. tax laws. Private speculation offered up by one particularly zealous Deter-ite was that the democratic government would be overthrown within six months and Deter would oversee the new regime as a titular dictator. I was particularly saddened to hear this was a country having several large soccer stadiums.

I had not spoken to Stromberg since our meeting at the cemetery, much to my relief. However, he has appeared to me in several dreams, floating just above the horizon, smiling wistfully. On mornings following those dreams, my life seems to go particularly well. But my life is going well these days anyway, so I am not conceding all the credit to Stromberg.

The End

www.ingramcontent.com/pod-product-compliance
Lightning Source LLC
Chambersburg PA
CBHW071951040426
42447CB00009B/1304